On *The Wire*

spin offs

A production of the Console-ing Passions books series
Edited by Lynn Spigel

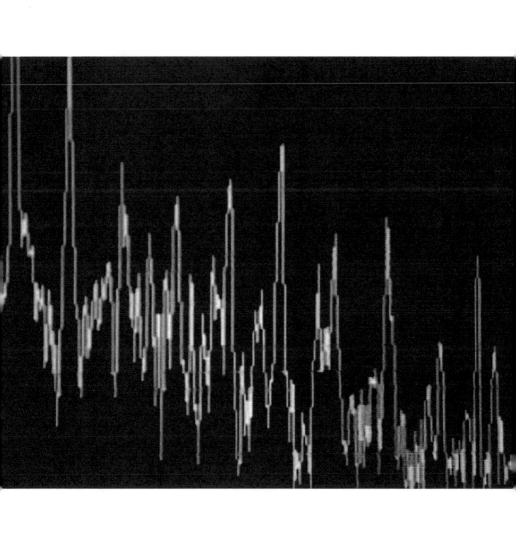

On *The Wire*

LINDA WILLIAMS

DUKE UNIVERSITY PRESS   *Durham and London*   2014

Cover art: Still from *The Wire*.
Courtesy of Photofest.

Library of Congress Cataloging-
in-Publication Data
Williams, Linda, 1946–
On the Wire / Linda Williams.
pages cm
Includes bibliographical references and index.
ISBN 978-0-8223-5706-3 (cloth : alk. paper)
ISBN 978-0-8223-5717-9 (pbk. : alk. paper)
1. Wire (Television program). I. Title.
PN1992.77.W53 W52 2014
791.45'72—dc23
2014000762

Contents

Acknowledgments

I owe thanks to three different classes on *The Wire* that I was fortunate to teach at UC Berkeley after the series ended. The first was a senior seminar that also served as my own initiation into television studies. The second was a large lecture class whose discussion sessions were extremely helpful to this book. The third was a graduate seminar on serial television featuring *The Wire* as a case study in which I tried out some of the ideas on seriality and melodrama. Many insights were sparked by the students in these classes and in countless discussions with friends. Special thanks go to three wonderful research assistants and editors: Jonathan Lee (who led the way), Kelsa Trom (wise beyond her years), and Irene Chien (without whom I would still be mired in research). I am also indebted to Christine Borden, who taught me the importance of Simon's journalism; Nikhil Krishnan, who understood the lure of technology; Mallory Russell, who counted many beats; Zeynep Gürsel, who knew about ethnography; Maryam Monalisa Gharavi and Catherine Zimmer, who were both smart about surveillance; and Elisabeth Anker, who told me to keep my eye on the series itself. I dedicate this book to all of these friends, colleagues, and students who showed me new facets of the series. Especially heartfelt thanks go to the three people who first made me watch *The Wire*: Edith Kramer, J. P. Gorin, and Quinn Fitzgerald.

Introduction

But to tell the truth, I no longer watch many
films. . . . I feed my hunger for fiction with what is by
far the most accomplished source: those terrific American TV
series like *Deadwood, Firefly*, or *The Wire*. . . . There is a knowledge
in them, a sense of story and economy, of ellipsis, a science of
framing and of cutting, a dramaturgy, and an acting style that
has no equal anywhere, and certainly not in Hollywood.
—Chris Marker, *La Jetée / Sans Soleil* DVD booklet

Who knew that the movie business would disappear. It disappeared
instantaneously. . . . There will be festival films, there will be a way to live,
where a movie like '[Michael] Clayton' gets made if you get a movie star like
[George] Clooney to waive his fee, there will be exceptions for decades. But
as a rule, the middle class drama, ambitious drama, it's on TV. Everybody
knows that, it's why TV is so great right now, they've got it.
—Tony Gilroy, *The Playlist* website

In the summer and fall of 2007, I was laid up in bed. For the first time
in my life since childhood I had time to feed my "hunger for fiction" via
television. A friend had brought me an inspired gift: bootlegs of the first
three seasons of *The Wire*. I proceeded to watch an episode each eve-
ning until I ran out. As soon as I could, I purchased the last two seasons
and continued to steadily feed a growing habit. The series ran weekly on
HBO from 2002 to 2008, but ran in a more concentrated, nightly form
on my bedroom TV from 2007 to 2008. By the time I finished watch-

ing, I was more than a fan—I was a convert. The project of this book is to understand to what I had been converted.

Through the microcosm of one decaying American city, *The Wire* reveals the interconnected truths of many institutional failures: a rampant drug trade that police cannot curtail, the devaluation of work measured in declining unions, a cynical city government that raises and then crushes the hope of reform, the poignant waste of schools and the failure of education, and, finally, a media that cannot report on the truth of any of the above, let alone see the connections among them, although *The Wire* itself does. The exemplary writing and plotting draws on the expertise of some of America's best contemporary writers of urban crime fiction—George Pelecanos, Richard Price, Dennis Lehane—but within the television serial form. The series digs deeply into character without making private virtue or evil the final cause of narrative outcomes, thus putting an unusual spin on melodramatic conventions. I have never seen anything so absorbing, so complex, so simultaneously challenging and gratifying coming from either the big or little screen.

Subtle nuances of race, class, and language are made possible by a locale in which blacks are the majority of the citizens, yet fixing things is not a matter of simply electing more black politicians. The usual racial melodramas of black versus white are thus not the crude affairs they have tended to be in most movies and television. Race, for example, cannot be reduced to a problem of "racism." It is inseparable from class, the plague of drugs, the decline of work, and the failures of government, education, and media. Nevertheless, the series tantalizingly holds out the hope of change, the hope of a better social justice. Indeed, it is simultaneously animated by the quest for this justice and deeply cynical about its achievement. A profound understanding of education both in and out of school makes learning, as it should be, the key to change, while a distinctive rootedness in the specific locality of Baltimore gives the series a social solidity lacking in any other work on television.

During and after the series' run, many television critics, not to mention the president of the United States, cited *The Wire* as the best television series ever.[1] Many other critics claimed it transcended the very form of television. Journalist Joe Klein claimed in the DVD commentary on the final episode that, "*The Wire* should win the Nobel Prize for literature!" Simon himself called the work a "visual novel"[2] (though just as often a Greek tragedy). Literary critics such as Walter Benn Michaels have followed Simon's lead. In a lament about the failure of the American novel to tell stories that matter to the neoliberal present, Michaels has claimed that *The Wire* is the "most serious and ambitious fictional narrative of the twenty-first century."[3] Sociologists Anmol Chaddha and William Julius Wilson also see the series as literature, arguing that it "is part of a long line of literary works that are often able to capture the complexity of urban life in ways that have eluded many social scientists."[4] They cite novelists Richard Wright, Italo Calvino, and Charles Dickens as models, while Michaels cites Émile Zola and Theodore Dreiser.

The series has the ability, like Dickens, Wright, Zola, and Dreiser, to give dramatic resonance to a wide range of interconnected social strata, and the different behaviors and speech of these strata over broad swaths of world and time. Yet at the same time it seems feeble to describe *The Wire* as our greatest novel (never written) or, as Fredric Jameson does, to extol its "refusal to be 'realist' in the traditional mimetic and replicative sense."[5] Like the comparison to Greek tragedy, much of this praise borrows a literary prestige that corresponds to the series' excellence but not closely enough to its actual serial television cultural form.[6] Before making these more exalted comparisons, then, it may help to see how *The Wire* grew and what it grew out of—first as a form of journalism, then out of the conventional melodrama of crime genres and soaps.

Although I find this particular television serial exceptional, it will not be my intention to laud its exceptionality as a rare flowering in the "wasteland" of television, for as both my epigraphs indicate, television today is hardly a wasteland. Nor is it my intention to follow the lead of *The Wire*'s prime mover, David Simon, who has certainly created great television but is not a particularly insightful critic of his own work. Rather, in seeking to articulate what is so exceptional about *The Wire*, I shall argue that it is first necessary to appreciate what is conventional about it: seriality, televisuality, and melodrama.

For twelve years David Simon worked as a journalist digging increasingly deeper for social context. But he quit the newspaper business in anger—accepting a buyout with a substantial severance package even though he was offered a raise to stay on—and began writing imaginative teleplays for the television series *Homicide*. In both of these apprenticeships, Simon absorbed a craft of writing that would serve him well in the leap into the less well-charted territory of *The Wire*.

A key first argument of this book will thus be that although *The Wire* may be sui generis, it does not transcend its mass culture bases in city desk journalism and television melodrama; rather, it is woven out of this very cloth. And the fundamental warp of this cloth is the (sometimes preachy) journalism Simon practiced at the *Baltimore Sun* along with long-form "new journalism" with novelistic gestures, culminating in the experiment of his miniseries dramatization of the lives of real people in *The Corner*. Its weft is fictional storytelling based on fact, which episodes of *Homicide* and *The Corner* awkwardly negotiate, but which *The Wire*, breaking more completely with the righteous tone of editorializing journalism, weaves together perfectly. Out of the warp and weft of the nonfictional and the fictional elements of this cloth, Simon expanded his craft into the sixty hours of serial television that constitutes *The Wire*. The genius of this series was thus neither, as Simon saw it, a novelistic rebellion against journalistic or televisual constraints but a slow genesis that learned a great deal from the discipline of these fundamentally melodramatic forms of mass culture.

A second part of the book takes up the most common praise given *The Wire*—that it is a modern tragedy—and turns it on its head. While the series is obviously a generic "cop show," clearly it is also something more. David Simon would like that something more to be tragedy. I argue instead that it is superior serial melodrama. Simon writes: "We have ripped off the Greeks: Sophocles, Aeschylus, Euripedes. . . . We've basically taken the idea of Greek tragedy, and applied it to the modern city-state." Instead of the Olympians, "it's the postmodern institutions . . . those are the indifferent gods."[7] Simon's claims are borne out by many examples, but perhaps the most important connection to tragedy, and especially to *Greek* tragedy, is the constant theme of injustice. Tragic heroes may rail against injustice, but in the end they must accept their fate. This, I argue, is not what *The Wire* does. It is much more concerned, as all melodrama is, with finding a more immediate, less cosmic justice. Melodramatic heroes suffer injustice; sometimes they overcome it by brave deeds, and sometimes they simply show their virtue by continuing to suffer. The two chapters in this section are about *The Wire*'s attempt to be "classical" tragedy and its ironically greater accomplishment in developing something more ambitious than the conventional melodrama we love to deride. Melodrama demands justice, while tragedy reconciles us to its lack. But justice itself, as we soon learn, does not consist of catching dope dealers or solving homicides. Nor does it consist of thwarting surveillance. Rather, it consists of the larger question of what might be an equitable and just society in which dope and homicide would not be central activities. Real justice, we are allowed to imagine, would consist of genuine, creative work, democratic governance, education with "soft eyes," and better stories about them all.

However, if it is the demand for justice, in the stark face of its frequent failure, that draws Simon to the form of tragedy (and that causes him to make some of his more exalted claims for the series), it is the concern for those who suffer the failures of justice that keep us coming back to the series. We are made to care about those who strive and those who suffer the injustice of neoliberal institutions. I will argue that the "base" melodrama of crime drama is not "transcended" by the higher form of tragedy in *The Wire*. Indeed, one key to understanding the greatness of the series lies in the spectacular tussle of these two forms: one world-weary, screaming futilely against the injustice of the universe, the other reaching for the virtue of suffering innocence to restore the good "home" of America's past. Dramatizing both the necessity for, and the difficulty of, reform within each of the major institutions portrayed, *The Wire*'s melodrama operates at both the personal and the institutional level. I argue that it is the meshing of the individual and the institutional that allows it to picture the political and social totality of what ails contemporary urban America and to imagine what justice could be. No other television series or film "franchise" has accomplished this feat.

A final section of the book asks about the relation between real learning and surveillance. Who has the benefit of "soft eyes," and what does race have to do with the larger melodramas told? Police are "up on a wire" when they have court permission to listen in to private phone conversations. To "wear a wire" is to have even more ability to collect incriminating evidence. The lure of surveillance as a quick fix to crime keeps the cops tantalized throughout all five seasons of the series. If only they had *this* newest gadget, they imagine, they could catch and punish the criminals. Ultimately, however, the figure of the wire encompasses something altogether richer, something deeper and critically at the heart of our highly "disciplined" society, than one finds in the CSI-style glamour of so many police procedurals. For on the other side of "the wire" are the corner boys and kingpins who observe the discipline of avoiding all forms of communication that might be "wired" and thus thwart the electronic quest to pry with "hard eyes" into the lives of drug traffickers.

Over and over we see that the best police work done in the series is not the hard intrusive look of surveillance, but the "soft eyes," which can build a different and better kind of knowledge. Indeed, one of the greatest features of *The Wire* is its exploration of when and how people really learn, in a reconception of the familiar "school melodrama" of heroic teachers. In season 4 former cop and rookie teacher Roland Pryzbylewski is given a single piece of advice by a veteran teacher: "You need soft eyes" (4.2). As it plays out throughout this season, this enigmatic advice begins to establish an alternative to the prying "hard eyes" of police surveillance and ultimately a better way to learn. As Detective Bunk Moreland demonstrates through his own practice of police work, "soft eyes" can take in subtle, seemingly peripheral forms of information and creatively process them to successful effect. This is a kind of learning that represents the opposite of *The Wire*'s technological fix. It can only grow out of a perceptive, intimate experience of a given situation. It finds its greatest expression, in and out of the classroom, over the course of a fourth season that revolves around Tilghman Middle School.

A final chapter begins with the fact that this series is the only dramatic narrative in television or film to proceed from a world in which "integration" is not a liberal fantasy of "tolerant" interaction, but a necessary if uneasy cohabitation. Indeed, it is the presumption of a certain black power base and what George Lipsitz calls a "black spatial imaginary," what I also call a black linguistic imaginary with special eloquence and cultural power. What is thus refreshingly missing from the series, and what gives it its edge, is any assumption of de-ethnicized whiteness as a cultural or political norm. However corrupt or righteous this black political and cultural power base may be, it is the ground from which all else proceeds. It renders black culture the center rather than the margin of experience and makes the acknowledgment of race necessary in practical political ways that the liberal ideology of "colorblindness" cannot countenance. It also paradoxically takes the burden off race as the key difference and renders the role of class much more visible than it usually is in American television or film. Most importantly, it rewrites the conventional melodrama of black and white that has been dominant in American culture since *Uncle Tom's Cabin*.[8]

This long-running melodrama is manifest in powerful cycles of racial feelings acted out in mass culture and major media events going back to the most popular novel and play of the mid-nineteenth century, *Uncle Tom's Cabin*, and the most popular film of the early twentieth century, *Birth of a Nation*. The "Tom/anti-Tom" antinomies contained in these two determining cases of moving-image mass culture have continued to play out in American culture. But in *The Wire* they encounter a decidedly new turn. Institutional rather than personal melodrama, world-building seriality grounded in a black spatial imaginary results among other things in the construction of new kind of hero—the elusive and ubiquitous robber of drug stashes, Omar Little—who poses a relevant answer to the "magic Negro" of the white spatial imaginary.

PART I
World Enough and Time

THE GENESIS AND GENIUS OF *THE WIRE*

1 Ethnographic Imagination

FROM JOURNALISM TO TELEVISION SERIAL

David Simon only ever wanted to be a great journalist. However, his notion of journalism was grandiose, aspiring to a deep sociocultural understanding of the lives of the people whose stories he reported. If ethnography can be defined as a method of nuanced qualitative social research, "in which fine grained daily interactions constitute the life-blood of the data produced," then Simon's journalism at the *Baltimore Sun* can be described as ethnographic from the very beginning.[1]

Simon filed three hundred bylines at the *Sun* in his first year out of the University of Maryland reporting on the cop beat.[2] Starting first with short pieces, he soon developed strengths for writing longer, multipart series. His first such story, "Little Melvin Williams," published in 1987, was about a late eighties drug lord who had until recently been king-pin. In many ways Williams is the foundation for the character of Avon Barksdale in *The Wire*.[3] This story was published in five parts after Simon took a leave to write the book *Homicide: A Year on the Killing Streets*, where he developed a knack for even longer stories. Based on cases occurring in 1988, the book was finally published in 1991 at 646 pages.[4] Simon was allowed to follow the lives and cases of the Baltimore Police Department's homicide unit on the condition that he did not communicate what he witnessed to his newspaper and did not quote anyone by name unless they agreed to go on the record.[5] The twenty-something Simon hung out with selected shifts of police and followed the progres-

Simon's *Baltimore Sun* "Easy Money" series on "Little Melvin" Williams, model for Avon Barksdale

sion or impasses of their many cases, most frustratingly the rape and murder of a young girl that was never solved.

After completing *Homicide*, equipped with deeper knowledge of the police and criminal justice system, Simon wrote another series for the *Sun*, "Crisis in Blue," a four-part article about the increasing dysfunction within the Baltimore Police Department. In this series he revealed that the failure at the heart of the system was institutional and far from individual.[6] In 1993 he took another year off, this time with former cop–turned–schoolteacher Ed Burns (who had been a frequent source in his crime reporting), to investigate the cops' antagonists: drug dealers and drug addicts in West Baltimore. The resulting book, *The Corner: A Year in the Life of an Inner-City Neighborhood*, reports on an extended West Baltimore family (crack mother, heroin-addicted father, crack-dealing son, and their friends, lovers, and associates). This 543-page tome was published in 1997, after Simon had abandoned journalism.

Both of Simon's long books employ the basic methodologies of ethnography: a long term—one year—stay in a field where a particular set of social relations can be observed. The observer learns the ritu-

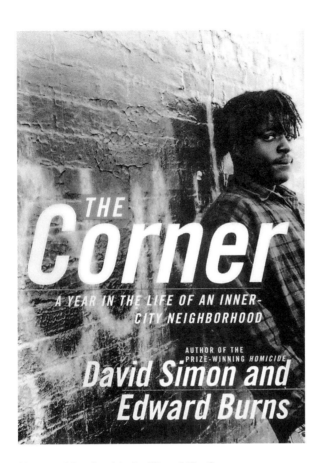

Simon and Burn's original edition of *The Corner*

als and habits of the culture by following selected individuals in their
work and daily lives. Simon's goal in both books was to understand and
depict the deeper workings of police culture and drug culture in inner-
city Baltimore through the eyes of their informants. In *Homicide*, they
were mostly cops investigating murders, along with some witnesses and
victims' families. In *The Corner* the informants were drug dealers and
users. In this latter case Simon and Burns had no official sanction to
observe what could, after all, be criminal acts. They simply hung out
on the West Fayette Street neighborhood corners practicing what they
unpretentiously call "stand-around-and-watch journalism."[7] This jour-

nalism transmuted into ethnography at the point at which the two men had been there long enough to become regular fixtures on the scene.

Ethnography is essentially a more systematic extension of "stand-around-and-watch journalism."[8] Field techniques are rooted in the idea of participant observation, in which data is regarded as a gift from willing informants. Simon was not a professional ethnographer; indeed, in studying the cops he may have been too enthusiastic, may have identified with his subjects too deeply, for the level of meticulous observation and precision that ethnography requires. He admits he simply loved "these guys"[9]—their language, their procedures, their tough and sometimes tender ways. Studying the corners, on the other hand, he and Burns were more measured, a bit more scientific. Their model was Elliot Liebow's classic, *Tally's Corner: A Study of Negro Streetcorner Men*, first published in 1967. While on the corner Simon and Burns adopted Liebow's principal rule: to limit loans of money or other favors to what each asker would have gotten from another friend. Thus they would occasionally drive a sick addict to a clinic or loan a little money for a fix.

Ethnographer George Marcus argues that there is an inherent problem with the ethnographic method when it concentrates solely on a specific location of study. How do you indicate the existence of the larger system that affects the micro-level of the community studied? To do so, he argues, ethnographers of a "single site" inevitably have recourse to a larger whole that has not yet been studied in so deep or systematic a fashion. As a result, researchers do not have data for the whole, which is often more assumed than observed. Marcus calls this recourse the "fiction of the whole," and "the whole" usually amounts to some abstraction: "the state," "the economy," "capitalism," and so on.[10] This fiction enables the telling of the ethnographic tale; it enables some kind of closure: "However slightly developed or imagined . . . the fiction of the whole . . . exercises powerful control over the narrative in which an ethnographer frames a local world."[11] Even the most scrupulously factual of ethnographers must presume that the micro-worlds of (say) homicide cops or drug corners exist within a larger system—a fiction of the whole that the micro-level community illustrates. Thus Marcus and others have developed the ambition to undertake a "multisited" ethnography—one that can approach the system as a whole by studying more of the sites that compose it.

Since the 1980s, multisited ethnography has expanded traditional single-sited ethnography to give greater breadth and scope to the discipline. In place of the classic concern with the unique perspective of local cultures (especially those of colonial subalterns or the underclass), some ethnographers have sought to identify a more "diffuse time-space" of study that expands beyond the single site. This method maps a more complex thread of interconnected cultural processes in a related world system of geopolitical interaction.[12] Through the discovery of the relations between various communities, the ethnographer attempts to "bring these multiple sites into the same frame of study and to posit their relationships on the basis of first-hand ethnographic research."[13]

The only problem, as Marcus freely admits, is that no single ethnographer has enough knowledge of enough worlds or enough time to map this constantly evolving world system. Admitting that multisited ethnography might be more of an ideal than a reality—the sort of imaginary "world enough and time" to which the poet Andrew Marvell long ago alluded—Marcus and his colleagues nevertheless hold out an ideal of an "ethnographic imaginary."[14] He writes, "I am looking for a different, less stereotyped and more significant place for the reception of ethnographically produced knowledge in a variety of academic and nonacademic forms. . . . Tracing and describing the connections and relationships among sites previously thought incommensurate is ethnography's way of making arguments and providing its own contexts of significance."[15]

Given the word "imaginary" and the ambition to reach beyond "academic forms," it may not be surprising that the place where the knowledge of the world of cops and the world of the corner converge to provide their own "contexts of significance" proves to be Simon's unique fabrication of ethnographically informed serial television melodrama, *The Wire*. Here, at last, there is "world enough and time" to make the arguments and set up the contexts that could not be managed in journalism. Serial television melodrama makes possible the larger canvass of the ethnographic imaginary.

When Simon found a way to combine the factual, ethnographically observed, and detailed worlds of cops and corners into one converged fictional world, he had discovered the genius of the series, already glimpsed in the 2000 script he peddled to HBO, entitled *The Wire: A Dramatic Series for* HBO. There had been plenty of long-running police procedurals on television, both episodic and serial. There had also been plenty of movies about gangsters or "boyz" in the hood, but with the exception of Spike Lee's 1995 adaptation of Richard Price's fine novel *Clockers* (1992), there had never been a film or a television series that had given equal time to both sides of the law and that had compared them as systems in and of themselves. Indeed, not even Price or Lee's *Clockers* had managed to capture the day-to-day workings of law enforcement and lawbreaking over a sustained period of time.

In the first season of *The Wire*, cops and drug dealers/users inhabit the first two worlds of the series's initial frame. Unlike most traditional genres, in which cops are posited as either morally better than the "robbers" they police, or occasional bad apples, here both sides are equally caught up in the contrasting procedures and disciplines of their work. The first is a homicide investigation, though one that does not seek the "solution" to that crime. In it we observe the routine of Detective Jimmy McNulty, who casually stops in on an unrelated court trial in time to catch a state's witness who fails to testify against a defendant in the dock. So far, this is what we might expect from a single-sited police procedural: the handsome (white) detective keeping an eye on cases involving black defendants and witnesses. What we don't expect is the episode to ignore the investigation of the crime scene with which it began, nor do we expect the focus to shift so thoroughly to that of the cop's antagonists: the drug dealers.

Indeed, we can measure the exact moment when *The Wire* becomes multisited and ceases to be an ordinary police procedural. At 24:04 minutes into the first episode of the first season ("The Target") the black defendant in the previous courtroom scene, D'Angelo Barksdale, who has just been acquitted, is driven to a strip club by Roland ("Wee-Bey") Brice, his uncle's main enforcer, in order to celebrate his freedom. While a typical cop show might allow us to glimpse the exultation of the acquitted party as a brief interlude before returning to the procedures of

McNulty observes
trial of D'Angelo

the cops, we now pay equal attention to the procedures of the recently acquitted defendant and the gang to which he belongs. On his way to the bar where the celebration will take place, D'Angelo violates the rule against speaking of business in a vehicle that might be bugged (the first introduction of the theme of "the wire"). Wee-Bey stops the SUV and out on the sidewalk lectures D'Angelo on the rules of silence. In the following scene, twice as long as any other in the episode, we are introduced to D'Angelo's uncle, kingpin Avon Barksdale, at the strip club that fronts for his drug-dealing organization. Here D'Angelo receives another lecture about discipline, in this case about the unnecessary murder for which he was just acquitted. Two scenes later, we learn that for this lack of discipline D'Angelo has been demoted to work drug sales in low-rise apartments instead of the more lucrative high-rise projects he once worked. The equally important procedures of cops and dealers are thus established, from this moment on in the first season, as the two fundamental "sites" of the series.

The ethnographic knowledge of the worlds of cops and drug dealers comes both from Simon's reporting for the *Sun* and from his two books of long-form journalism—*Homicide* and *The Corner*. However, the parallel unfolding of these microsites, which this season as a whole carries out, enables a rich thematic comparison of the two institutions: cops who try to be "good police" and cops who just want to bust heads; and drug dealers who either possess or lack the discipline to avoid capture. The paradox of Simon's expanding ethnographic imaginary in *The Wire* is that the move to fictional storytelling allows him to abandon the "fic-

D'Angelo's first lecture
about silence

D'Angelo's second lecture
about discipline

tion of the whole" by instead building generalizations grounded in the procedural knowledge of his two initial sites. In other words, by moving to the form of serial fiction, *The Wire* itself, by multiplying "sites" from season to season, adding to the contrast in cops and dealers, builds its own "fiction of the whole." Serial fiction, based upon the contrasts of two related institutions, thus solves the problem of single-sited ethnography by building larger multisited (albeit fictional) worlds.

Each new season of *The Wire* accretes a new ethnographically observed world to the initial one of cops and corners. The following season adds the world of a predominantly Polish dockworkers union (the only narrative thread not continued throughout the series). The third season adds the world of city politics to that of cops and drug dealers and builds further parallels between the efforts of city government, police, and drug dealers to reform themselves: a reformist (white) candidate runs for mayor; drug dealers form a cooperative, and one rogue police major undertakes his own brilliant reform of a drugs-permitted zone ("Hamsterdam"). A remarkable fourth season focuses on a new generation of corner boys and drug dealers within the added institutional site of Tilghman Middle School, where a former cop now teaches. The fifth season keeps all but the docks of the second season in play, adding the new world of the *Baltimore Sun* and its persistent failure to report the real city news while cops continue to police a more ruthless new generation of drug dealers.

As the series cuts from one site to the next, rarely stopping to recap or reiterate, it approaches what the ethnographer could only dream of: a multisited ethnographic imaginary that no longer needs to depend on allusions to abstract ideas of "the state," "the economy," or "capitalism" as its "fiction of the whole." Its many sites add up and reveal a vivid picture of that whole that needs no economic theory of neoliberalism to be self-evident. The vivid and accessible interlocking stories from so many concrete ethnographic sites is what fiction affords, what ethnography aspires to and what newspaper journalism can only rarely achieve.[16] What, then, enabled this former journalist to make the leap from reporting fact to a fictional ethnographic imaginary? Simon himself would like us to think that he was inspired by both tragic and novelistic forms. I argue, instead, that it would be two experiments with television that would hone the skills of this dyed-in-the-wool journalist and allow him make the leap from reporting fact to writing fact-based multisited fiction. But for this to happen Simon had to quit the business he loved and turn to a certain discipline of television that he has never quite admitted embracing. To this day, he remains furious at the newspaper business for rejecting his brand of reporting, but he must know by now that it was the best thing that ever happened to him.

Rifle-Shot Journalism

As a journalist, Simon evolved in the direction of New Journalism's more novelistic way of reporting. The New Journalist is so "saturated," as Tom Wolfe has put it, with the situation of a given subject that he

(LEFT)

Polish dockworkers' church gift

City politics: Thomas Carcetti, the white reformist

Drug dealers reform

(RIGHT)

Major Colvin reforms police

Corner boys of Tilghman Middle School

Baltimore Sun city desk

or she feels entitled to get inside characters' heads—to say what they think.[17] Of course New Journalism is no longer new. It is well entrenched in journalism and is not only represented by a figure like Wolfe but by some of the best nonfiction writers now working. Structurally, however, it is often more like a movie than a novel: it "proceeds scene by scene, much as in a movie"; it incorporates "varying points of view, rather than telling a story solely from the perspective of the narrator."[18]

"Whole scenes and stretches of dialogue" are precisely what we get in Simon's September 3, 1995, *Baltimore Sun* story "The Metal Men"—the story that would cause him to quit journalism. Unlike a much earlier five-part story on the drug kingpin, Little Melvin Williams, this one is New Journalism through and through. It begins by setting the scene of a crime and establishes a point of view: "Kenny wipes his mouth, passes the wine and stares into the shopping cart, his mind managing a quick calculation." He calculates how much he and his brother Tyrone might get for certain quantities of copper pipe and other pieces of metal scavenged from a vacant house. Kenny and Tyrone are in the middle of a heist, ripping out metal from a Fulton Avenue row house in West Baltimore. Tyrone goes deeper into the guts of the building with a hacksaw, thinking, "Get the metal now or someone else comes behind you to grab it." He and his brother emerge with a shopping cart full of stolen metal. In their rattling cart they "shoot down Fulton and cross Fayette where the corner boys are touting a fresh heroin package. . . . There is no way to sense the speed involved unless you're with them, cantering beside a full shopping cart, making for the scales in absolute earnest."[19]

That's our excited reporter "cantering" right alongside them. And this is our reporter in the next section, pronouncing upon the meaning of the scene:

> Behold the ants. . . . Day after day, they rattle back and forth with their shopping carts, crowbars and mauls at the ready, devouring Baltimore bite by bite. . . . Right now they're taking the downspouts from Westport's public housing, and the metal handrails from a Wilkens Avenue rowhouse. . . . On Lafayette Square, there's a church that closed on Friday with copper flashing adorning the room; come Sunday, it rained in the house of the Lord.

Sun Magazine

THE BALTIMORE SUN   SEPTEMBER 3, 1995

Heavy Into Metal

Aluminum, iron, copper and brass —
you name it, they'll steal it

BY DAVID SIMON
PHOTOGRAPHY BY MICHAEL LUTZKY

"The Metal Men" as it appeared in the *Sun*

As the metaphor of the ants suggests, our reporter is more than a little in awe of the sheer energy and speed of the dismantling, even as he acknowledges the cannibalizing waste:

> The metal men know that it's late in the game—that the neighborhoods around the scrap yards have been stripped bare of the best stuff. Now, a good afternoon's work can be dragging a pair of 250-pound radiators for 12 blocks in the hot summer sun. But still, that's $10. And $10 will get you a vial of heroin and a cap of cocaine to go on top.
> The ants are here; the picnic is us.[20]

The story shifts to the repercussions of metal scavenging located at other sites: the director of a nonprofit cooperative seeking to rehabilitate rental units for low-income residents surveys the devastation of a gutted shooting gallery that is beyond the point of restoration; the housing commission seeking to quickly restore housing units by using bidless contracts is encouraged to engage in corrupt deals and high prices; the company that buys the stolen metal is indifferent to the obvious illegality of its source; a police colonel, Ronald Daniel, lacks officers to police the problem. A later scene introduces a character who was not present at the initial scavenging but is also a metal man; his name is Gary. He hovers around the edges of the story and chimes in whenever Simon's story demands a more articulate and moral voice, the voice of someone who knows that scavenging is wrong, who would like to earn a more legitimate dollar but who, like the others, can't work for that "wait-for-Friday money" because he needs his daily fix.

A final scene in this six-section story has the original metal men, Kenny and Tyrone, and a cohort getting high in the wrecked basement of what was once their neighborhood's after-hours club. Again here Gary comes into the story as a commentator. The story concludes:

> And Gary—he's a hard-core metal man only in the cold months, when business gets weak at the crab house where he's been working and they cut him back to a day or two a week. Come warmer weather and he's back in the kitchen, where the crab house pays cash every day—same as at the scales.
>
> They all claim to pull carts because a job isn't available, because the jobs are gone and this is a way to make money from nothing. But in the same breath they admit they can't work for that wait-for-Friday money. These are desperate lives that can stand no structure, though that's not to say there's anything fleeting or temporal about the game itself. Metaling is now a fixed part of the city's drug culture, certain to endure for as long as the scales stay open and the dealers want cash for vials, for as long as some unguarded part of Baltimore can be pried apart.
>
> The ants will see to it. Grant them, at least, some small due for creating wealth by destroying wealth, for going beyond the stereotype that says a dope fiend stands on a corner all day, scratching and nodding. Hard work doesn't scare a metal man.
>
> "Sometimes," says Gary, "getting high is the toughest job there is."[21]

Viewers of *The Wire* and readers and viewers of *The Corner* (book 1997; miniseries 2000) may recognize a number of features in this multipart work of journalism that would end up in the series: Daniel, the police colonel with no staff to foil the metal men, is surely a prototype of Lieutenant—and then Major—Cedric Daniels; they will certainly recognize in Gary more than a glimmer of one of the series's most beloved characters, Reginald ("Bubbles") Cousins— metal man and scam artist extraordinaire. With antlike persever- ance, this sometime criminal informant, metal scavenger, and ama- teur philosopher is found, halfway through the third season of *The Wire*, converting his metal-scavenging shopping cart to a quasi-legal traveling emporium to sell T-shirts and discarded cell phones in Hamsterdam; in the fourth season he turns up at the middle school trying to enroll his latest, and youngest, partner in crime. By the end of the fifth season he has been clean for a year and is selling the *Baltimore Sun* on the street while serving as the subject of a jour- nalistic profile in the very paper he sells. Bubbles, as a character, is the fictional device that allows Simon to develop and expand the ethnographic observation of his two initial sites of cops and corners into a multisited system. His pathos, his enterprise, his addiction, his doomed relationships with younger comrades, all grow out of the thick descriptions of Simon's previous reporting. Yet no one figure of that reporting could do the emotional and ideological work of this one character. Bubbles is fiction, but he grows out of an amalgam of two real men: a twenty-year criminal informant called Possum and Gary from "The Metal Men."

Gary turns up in the *Sun* article "The Metal Men" because he was then being exhaustively researched as one of the main characters of Simon and Ed Burns's ethnographic nonfiction, *The Corner: A Year in the Life of an Inner-City Neighborhood*. He is the son of a church- going family who came to Baltimore in the Great Migration from the Deep South and briefly prospered. Gary too prospered. But instead of leaving home like his siblings, he stays in the neighborhood, marries Fran, and has a son. Fran becomes a hard-core addict, and eventually Gary does too. He is the mostly absent father of D'Andre, an up-and- coming young dealer. Gary is not an overt victim of social circum-

(LEFT)
Daniels, from Daniel in "The Metal Men"
Bubbles and Johnny race for the scales
Bubbles on a scam

(ABOVE)
Bubbles selling T-shirts in Hamsterdam

stances. He does not lack education or a moral upbringing. As a result, however, he has never been street hard, and the failed Baltimore neighborhood he sticks to is the worst environment he could possibly find himself in. We meet Gary early in *The Corner*, getting high in the empty three-floor Victorian he once owned, recalling the day's earlier caper scavenging copper right out of the basement of an occupied house. Gary's metal-scavenging escapades punctuate the book; they embody what is left of his work ethic and optimism—an optimism that will eventually fuel the creation of the fictional and even more effervescent Bubbles.

Though the real Gary can beautifully represent his own doomed world, and though he can provide the phrase "Leave it to Beaverland" to describe the foreignness of the world of suburbia, he cannot, like the fictional Bubbles, lead us very far into these other worlds. Gary cannot pivot between cops and corners; he cannot visit "Leave it to Beaverland" except to get arrested; he cannot put hats on the major dealers so the cops can ID them. Simon clearly loves Gary, but, restrained by facts, he cannot make him either as perceptive and insightful or as sympathetic as Bubbles. He cannot use Gary, as he uses Bubbles, to silently witness the totality of what transpires not only on the corner but also with the cops, in the schools, or even as a media story himself. He cannot use Gary to witness the folly and the grandeur of the fictional experiment that was Hamsterdam. Neither can he redeem the historical Gary. Gary dies of an overdose, and Possum, the other factual basis of Bubbles, dies of AIDS. Both of these fates clearly haunt Bubbles too, but Simon chooses to portray Bubbles's life as one of the few moderately hopeful stories in *The Wire*.

The point is not that Simon's Bubbles is a more sentimental and hopeful version of Gary (and Possum) and therefore that *The Wire's* fiction softens the otherwise too realist ethnography. Such an argument implies that only an irredeemably bleak picture of the multiple sites of the city are the "true" ones, as if this one strand of "happy ending" negates the realism of the rest. This would be a definition of realism that opposes things as they are to things as we might want them to be and that sees melodrama as diametrically opposed to realism, an impression I hope to correct throughout this book.

Bubbles performs the fictional function of the typical Dickensian underclass character—which is not only to make us love him despite his foibles but also to connect the different sites of serially unfolding social worlds via his movement through them. However, Simon's ethnographic imaginary does not permit him, as Dickens once used his sympathetic lower-class characters, to use Bubbles to orchestrate melodramatic happy ends. Nor does it permit him, as Dickens frequently did, to drop this connector after he has served his purpose of uniting the more "central" middle-class characters. Bubbles is as central a character as one can be in a serial melodrama with some thirty-five crucially important characters developed over five primary sites, for the dramatic form forged out of the multisited ethnographic imaginary of this sixty plus hour work can best be described as serial melodrama with occasional overtones of tragedy. What is different about this serial melodrama from most of what we see today on television is not so much that it is consistently based on "real events"—after all, the drugs-are-allowed scenario of "Hamsterdam" is hardly a real event—but the very detailed multisited ethnographic knowledge that goes into the construction of the tale as a whole.

From Op-Ed Rant to Ethnographic Serial Melodrama

"The Metal Men" is a late and decisive work in Simon's career at the *Baltimore Sun*. It begins as a story about the scandal of scavengers in the voice of an outraged but unquestionably classed and raced citizen ("The ants are here; the picnic is us"). Although the story of the ants is told with great sympathy, there is no mistaking the white middle-class "us" on whom those ants are feasting. Simon strains to tell the larger economic story of absent jobs and the need to fill this absence with a vocation of a sort. And it is precisely this larger economic situation—the complexity of the connections between metal men, housing commission, cops, and metal dealers—and the story's obvious sympathy for the metal men themselves that supposedly caused Simon's editor, John Carroll, at the *Sun* to attempt to "kill" the story.[22] In the end, however, the story ran prominently, all in one piece, in the *Sun Magazine*, occupying nine pages and with many accompanying photos. According to Lawrence Lanahan, another editor, Jan Winburn, convinced Carroll to print it. But by this time Simon had had it. He had already had a series on race rejected, and he felt his book journalism should have earned him a raise. He took a buyout and pursued a standing offer to write for the television series based on his earlier nonfiction book *Homicide*.[23]

Sun editor John Carroll would later contend that Simon's "Metal Men" was too similar to the work he was doing for *The Corner*, which probably means that it had too much New Journalism insight into characters and not enough fact-based original reporting. Simon refutes this, arguing that he did original reporting with mostly newfound sources, and that Carroll's contention ignores the fact that *The Corner* would not be published until two years after the "Metal Men" story. Simon's other boss at the *Sun*, Bill Marimow, also objected that the piece ennobled the thieves who were stripping the city of its infrastructure.[24] Marimow would have preferred a simpler story about the scandal of the scavenger.

Simon is still angry and calls his editors "venal," citing their "tumescence" at the very word "Pulitzer" (which he never, and they both, received).[25] The quarrel with his editors certainly raises the question of what journalism should be. More tellingly, for us, however, it points to what *The Wire* would become. Simon believed that newspapers should adopt a "broad sociological approach"; Carroll and Marimow believed they should aim a "rifle shot" at narrower stories and individual problems. Simon derides the rifle-shot approach as follows: "Surround a simple outrage, overreport it, claim credit for breaking it, make sure you find a villain, then claim you effected change as a result of your coverage. Do it in a five-part series, and make sure you get 'the *Baltimore Sun* has learned' in the second graph."[26] At issue is how much you report only on the narrow individual story—often necessarily reduced in short-form journalism to the melodramatic story of villainy or victimization—or how much you explain the whole system that leads to the story. As Simon put it, "one story is small, self-contained and has good guys and bad guys, while "the other one is about where we are and where we're going as an urban society and who's being left behind, and it's harder to report."[27] "The Metal Men" seeks to explain the system and is indeed more ambitious and complex than the usual expose-a-simple-wrong rifle shot or even than Simon's excellent early reporting in the Little Melvin Williams story, but there is also no doubt where Simon's sympathies lie: not with the police colonel, not with the housing commissioner, certainly not with the scrap metal companies, but with Gary as the eloquent voice behind the deeds we actually see Kenneth and Tyrone commit.[28]

Simon sees himself on the side of "a nuanced world with complex human beings," while Carroll and Marimow see themselves as performing a public service that cannot reach for the larger ethnographic complexities when they have a victim to champion or a wrong to expose. Cast this way, the argument seems to be about Simon's nuance and complexity versus the black-and-white outlook of his editors. With the hindsight of the achievement of *The Wire* it is tempting to side with Simon against the Pulitzer lust of the newspaper business and to place him, as even his former editor John Carroll puts it, "on the side of the angels."[29] However, this would be to succumb to the simplistic vilification of melodrama itself as precisely the story of good and evil that Simon claims to have renounced. Furthermore, it would be to misunderstand the deeper value of the new kind of television serial melodrama that can juxtapose dramatically different worlds over time, allowing situations to ripen, characters to change, history to unfold.

To put Simon's argument with his editors into televisual terms, the good guys and bad guys' "rifle-shot" reporting is like an hour of episodic television whose world is necessarily narrow and whose time is limited to a half hour or hour. In contrast, it is the expanded world of many sites, and it is time—that extra time in 2007–2008 that I had to watch television, the extra time that *The Wire* takes to develop and interweave plots, and to prepare the significance of a character and his or her place in an institution, the extra time that Simon had to unfold the story of Baltimore over five seasons and five years of narrative time—that enabled him, as Lorrie Moore puts it, to "transform a social type into a human being, demography into dramaturgy."[30] With "world enough and time," it becomes possible, as Walter Benn Michaels puts it, for the series to be "about the world neoliberalism has actually produced rather than the world our literature pretends it has."[31]

Simon was a tenacious reporter because he did not just want to get facts and expose a "simple outrage." He wanted to expose the larger institutional and systemic ones. In "The Metal Men" those outrages were not just the scavengers but also the lack of work, the corrupt scrap dealers, an overwhelmed police department, a corrupt housing commission. We can appreciate how Simon strained against the limits of the *Baltimore Sun*, but we can also see how the short "graph" and the relatively short punchy story represent the fundamental discipline of reporting that Simon absorbed from journalism and that would help him build the greater scope and institutional complexity of *The Wire*.

Still, Simon's editors did have a point. You can lose your reader if you go off—as Simon often does go off in *Homicide* and *The Corner*, and even in "The Metal Men"—into long sociological arguments about what's wrong with the culture that produces dope fiends instead of citizens. You can lose your audience when an ethnographic story tips over into an overlong op-ed—or what can only be called the Simon rant.[32]

In all Simon's journalism—both the long and the short forms—the editorial comments are presented in his own white, middle-class, educated, impassioned voice—the kind of male voice that can boom out with mixed admiration and outrage. Given the extended length of a book like *The Corner*, this is a voice that can rage on and on about the futility of "the war on drugs" in an impassioned and royal "we":

> We can't stop it.
>
> Not with all the lawyers, guns, and money in this world. Not with guilt or morality or righteous indignation. . . . No lasting victory in the war on drugs can be bought by doubling the number of beat cops or tripling the number of prisons. . . . Down on Fayette Street, they know. . . . In the empty heart of our cities, the culture of drugs has created a wealth-generating structure so elemental and enduring that it can legitimately be called a social compact. . . . At Monroe and Fayette, and in drug markets in cities across the nation, lives without any obvious justification are given definition through a simple, self-sustaining capitalism. The corner has a place for them. . . . Touts, runners, lookouts, mules, stickup boys, stash stealers, enforcers, fiends, burn artists, police snitches—all are necessary in the world of the corner. . . . In this place only they belong. In this place only, they know what they are, why they are, and what it is that they are supposed to do.

Here, they almost matter. . . . We want it to be about nothing more complicated than cash money and human greed, when at bottom, it's about a
reason to believe, that it's all about the addictive mind, when instead it has
become about validation, about lost souls assuring themselves that a daily
relevance can be found at the fine point of a disposable syringe.[33]

Eloquent, passionate, ironic, angry; this is the voice of David Simon in
an "editorial" about Gary and his corner world that goes on for eigh-
teen pages, turning into a history of the drug trade in Baltimore from
the time of the heroin-using fringe hipsters of the late fifties through the
cocaine revolution and into the early nineties, when the mothers—once
the bastions of the community—became dope fiends also.

This editorial voice speaks *on behalf* of the victims of a dysfunctional,
drug-addled society, but it is not *of* them. Because it has done its ethnographic homework, it feels entitled to speak as a royal "we." Simon's
other long argumentative essays include a beautiful set piece on "the
quiet genius" of "the paper bag"—"a staple of ghetto diplomacy in all
the major American cities." This bag disguised the public consump-
tion of alcohol and made it possible for the government to ignore "the
inevitable petty vices of urban living and concentrate instead on the
essential." But since there is no equivalent of the paper bag in the war
on drugs, our editorialist explains, there can be no "accommodation
between the drug subculture and those policing it. . . . Rather than accept the personal decision to use drugs as a given—to seek out a paper-
bag-solution to the corner's growing numbers—we tried to live by mass
arrest."[34]

Other such "editorials" in *The Corner* treat the scandal and waste of
prisons, the lack of real training for police, the economic failure of the
American Dream, and the reason the schools, once "the way out for us
and our parents," can "no longer save us." These public schools "that
launched the immigrant masses out of the pushcart ghettos and into
manicured suburbs hold a place of honor in the American mythology,"
but not, this editorial goes on to tell us, in the American reality of West
Baltimore. Yet another editorial offers an argumentative essay on teen
pregnancy ("accident is not at all the word for it"),[35] while another
compares the school system's "juking the stats" to give students higher

scores to the police department's reclassifying crimes to make them seem less sinister.[36]

A final editorial represents the apotheosis of this impassioned white middle-class op-ed: what if "we" were in "their" shoes?

> We'd persevere, wouldn't we? . . . Come payday we wouldn't blow that minimum-wage check on Nikes, or Fila sweat suits or Friday night movies at Harbor Park with the neighborhood girls. . . . We'll head off to our college years shining like a new dime, swearing never to set foot on West Fayette Street again. . . . We would rise above the corner. And when we tell ourselves such things, we unthinkly [sic] assume that we would be consigned to places like Fayette Street fully equipped with all the graces and disciplines, talents and training that we now possess. . . . We would be saved and as it always is in matters of salvation we know this as a matter of perfect, pristine faith.
>
> Why? The truth is plain:
>
> We were not born to be niggers.[37]

Fans of *The Wire* will recognize in the preceding "op-ed" rants many of the crucial themes of the series, as well as the genesis for many of its greatest dramatic actions: the futile "war on drugs" that will be repeatedly compared in the post-9/11 context to the equally futile "war on terror;" the deep embeddedness of drugs as the only viable source of income and the only reliable diversion; the paper bag that police Major "Bunny" Colvin will hold up in a district meeting, calling it a "great moment of civic compromise." Colvin's speech (3.2) lays the moral groundwork for his subsequent "Hamsterdam" experiment—to create the equivalent of a paper bag for drugs (3.4–3.8). The failure of schools will find its greatest expression in the focus on Tilghman Middle School in season 4 when former police officer Roland "Prez" Pryzbylewski notes that the schools operate with the same set of procedures as his old police bosses, by "juking the stats."

We are relieved of Simon's most impassioned "op-ed" rants because in *The Wire* they have been spoken from the mouths of characters in dramatic situations. In this form we don't feel lectured at. The op-ed transmutes into drama spread out over the course of the five seasons, and the point of view expressed in "We were not born to be niggers" is

Bubbles "schools"
Sherrod among the
ruins of Hamsterdam

fortunately no longer necessary. At its very best, "we" ceases to be "us" trying to understand "them."[38] What Simon discovers when he turns to the melodramatic serial is a way to let one "site" function as the commentary on another. He no longer needs to pronounce in an editorial voice on the dysfunctions of any one system.

For example, in the last scene of season 3 we find Bubbles and his latest protégé scavenging metal with his shopping cart amid the piled-up ruins of Hamsterdam. The city has torn down the "paper-bag" experiment where drugs were tolerated, the experiment that ended Colvin's police career. It has also ended Bubbles's incipient retail career, conducted, just as metal scavenging is, with the aid of his ubiquitous shopping cart. Bubbles teaches a new scavenging partner the value of aluminum that he pulls out of the rubble. He also gives advice to his inexperienced colleague: "You green; you think you brown but you green. . . . I hope you listening because I'm trying to school you here" (3.12). Here we catch Bubbles in a pattern of repetition, tutoring another younger man the same way he did Johnny in the first scene. Like the real Gary before him, he is excited about the possibilities of earning enough for a fix through this scavenging hustle. (But in this case he is also preparing us, thematically, for the next season's shift to the new site of the school.)

Bubbles suddenly pauses as he spies Colvin standing alone in civilian garb, before the bulldozed ruins of his former experiment. Neither knows the other. Together they silently contemplate the deserted scene, each for his own reasons regretting what once had been. Finally Bubbles says to Colvin: "That's something, huh . . . like someone took a big eraser

"Like someone took a
big eraser and rubbed
across it"

"It was a good thing, huh?"

and rubbed across it." Colvin, defeated, just looks at Bubbles. Bubbles continues, "But before, a dope fiend come down here, cop a little somethin'—ain't narry a soul hassle him—they just let him be." Colvin cautiously asks, "It was a good thing, huh?" Bubbles, equally cautious, backpedals, "I'm just sayin,'" but as he walks away to join his partner and continue along with his shopping cart, he explains his regret at the loss of the great experiment: "You probably don't know, but its rough out there, baby; cops be banging on you; hoppers be messing with you." Colvin stands alone again before his failed experiment as Bubbles moves away, and says, "Yeah, thank you."

If Simon had still been writing journalism, this would be the place where his op-ed would dilate upon the ruins of a noble social experiment—the equivalent of a "paper bag for drugs." It would be the place where he would pronounce upon the good of Colvin's attempt and the evil of the police and city government officials who shut it down; it

Crane up and back in a
rare end-of-season flourish

would also be the place to expound upon the many reasons for the inability to solve the problems of a drug-wracked neighborhood. Instead we are given this quiet acknowledgment of the "good thing" that was Hamsterdam—the dramatic and failed solution to these problems—by the one person able to recognize it because he lived it. But we should not let the understated nature of the scene fool us. This is one of those wonderful melodramatic coincidences when two characters we have grown to love and admire, coming from very different social worlds, coincide and, however briefly, understand one another. This is also what melodrama scholars have called a "recognition of virtue." In an old-fashioned melodrama it might be that moment when the woman rescued from an ice floe, formerly banished from the community of the "good," is recognized for her suffering—say, Lillian Gish at the end of *Way Down East,* when she even forgives the villain who deceived her.[39] The point of suffering in melodrama is usually to enable an otherwise invisible "moral legibility."

In David Simon's journalistic op-ed rants he would pity the victims of adverse social conditions, even if they were drug addicts, and he would condemn the city, the police, the general lack of understanding that simply blamed them for their addiction. Here, however, he has discovered a new way of doing what the newspaper business (in his ideal vision) should have been doing but was not. In this switch from telling to showing, from telling us how *he* feels about some outrage, he now makes us feel the outrage as it impinges upon characters. In other words, and thankfully, compared to the op-ed, not in *so many* words, as the camera cranes up and back in a rare flourish, and as we hear the rare melos that marks the end of an episode (and in this case the end of a season), we understand that we have just seen the one person in the series qualified to pronounce upon the "good" that *was* Hamsterdam and thus the good that *is* ex-Major Colvin. The "moral legibility" of melodrama is served.

David Simon may have quit the newspaper business, but the newspaper business did not quit him. In place of the five-paragraph rifle-shot story, he would eventually create a five-season cumulative serial whose primary outrage—a futile war on drugs—encompasses myriad others. These outrages are never simple; they are multiple and compounded. In place of the credit to the *Baltimore Sun*, the credit will go to HBO. In place of a tone-deaf editorial voice of "dissent," he will disperse the dramatic voices of characters from across the spectrum of Baltimore life, opting for a multisited ethnographic imaginary where serial melodrama can show us, in a way sociologists and ethnographers cannot, how much, as Detective Lester Freamon puts it, "all the pieces matter."

2 Serial Television's World and Time

THE IMPORTANCE OF THE "PART"

> Sometimes the weakest shit in a story is the stuff
> with quotation marks around it. You got a guy telling us how
> rough it is on the street. . . . That doesn't have much pull; but
> if you can describe how it really is, *tell his story in moments*. . . .
> — Gus Haynes, season 5, *The Wire*

When David Simon left the newspaper business to write occasional scripts for the weekly cop show *Homicide: Life on the Street* (NBC, 1993–1999), based on his own nonfiction book, he had to first learn to write for television.[1] Simon's publisher had sent the book to the film director (and Baltimore native) Barry Levinson hoping it might become a film. Levinson realized that the premise of the book—a group of grumpy, eccentric black, white, and ethnic homicide cops who do not always solve their crimes—could last much longer than a single "year in the life of the killing streets"—as the subtitle of Simon's book put it. The subtitle was thus changed to the slightly more upbeat *Life on the Street* and the situation was adapted to hour-long episodes of serial television. As in most cop shows on television, the cops would be there each episode but the perpetrators and victims would change. Thus, even before Simon began to argue with his bosses at the *Sun* over the value of his "Metal Men" series, the pilot of *Homicide: Life on the Street*, directed by Levinson, written by Paul Anastasio, aired on January 31, 1993.

The series began as a relatively "strong" serial with many ongoing subplots extending over several episodes. It completed its first nine-episode season and eventually won a Peabody Award for best drama. Often shot on location with a purposely jerky, hand-held 16mm camera, the series was praised for its authentic view of crime, neighborhoods, and calloused but interesting cops. But the series did not do well in the ratings and a second season was only begrudgingly granted by NBC. It was among the shortest ever scheduled—only four episodes. By this time David Simon was eager to join the action. He and his old newspaper colleague David Mills wrote what was originally intended to be the last episode of this short second season, based on a story by Tom Fontana. For this season, producers Fontana and Levinson had been ordered by NBC to brighten the mood, to eliminate multiple subplots, and to concentrate on a more satisfying main story that would conclude in each episode. Ironically, then, Simon's first assignment writing for television charged him with turning a police procedural known for its ethnographic accuracy and deeper contextualization into something more like the dreaded "rifle-shot" approach that he had left the *Sun* to avoid. Novice that he was, Simon complied. The resulting script, which opened the season, attracted a higher caliber of guest star than previously featured in the person of Robin Williams. With these concessions toward the televisual version of the "rifle shot," *Homicide: Life on the Street* became a modest hit and would endure for seven seasons. *Homicide* thus served as Simon's second apprenticeship building skills that he would contribute to *The Wire*. Like it or not, as with his first apprenticeship, Simon learned to hone the craft of efficient televisual writing.

However, before he embarked on *The Wire*, he served a third apprenticeship in the televisual adaptation of his own long-form journalism in the miniseries *The Corner* (HBO 2000). This time he was not adapting ethnography into fiction, but dramatically rendering the documentary "truths" he had already recorded in that book. The series won a Peabody Award and was nominated for several Emmys. The prestige of these awards helped put in place a great many of the essentials that would benefit *The Wire* two years later: including a cohesive production team working with a cohort of remarkable black actors in a story of drugs in inner-city Baltimore; and the benefit of the aegis of HBO, the most "premium" of the premium cable channels at a time when both cable and networks were pursuing stronger forms of seriality.[2]

HBO already had two of the most popular cable hits in 2000 with *Sex and the City* (1998–2004) and *The Sopranos* (1999–2007) when it produced *The Corner*. The miniseries was based on the true events of the 1997 book, which itself looked back to the year 1993, which Simon and Burns spent researching the West Baltimore neighborhood corner where West Fayette Street meets Monroe. Once again, it is the life of the real Gary, the addict who showed up in Simon's journalistic "Metal Men" article, that forms the basis of the story. Gary, his wife, Fran, and their son DeAndre, who himself soon has a child with the thirteen-year-old Tyreeka constitute the primary characters. All but the young DeAndre and Tyreeka are addicts.

Once again we find Simon, working with cowriter David Mills, learning to avoid the impassioned "op-ed" rants of his earlier journalism by locating the drama in the mouths of his characters. But now, with the greater temporal extension of a six-hour, six-part miniseries Simon and Mills could expand the narrow rifle shot of both journalism and the television series *Homicide* into an almost epic-sized canvas. In this case, we do not (quite) feel lectured at by the white, middle-class Simon and Burns in this dramatic rendition of the lives of real people acted by professional actors in a sometimes faux-documentary style because the black director Charles S. Dutton, standing in for Simon and Burns, serves as initial narrator and "host." Dutton himself stands on the corner, addressing the camera to attest to his own knowledge of this scene:

> I grew up and hung out on a corner just like this one . . . a corner like thousands of others across the country . . . the information center of the neighborhood. You want to know who's got the good drugs, who got killed last night and why and who did it, you come here. The contradiction of it is, on one hand the corner pulsates with life, the energy of human beings trying to make it to the next day. But also, it's the place of death, of addiction or the suddenness of gunshots. Thirty years ago when I was hanging out here it was bad, but then Maryland had only five penal institutions. Today there are twenty-eight. . . . There are a hundred open-air drug markets in Baltimore, thousands in America whether the rest of the country wants to

Charles Dutton stands
on "the corner"

think about them or not. This film is a true story of men, women, and children living in the midst of the drug trade. Their voices are too rarely heard.

Thus does Dutton's own reportorial voice seem to eliminate the us/them problem of Simon and Burns's white, middle-class op-ed. Because Dutton is a black man from Baltimore, he seems entitled to "report" on the life of the corner.

However, if Simon and Mills avoid the problem of the white authorial "us" and the black "them" of Simon and Burns's original ethnography it is only because they have provided a black surrogate by placing Dutton in the (fake) position of ethnographer following these stories that have already been followed by Simon and Burns. As a result, these beautifully acted and lovingly directed segments sometimes smack, especially in these introductory and concluding sequences, of a documentary didacticism that is not ameliorated by being "faux." For example, in the first shot of the first hour-long segment, "Gary's Blues," Dutton "interviews" Gary (played by T. K. Carter) as he walks fast down a back alley. As Gary walks forward facing the camera, we imagine the unseen Dutton and camera crew walking backward as if catching Gary on the fly. We hear Dutton's voice as he tries to get Gary to explain why he has fallen from his former entrepreneurial heights to his current abject state. This questioning continues, with Gary proud to boast of his former glory, until he arrives at the eponymous corner and Dutton asks, in empathic tones, "What happened [to make you an addict], Gary?" The ashamed Gary avoids answering by ducking into the corner Korean convenience store to buy a cigarette, while the camera pans clockwise from the doorway into which Gary has disappeared. A bravura, perfectly timed 360-degree survey of the entire scene of the corner follows, revealing the ravaged intersection of West Fayette and Monroe; some of the bystanders revealed stare at the camera, others greet Dutton. Just as the pan comes full circle, Gary reemerges from the doorway, a twenty-five-cent cigarette in hand. Once again Gary is confronted by the camera and Dutton's voice, still trying to understand "what happened" to bring Gary to the condition of buying his cigarettes one at a time. Avoiding the question, Gary is nevertheless still happy to reminisce about the old days when he used to work at this same store, giving Dutton advice as to whom else he should interview. When Dutton asks again what went wrong to bring Gary to this condition, he hustles off into the street, back now to the camera, apparently to seek the money for his next fix.

Fortunately, this long-take, perfectly rehearsed, faux-verite style is not sustained throughout the rest of the miniseries. It is deployed only at the beginning of each episode to help us "get into" the individual stories via documentary interviews, and then again at the end to get us out. The rest of the miniseries proceeds as a more normal fictional narration. The fates of the Gary McCullough/Fran Boyd families extend over the time of the year chronicled in Simon and Burns's nonfiction book. During this time, DeAndre begins dealing; his thirteen-year-old girlfriend gives birth; Fran, the matriarch, gets clean but occasionally falls back; DeAndre tries to "step up" to being a father but can't find legitimate work and so falls back into dealing and finally into using; gentle, proud Gary keeps hustling, showing glimpses of shame and conscience, and eventually finds a peaceful death in overdose.

At the end of the sixth and final episode, "Everyman's Blues," director Dutton reappears on the corner to introduce the real Fran Boyd, her son DeAndre (along with DeAndre's former girlfriend, Tyreeka, and Blue, another minor denizen of the corner who has survived). Dutton asks them what effect this movie of their lives has had on them. Predictably, all say it has convinced them to "be strong," to avoid drugs, and to be better models for their children—in fact, to be what Dutton's voice-over interviews have been urging them to be all along. Subdued, and less vibrant than the actors who played them, and with the marked

Dutton asks Gary, "What happened?"

Gary reminisces about working in this corner store

Gary eludes his questioner

The real Fran;
the real Tyreeka

absence of the deceased Gary, they are a sober, remorseful, and pathetic lot. Dutton ends the sequence by giving hugs all around.

Mixed bag that it is, *The Corner* was much praised for its authenticity and social realism by those critics who noted it. *Variety*, for example, praised Dutton for ensuring that "the audience at home feels the pain and inescapability of the streets," as if the audience at home could not understand or endure this pain without Dutton to explain it to them (the omission of such a buffer would perhaps be the most singular achievement of *The Wire*). It then offered the predictable praise of actors, "all of them in roles that can't be pitied or hated [who] . . . turn in top-notch perfs. . . . In an arena where it is so easy to overact, this ensemble keeps the action tight and focused."[3] However, the series, like *The Wire* later, was not popular; it was not until *The Corner* won a Peabody, three Emmys (best miniseries, best writing, and best directing), and emerged three years later on DVD that it began to earn something more than a dutiful "this is a social problem we need to face" kind of criticism. And one reason for the greater enthusiasm of these later reviews is that by then *The Corner* could be recognized as the crucible out of which the much less didactic and dutiful *The Wire* had grown. In other words, if today we find Dutton's sympathetic docudrama over-earnest and even condescending (as, for example, in his off-camera prodding of Fran to be a better mother, or in his efforts to pull platitudes out of their mouths and to deliver hugs to the survivors at the end), it may be because *The Wire* has shown that (at least HBO) audiences do not need host-buffers

Roots: the only previous television serial with a majority black cast

between, as *Variety* put it, the "home" audience and "street" addiction to pander to them. The point, however, is that even the ambitious HBO, as well as the writers adapting the book, Simon and his friend David Mills, *thought* there was a need.

In the tradition of race-oriented television miniseries, we have to go all the way back to Alex Haley's *Roots* (ABC, 1977) to find a moment when television trusted that the serialized concerns of a black family broken by slavery could sustain viewership for more than the usual episode of conventional television, though of course *Roots* only did so with the added attraction of cameos by many white stars and with the appearance of Alex Haley at the end as its very own host-buffer. Twenty-three years later, HBO's *The Corner* offered another TV miniseries, also based on the model of a black family saga—this one broken not by slavery but by poverty and drugs. Dutiful, overempathic, and crudely melodramatic as it seems today (and *Roots* looks even worse), there is no question that *The Corner*'s critical success helped make the much bolder *The Wire* possible. Neither *The Corner* nor *The Wire* would be popular during their initial airing, even among HBO's purportedly hip, elite, and often black viewers. Indeed, David Simon's famous "Letter to HBO" urging them to go ahead with production of his initial scripts for *The Wire* counted on the cable channel's willingness to take the kind of chance they had already taken with *The Corner*.[4] Simon argued that as with *The Corner*, "the critics will be discerning if the quality is there." And as with *The Corner*, Simon strategized, it would be possible to film the whole season and thus offer the critics the "entire package" or most of it at the premiere so that no one could "possibly miss the point." That "point," most reviewers seemed to think, was the authenticity of the portrayal of (broken) family life in the drug-ravaged inner city. At some level, authenticity is indeed the "point" of *The Wire*. It was also the point of Simon's 1995 *Sun* article, "Metal Men": that sometimes "getting high is the toughest job there is." But authenticity can only take us so far in the discussion of these televisual forms.

Television Serial

Remarkable as it is, *The Wire* is not exempt from the structure of serial television melodrama manifest in the rest of popular television since the eighties, no matter how hard HBO might have tried to convince us that "it's not TV." We saw in chapter 1 how *The Wire* grew out of and improved on Simon's long-form journalism. Here we will see how it grew out of and improved on a televisual form whose original lingua franca was episodic melodrama, now becoming longer in miniseries, and then in open-ended multiseason serials. What would prove most remarkable about *The Wire*, however, is its move away from the tried-and-true family-saga melodrama into what I will call the serial melodrama of institutional connections.

The term "melodrama" was missing in the critical discourse about *The Corner*, and it has been mostly missing in that on *The Wire*. The "authenticity" for which both have been praised and that *The Wire* particularly prized has seemed contradictory to melodrama, traditionally considered a theatrically tinged, passé genre of vivid emotions conveyed as much through mise-en-scène and music as through dialogue. Yet if we return to the moment when television began to explore seriality beyond the obviously melodramatic soap operas, we find that the term was once much in evidence. In the 1980s, when network serials had their widest popularity with the long-playing, prime-time serials *Dallas* and *Dynasty*, there was no denying the big-emotion, good-evil melodrama of these particular family sagas. *Dallas*, for example, began as a five-part miniseries in the tradition of *Rich Man, Poor Man* or *Roots*—that is, as family saga melodrama. It was such an instant hit that it was soon continued as an outright serial on the model of the daytime soap opera with no predetermined end. And continue it did, from its 1978 debut throughout the 1980s and into a grand total of fourteen seasons. When it finally ended in 1991, it would be counted second only to *Gunsmoke* as the longest-running American television series.

During the 1980s, under the influence of these network "prime-time soaps," many familiar genres—cop, private eye, sci-fi, and doctor—were adapted into serial melodramas. These series/serials were what Jeffrey Sconce, borrowing from Horace Newcomb, calls "cumulative" forms of storytelling.[5] While many of these series afforded strong closure of individual episodes, most had the ability to keep at least some narrative threads unresolved. For example, the hospital show and its different "crisis of the week" would now be interwoven with longer-term story lines that could recede or emerge any given week. Sconce writes "by focusing less on episodic treatments of crooks and patients and more on the serial development of *melodrama* involving the private eye, cops and doctors," the series/serial could become more complex.[6] With these changes, the serial accumulation of narrative that had once been reviled in soaps and other "low" genres increasingly becomes a source of praise; instead of being compared to soaps, the newer serials were dubbed "prime-time novels," and their soaplike narrative "convolution" was recast more positively as novelistic "complexity."[7] Within such a critical framework it is not surprising that the very term "melodrama," laudably still prominent in Sconce's description above, has very often been muffled in favor of the seemingly more realistic authenticity and presumably higher literary form of the novel. Of course there is also a strong gender component to the devaluation of feminized soap operas and (presumably more masculine and realistic) novels. I am even willing to speculate that part of the reason for the masculine dominance of so many contemporary serials from *The Sopranos*, through *The Wire*, *Breaking Bad*, and *Mad Men* is the desire to disassociate such work from the taint of the feminine family melodrama and their earlier soap-opera origins.

Given the mostly negative connotations of the term, it is not surprising that "quality television" of the sort represented by the above serialized dramas prefers not to be called melodrama. The following two chapters will probe this term further to explain why I think it is important to recognize the melodrama of a serial like *The Wire*, or indeed, most of the serials belonging to what some have called the Third Golden

Age of television and the "signature American art form of the first decade of the twenty-first century."[8] For the time being, however, let us simplify by saying there are two kinds of serial melodrama to be found on television and that both are descended originally from nineteenth-century serial fiction, radio and television soap operas, family saga miniseries, and the prime-time network serials mentioned above. The first kind, more readily found on one of the four networks, will usually acknowledge that it is melodrama by name and will come with numerous commercial interruptions. The second kind, the kind that doesn't like to call itself melodrama (usually because it considers itself too "authentic" or "novelistic," or simply "better than television") will usually come with fewer commercial interruptions on premium or basic cable.[9] The first kind usually builds sufficient redundancy into the program for the viewer who only occasionally tunes in to follow the story. The second kind rarely acknowledges its relation to melodrama, does not have as much built-in redundancy or compelling miniclimaxes designed to bring us back from the refrigerator over commercials—and many of them, the most "premium" of the cable channels, don't even have commercials.[10] These serials are often more demanding; they count on viewers to remember the narrative from episode to episode and season to season (exemplified as I write by *Breaking Bad*, but from 2002 to 2008 by *The Wire*).[11] Both kinds of serial melodrama can have varying degrees of seriality: at one end of the spectrum are episodes that may leave only a few threads of the ongoing narrative open. In the middle are the miniseries that may extend for several episodes but whose completion after four six or eight is usually foreordained (unless, like the network *Dallas* in the 1980s or the BBC/PBS *Downton Abbey* in the 2010s, it converts from a minseries into a serial). At the far end of the spectrum are episodes that do not resolve themselves and whose seasons are designed to continue, though unlike soaps not forever. These are what television critics call "strong serials."

What makes it possible for a serial—on network or cable—to hold our attention in an era when our multitasking attention spans, due to constant interruption by other media, have only grown shorter? If serial television lacks the spectacle inherent in cinema to *grab* our attention (and of course it does not entirely lack spectacle as its screens get larger and as it mixes old and invents new popular genres), it nevertheless manages to *hold* our attention for a remarkably long time. What is the secret of its ability to keep us glued to the screen, attending carefully to every detail and nuance of what transpires? The answer rests in the fundamental paradox of contemporary serial television. By parceling itself out in small "parts" it gains "world enough and time" to spin longer stories over possibly many social worlds. But unlike the daily soap operas or even the network primetime soaps that did not trust their viewers to pay attention, the extra attention required by viewers in the fewer episode-per-season cable drama is often rewarded both emotionally and intellectually by well-crafted narratives that used extra world and time to go deeper into problems, situations, and characters. Here was television that did not call for distraction and that did not feel like a waste of time.

"World enough and time" is what the poet in Andrew Marvell's famous carpe diem poem complains he does not have for the proper wooing of "his coy mistress": ("Had we but world enough, and time, / This coyness, Lady, were no crime").[12] Serial television, especially that shown today on premium cable, unlike Marvell's highly compressed poem, *does* have world and time, and not only for wooing. In it, any number of related storyworlds becomes part of an ever-shifting, still-developing whole, enjoyed as much in its many connected parts as in its finally resolved whole. Indeed, it is this very extended experience of world and time that is so seductive about the kind of serial television that rewards attention.[13] Thus, the more competition there is for our attention with computers, cell phones, and tweets, the more it has lately come to seem that seriality blooms. Put another way, the less time we have, the more time we spend watching in the parceled out mode of seriality. Stories composed and delivered in parts can be consumed in relatively short spans of time, making it possible to keep on reading or watching for an overall longer time, "hooked" on not so much a single story but the intertwining and unfolding of many stories.[14]

It is perfectly possible for a television showrunner to not take advantage of this greater world and time, to stick to a narrower world and a more delimited time, and only to develop what television writers like to call A- and B-level characters—major plots and secondary subplots.

The Sopranos is an excellent example. However, as Dickens showed with his last serial publication, *Our Mutual Friend* (1853), and as *The Wire* amply demonstrates, it is also possible to disperse and interweave narrative threads so thoroughly through so many different worlds that it becomes difficult to distinguish between A or B, C or D levels. Indeed, it can become nearly impossible to say who *is* a main character—in *The Wire* it is really not Detective Jimmy McNulty. When this happens, seriality performs an enlarged understanding of the idea of suspense, not as cliff-hanger but as one strand of narrative is suspended to make way for another and yet another.

Series/Season/Episode/Beat

In scripted television serial drama the length of a series is variable. Some unfortunate serials are not renewed or canceled midseason and thus cannot come to fruition. Such seemed to be the fate of the originally strong serial *Homicide* at the point Simon and Mills began to write for it (see chapter 1). The solution then was to change it to a weaker serial and to stick very close to those "killing streets." Others, like *Battlestar Galactica* (Sci-Fi 2004–2009) or *Lost* (ABC, 2004–2010), extravagantly expanded their (quite literal) storyworlds and were granted time to plan their conclusions (however disappointing some of us might have found them). The length of a season is also variable. Network seasons tend to offer up to twenty-four hour-long episodes including commercials (usually forty-three minutes of drama, seventeen minutes of commercials), while most premium cable series are twelve or thirteen commercial-less fifty-minute to hour-long segments, or even fewer. What is fairly constant in both, however, is the convention of the fifty-minute to sixty-minute "hour" as the basic unit of viewing time, with or without commercials, even though season premieres and finales sometimes extend to more time.

Why an hour? There are, of course, many popular half-hour shows, and certainly some of them are serialized. But most of these are comedies without particularly strong through stories: for example, Larry David's *Curb Your Enthusiasm* (2000–), *Parks and Recreation* (NBC, 2009–), *30 Rock* (NBC, 2006–2012), and *Two and a Half Men* (CBS,

2003–). The half-hour show tends to cater more to occasional viewers, while the television unit that tends to command the more serious critical attention is the hour. In the hour serials, the perception of constant flow is made possible by the organization of precisely timed short parts. The short part then makes possible the longer serial time of the season and the series. Today that shorter piece is the hour-long segment (just as for Dickens it was a two- or three-chapter installment). A network serial like *24* (Fox 2001–2009) was emblematic of the temporal sensibility of the hour segment. Each season was organized into twenty-four one-hour segments of "real time"—the first hour of the first episode is called "12:00 AM–1:00 AM," the second episode is called "1:00 AM–2:00 AM," and so on. Thus each episode provided an acute sense of the pressure of time–deadlines, fast action, and suspense–in the busy life of Jack Bauer, counterterrorist. Each episode acted as "an extended temporal signifier" in which the allotted time is experienced acutely in the mode of suspense.[15] Watched on television, the miniclimax is designed to pull us back over the interruption of the commercial and to make us feel the pressure of the hour as container for the weekly dose of suspenseful melodrama. Watched on DVD or DVR without the commercials, one has the sense of redundancy caused by the little backtracks in time necessary after the break of a commercial. Watched either way, one has an acute awareness of time itself.

Even when there is not such an overt melodramatic structuring of suspense in a literal countdown to a deadline, we nevertheless feel the "pressure of the hour" in each hour-long episode of a serial. This hour becomes distinctly more tangible in comparison to the longer and often less regular rhythms of feature films.[16] What is perhaps remarkable, however, is that we even feel this temporal pressure in series that do not have commercials. We feel it, in other words, whether we watch fifty-nine minutes of uninterrupted premium cable or forty-three minutes interwoven with seventeen minutes of commercials on a broadcast serial. We feel this temporal rhythm, I believe, because it is the very essence of television. Indeed, it is not television's smaller budgets or smaller screens that mark its difference from movies but this rhythmic adherence to regularity of segmentation, or what one television scholar writing about television in general has called a "dialectic of seg-

mentation and flow" and what another has called the poetics of seriality, basically "the old, the new, and the gap (or the 'between')."[17] This
latter scholar, Sean O'Sullivan, argues, for example, that in season 1 of
the *Sopranos*, the segmented quality of the serial's structure offers a
poetics that not only moves us from place to place but creates parallels,
contrasts, and interruptions, requiring us to see the pieces *as* pieces.
Such is television's distinct aesthetic form, and it contrasts with that of
cinema, whose viewing time does not need to obey "the pressure of the
hour" and whose segments are longer and whose rhythms can be much
more various.

The regularity of the hour is matched by the regularity of the smallest
segment of the televisual hour: what television writers call the beat.[18] A
beat is the smallest unit of television space-time; it is the basic building
block of television drama and part of what television scholar Michael Z.
Newman calls the "group style" of commercial television storytelling.[19]
This style is forged partly by the need to produce a miniclimax before
each cut to commercial to give viewers a compelling reason to return
to the set. But perhaps more fundamentally it is forged by the way television, unlike film, must parcel out narrative information in urgent,
often melodramatic units that more overtly grab attention. For Newman it is not "in spite of television's commercial logic but because of
it" that a work achieves its effects. Whether one agrees with the bene-
ficial aesthetic effects of the need to cut to a commercial, the larger
point that television, so long viewed in a state of distraction and so
long interrupted by commercials strives for "accessibility and ease of
comprehension" seems irrefutable.[20] Television is assuredly "the most
pervasive and efficient system for the management of attention."[21] The
network prime-time serial commands attention via what Newman calls
"clear, ongoing stories about compelling characters facing difficult obstacles."[22] The basic rhythm by which these melodramatic serials orga-
nize themselves is that of beats—very short segments of action, or emotional reaction, that do not strain attention spans, that enable the longer
arcs of ongoing stories.

"Typical television"—let's say an hour-long segment of episodic network broadcast drama with commercials—is thus a "rapid succession
of short segments," each organized into an "act" that leads up to a com-

mercial. Each of the four acts (now five with the addition of yet another commercial) usually contains at least six beats, with the final act leading up to some kind of closure. Such television is by definition not like long-take, uneventful art cinema—nor is it like the bravura, hand-held reverse track and pan described above in *The Corner*. It is clearly segmented and thus interruptible. And even if it is not interrupted by commercials it interrupts itself by cutting from one small unit of space time to another, proceeding always in short segments. Thus, Newman concludes, "by demanding that beats (scenes) be short, the networks create the conditions for a sophisticated mode of ensemble storytelling."[23] Within Newman's logic, short beats can allow for more complex weavings in a longer serial as long as the storytelling remains clear.[24] Sophistication, however, is a relative judgment. Newman admits that there is no "natural reason" for the segmentation of the narrative to be in four equal portions with breaks each quarter hour, beyond the need to intersperse commercials, but he nevertheless asserts that the four-act structure "achieves a sense of proportion and symmetry, ensures steadily rising action, and organizes patterns of attention and expectation, with first acts opening causal chains . . . to be resolved (at least partially) in the fourth."[25] I would argue that a more "complex" serial might not ensure steadily rising action and sure resolution of all causal chains. However, Newman offers an apt description of the regular rhythms of the American television single episode and serial (melo)drama of the last twenty-five years—a rhythm all television viewers know in their bones but which serial television has learned to extend via the short beat into longer story arcs.

Now we might expect that all of this segmentation and industrial "group style" is precisely what the premium cable serial is free to disdain, since its viewers buy subscriptions that pay for the programs outright rather than endure commercial interruption (in which the sponsor effectively pays for viewer eyeballs). The absence of commercial interruption might seem to enable a more varied rhythm, and to a degree it does. *The Corner*, for example, takes advantage of this freedom, though perhaps to its detriment since its stories do seem to drag. For the most part, however, the short beat, the hour episode, and the serial accumulation of story—if not the suspense before a commercial—are enduring televisual conventions that originated in broadcast television and have carried forward to cable serials that do not have to build toward commercials.

A comparison between the first episode of *Homicide* that David Simon wrote and an episode from the third season of *The Wire*, also written by Simon, should help illuminate the similarities and differences of an hour-long episode of these two different "cop shows," one aired on NBC January 6, 1994, and one that aired September 19, 2004 on HBO. Both are beginning episodes of their season. The episode of *Homicide*, called "Bop Gun"—starring Robin Williams—was originally intended to finish the short season commissioned after the weak showing of the series's first season. It was repositioned to the first episode of the short (four-episode) second season and attracted the series's highest ratings.[26] This ability to reposition an episode already suggests a weaker seriality than we will see in *The Wire*. As we have seen, it was this weaker seriality and concentration on the episodic guest star that Simon's writing helped inaugurate that made *Homicide* enough of a "hit" to survive. By adhering closely to the formulas of broadcast episodic melodrama, but also adhering to some elements of the ethnographic material of his original book and a weaker continuation of the stories of the homicide detectives, Simon's (and Mills's) script assured them both new careers in writing for television.

"Bop Gun" opens briskly with a white family, Robert Ellison (Williams), his wife, and two children, admiring the sights near Baltimore's Orioles Park. Nearby, three black men play basketball until one of them pulls a gun on the others as an intimidating joke. Soon they spy the tourists and leave the basketball behind. This one-minute, musically overlayed "cold open" (precredit bit of drama) is followed by what was already the series's standard, one-minute credit sequence, with canted, black-and-white images of a gritty Baltimore. The main cop characters are introduced, along with the names of the actors who play them. As is typical, the last credit introduces the name of the guest star.

The episode as a whole corresponds closely to Newman's description of the beats of a broadcast serial (with no beat much longer than 2.5 minutes). The rhythm is brisk; not counting the cold open, or the credits, there are eight short beats that efficiently build to a miniclimax

Bereaved family faced with
an onslaught of reporters

before the "curtains" of the first commercial: one minute is devoted to
the investigation of the crime scene, which reveals that Ellison's wife has
been killed in a stick-up. Homicide cops Beau Felton (Daniel Baldwin)
and Kay Howard (Melissa Leo, originally a male detective in Simon's
book) investigate the scene and immediately identify it as a "red ball"—
a high-priority crime that will receive ample resources for investigation,
in this case because the victim is white and middle-class. The second
beat shifts to the district office, where the police interrogate the traumatized family and the word "red ball" is used again (2 minutes 56 seconds). The third beat (roughly the same length) concerns the interrogation of the family's two children, the youngest of whom does not yet
understand that her mother is dead. The fourth beat (1 minute) shows
Felton and other cops obtaining clues of likely suspects. The fifth beat
shows detective Felton apprehending one suspect in his home. The sixth
returns to the police station, where Ellison, the bereaved husband and
father, overhears detectives chortling about all the overtime they will
make on this case. Furious, Ellison complains to their superior Lieutenant Al Giardello (Yaphet Kotto). The seventh beat ensues in Giardello's
office as he explains that the job of the detectives is to solve the murder, not to grieve for Ellison. Ellison gathers his children to leave, and
the climactic final beat before the commercial (33 seconds) shows the
onslaught of reporters, alerted to the red ball, shouting questions and
snapping photos as the family attempts to leave the building.

Much of the rest of the forty-five-minute episode[27] is devoted to the
police interrogation of the three black men seen at the episode's begin-

"The lady wouldn't give up the locket."

ning, all suspects. The case is complicated because the one who finally confesses to the crime, Vaughn, is the youngest of the three and seemingly the least prone to violence. Even after he has been identified as the shooter and is sentenced to life without parole, Detective Howard believes Vaughn to be taking the fall for one of the older ones. Above and beyond the call of duty, she visits the county-dwelling, law-abiding, churchgoing aunt who raised him, as well as the inner-city addicted mother who once abandoned him but to whom he had returned. Still unconvinced of his guilt, she visits Vaughn himself in prison. What she learns is both heartbreaking and typical of the tough attitude of the series as a whole: Vaughn indeed shot Ellison's wife point-blank in the face to get her locket. However, he had initially taken control of the gun because he believed that if he possessed its "power," he, unlike his trigger-happy older friend, would be able to keep everybody safe. The only problem was that the "lady wouldn't give up the locket."

Rather than reveal the innocence of the presumed shooter, the climactic "curtain" of the final fourth act reveals how good intentions went awry in Vaughn's mistaken belief that he could prevent violence by commanding the gun. This false "power of the gun," which Simon has now learned to embed in his drama rather than to voice directly as a "gun-control" op-ed, is thematically echoed in an earlier scene when Ellison, the husband, ashamed of his own powerlessness in the face of the killer's gun, begs to hold a cop's gun just to know what it is like to have that kind of power. A thoughtful disquisition on the fickle and destructive power of the gun, "Bop Gun" ties up its narrative threads neatly at the end and observes the four-climaxes-before-each-commercial rule of '90s television drama. The crime is solved in the course of the episode, with the "realistic" twist that the kid we believe to be a railroaded victim of the judicial system admits his guilt and accepts his punishment of life imprisonment. Vaughn writes a regretful letter to the bereaved husband who is too bitter to read it. The illusory power of the gun is exposed, as are the unfortunate racial politics of policing that give priority to the red ball when the suspects are black and the victims white.

Robin Williams as Ellison displays frustrated impotence, a prepubescent Jake Gyllenhaal plays his traumatized son, Melissa Leo as Detective Howard shows persistence and empathy, the older black perpetrators display hardness and rage as they are sentenced to thirty years, and the "good kid" who did it finally articulates remorse as he faces life in prison—all in forty-five minutes at an average beat of 1.6 minutes. No beat is longer than three minutes, with the exception of the final climax, in which Vaughn, the killer, overcomes his hardened, Muslim Brotherhood exterior to express his regret for the crime to Detective Howard. This final scene—the curtain—brings in Buddy Guy's blues song "Feels Like Rain" over parts of the scene to lend a strong sense of finality. As for the tough but not unfeeling cops, they will be there next week, after this "red ball" closes, when a new guest star arrives and the next body falls.

Placed in the time slot previously occupied by *L.A. Law*, offering a "disciplined" rifle-shot exposé of the need for gun control but without overt editorializing to this end, this 1994 opening of the second season of *Homicide* succeeded in ratings where the previous season had not, whether through the quality of the writing or the fame of the guest star. Seen by 33 million, it received a respectable 18.0 Nielsen rating and many awards, including an Emmy nomination for Williams for Best Guest Actor in a Drama Series, and a Writers Guild Award for Simon and Mills for Best Screenplay of an Episodic Drama. And episodic it certainly was, with its strong ending and nothing but the work of homicide continuing.

Now compare this *Homicide* episode to the opening episode of the third season of *The Wire*, "Time after Time" (3.1), from September 19, 2004. I chose this episode because the first episodes of the first and second seasons have already been much discussed and because it allows us to study this serial's apportionment of "world and time" right in the middle of this five-season series exactly where "the plot thickens" with a more overtly political narrative thrust that becomes the hallmark of the serial. It is in this third season that *The Wire* definitively distinguishes itself from other series and serials and becomes much more than "a cop show." Having already elaborated the problems of police, the losing "game" of drug dealing in the first season's story of D'Angelo (a character who develops partly out of *The Corner*'s DeAndre), and the diminishing work of unionized labor in the second season on the docks, it now moves to the crucial question, never confronted in previous "procedurals"—whether cop shows (like *Dragnet, Hill Street Blues, Homicide,* and NYPD *Blue*) or legal shows (from *Perry Mason* to the many incarnations of the combination cop show/legal show *Law & Order*)—of how to remedy these problems: how to reform a police force that fails to reduce crime; how to better an inner-city underclass where honest work is so underpaid and the alternative drug "game" uses up its players before they reach maturity; how to reform a legal system that overwhelmingly incarcerates black men; how to reform a city government that can't decide whether to give resources to police or schools. In this season the world of the docks is not kept in play and in retrospect, seems less a part of the whole that is *The Wire* than the other seasons do. Below I offer an overview of the major "events" and locations of this episode before turning to the actual rhythm of its "beats."

The first episode of season 3 is called "Time after Time." It finds cops, drug dealers, and their dependent addicts at their usual cross purposes. A sense of futility on the part of the police fuels the main arc of action that will transpire over the course of this entire season: Major Bunny Colvin's decision to institute Hamsterdam (a mishearing of Amsterdam)—as a few selected neighborhoods where drug sale and use will not be prosecuted as a trade-off for law and order in the rest of his district. As in *Homicide* and most serials, a "cold open" begins every episode. In *Homicide* it efficiently set up the collision between the family from Iowa visiting the city and the young men playing basketball without actually showing us the robbery and murder. In *The Wire* it is comparatively inefficient—it neither advances the plot nor sets up later conflicts. But it is richly thematic.

The fall of the towers
Poot and Bodie transfixed

The mayor of Baltimore, flanked by developers in suits and hard hats, makes a speech and ceremoniously presses a lever as a gathered crowd witnesses the razing of the two Franklin Terrace Towers housing projects where the Barksdale drug gang once ruled. Black Mayor Clarence Royce promises that better low- and middle-income housing will soon replace the current blight. The mostly black crowd applauds. However, as the towers fall, the destruction meant to signify progress almost immediately backfires as smoke, dust, and debris blow back onto the street and choke the gathered crowd, pointedly recalling the fall of two other, taller and still-inhabited towers that fell in Lower Manhattan on 9/11.[28]

In the crowd watching this spectacle are three "corner boys," two of whom—Preston ("Bodie") Broadus and "Poot" Carr—we remember from the low-rise "pit" where they dealt drugs in seasons 1 and 2. The cold open begins with their quick march to the event. Poot, the youngest, is nostalgic for the project home where he lost his virginity in the seventh grade. Bodie, who is older and more cynical, reminds Poot that it is also the place where he repeatedly contracted VD. In a line that forms the epigraph for this episode he issues his judgment to Poot: "Don't matter how many times you get burned, you just keep doin' the same thing." Each cold open of each episode ends with an epigraph that is most often a quote spoken by a character in the episode. Though Bodie cynically avers that they will just build some "other shit" to replace the current housing, he is nevertheless transfixed by the spectacle of implosion, as if he too understands that the destruction of the towers foreshadows the loss of youth and hope. More practically, however, he also explains to Poot that the loss of these projects is the loss of prime drug-selling real estate: if you live in the projects "you aint worth shit, but you selling product there, you got the game by the ass."

This cold open is 3 minutes and 49 seconds, compared to *Homicide*'s 1 minute. It does not advance the plot or anticipate (except thematically) what is to come. The epigraph that ends it leads into a credit sequence that offers a tight montage of images and incidents taken from this particular season, emphasizing the newly incorporated world of real-estate development and city hall politics. These credits, at 93 seconds, are themselves 33 seconds longer than those of *Homicide*. And while they provide the names of actors, they do not signal which actor belongs to which character. In fact, the credit sequences of each of the five seasons avoid showing the faces of any major characters and never feature important "stars," concentrating instead on typical gestures—of dealers, cops, and now police and city government. The following section summarizes the major events and locations of this first episode of season 3.

1. In the "Special Detail" drug surveillance unit, Detectives Jimmy McNulty and Leander Sydnor surveil corner drug activities from a dirty vacant house. They are trying to discover what Joseph ("Proposition Joe") Stewart's East Baltimore drug outfit is up to. They use surveillance "on a wire" to learn more about the activities of higher-level drug dealers. At the same time, back in the detail office, Detectives Lester Freamon and Roland "Prez" Pryzbylewski listen in on the cell communications. After six months of wiretaps, they still have no real information on Proposition Joe's activities. After their long day's surveillance, Detectives Sydnor and McNulty return to the office to report to Lieutenant

Stringer Bell conducts
meeting according to
Robert's Rules of Order

Cedric Daniels. Rhonda Pearlman, the prosecutor, is there too (perhaps the first hint of the developing liaison between herself and Daniels). She believes it would be best to "charge what we have," but McNulty holds out hope of building a wider case.

2. In the "Western District" drug neighborhoods Detectives Thomas ("Herc") Hauk and Ellis Carver (a white/black team of detectives also familiar from the first two seasons) do what they have always done: ineffectively chase street-level dealers. Only now there is an element of farce as Herc, the dumb white one, plays Isaac Hayes's theme from *Shaft* on his car radio, posing as the cool cop on the case. Neither Herc nor Carver seems to have learned from the past two seasons that head bashing low-level dealers is ineffective policing. What's more, the teenage "hoppers" cleverly elude them. Carver ends the scene with futile exhortations from the roof of a police car: "We will beat you longer and harder than you beat your own dicks." It is obvious, though, that the young dealers are more organized and disciplined than the police.

3. In yet another part of town, Stringer Bell, who runs the drug operation for the incarcerated Avon Barksdale, conducts a contrastingly sober meeting of the gang in a funeral home, scrupulously following *Robert's Rules of Order*. His macroeconomics education at Baltimore Community College—briefly spied upon by Detective McNulty in the first season—allows him to explain the concept of quality product to his dubious minions, including Poot and Bodie. Quality product will be their new MO, says Bell; dead bodies only bring police.

4. At Western District headquarters, Major Bunny Colvin—only

Colvin tries to
orient new cops

briefly seen in the previous season and thus a new focus in this one—
orients two new beat cops with a lesson on knowing at all times where
they are. Detectives Herc and Carver affectionately rib the new officers
as they book the only suspect from their afternoon's wild-goose chase—
an obviously beaten fourteen-year-old charged only with loitering.
Colvin disparages their methods but seems unable to teach them better.

5. Meanwhile Bubbles (the fictional addict character developed out
of the real Gary) and his white younger friend Johnny attempt to heist
a cast-iron radiator to sell for scrap metal in a scene highly reminis-
cent of Simon's original "Metal Men" story from the *Sun*, reprised in
the nonfiction book *Corner*, and then again in the television miniseries.
The scene is now expertly woven into the larger thematic and narrative
arcs when their metal-heavy grocery cart crashes into Marlo Stanfield's
SUV. This is our first view of the dispassionate rival to the Barksdale
gang. Marlo's minions exact their revenge by leaving them pantless to
sell their radiator to the scrap metal dealer. By the end of a day's scavenging, after buying new pants and bargaining on the street for their
drugs, they have barely enough to share one hit, leaving the usually irrepressible Bubbles bitter.

6. In city hall, another new character, the white city councilman
Thomas Carcetti, holds a hearing in which he exposes the failure of
police to reduce crime, chiding the black police commissioner, Ervin
Burrell. Later he meets with Burrell in an effort to team up with him to
reform the department. When Burrell refuses, Carcetti calls the press
to observe the next meeting. Throughout this season, the energetic and

Avon (right) invites
Cutty to join his operation
when he leaves prison

Lieutenant Daniels
learns his promotion
has been held up

intelligent Carcetti rises to political prominence on the promise of reform, eventually running for mayor.

7. In the state prison, Stringer Bell's partner, Avon Barksdale meets with another new character, Dennis "Cutty" Wise, soon to be released, and recruits him to his operation. Cutty is evasive; after serving fourteen years he is reluctant to continue in "the game." Later Cutty emerges from prison, fails to find work, and also fails to get paid for the package of heroin he is given by the Barksdale organization.

8. Lieutenant Cedric Daniels, in charge of the special wiretap detail, meets with his boss, Commissioner Burrell, and discovers that his own promotion to major has been held up for political reasons. Daniels's wife, Marla, from whom he is now separated, is running for city council, and the current mayor is suspicious of her. The separation between Marla and Cedric has taken place in the gap between seasons, revealing the priority given to institutional over private life in this serial.

Jimmy and Bunk and kids
at Orioles game

9. Detectives Jimmy McNulty and Bunk Moreland, ex-partners in the Homicide Division, are seen in a rare moment of unlubricated leisure at an Orioles game with their kids. Jimmy jealously eyes his ex-wife sitting in much better seats with a new boyfriend. Bunk is called away to investigate a new murder.

10. At a "Comstat" meeting police commissioner, Burrell, and his white deputy of operations, Bill Rawls, rake their district commanders over the coals for not achieving a drop in the annual felony and murder rate. Major Bunny Colvin questions the feasibility of the policy of reducing crime stats but not actual crime with a remark that will prove prescient for this and the next two seasons: "You can reclassify an agg[ravated] assault and you can unfound a robbery, but how can you make a body disappear?"

11. Detective McNulty argues with his boss, Lieutenant Daniels, who is reluctant to authorize any more wiretaps to pursue Stringer Bell. Throughout the first two seasons wiretaps have been the Holy Grail for both McNulty and his fellow detective, Lester Freamon. It has been their hope that police work that follows the money could reach up to the sources of the drug trade rather than to fruitless "buys and busts" of corner boys. In frustration, McNulty returns to the now two-year-old Barksdale case records, from season 1, searching for new leads. "If you don't look at what you did before, you do the same shit all over," he explains, sounding a lot like Bodie in the cold open.

12. In a final scene, Major Colvin drives his car through his district. While stopped at a red light a young dealer, the same dimwitted boy with the sideways hat we have seen in many previous seasons, is both brazen and stupid enough to try to sell Colvin some heroin. Not until Colvin shows his radio and puts on his hat does the boy realize he's police. In disgust Colvin slowly drives off.

"Time after Time" introduces many factors motivating the long arcs of character and action that will follow over the twelve episodes of this third season. The final scene, in particular, serves as one of the last straws for Major Colvin, who will soon initiate his own radical reform by permitting the sale of narcotics in portions of his district in an effort to actually perform police work in the other, drug-free portions. However, in this hour-long episode, nothing concludes and nothing, with the possible exception of Stringer Bell's "rules of order," and council-man Carcetti's improved manipulation of the press at his second hearing, comes to fruition.[29] The first half of the season's police narrative will be a variation on patterns of futile surveillance and clumsy chases that never catch the big fish. Now, however, we learn how the police cheat by "juking the stats" to make it seem they are actually deterring crime. And now we also learn about new dimensions of city government: the futile razing of the towers that will *not* change housing conditions for the poor, but which inaugurates the theme of development important throughout the series, and Tommy Carcetti's sparsely attended city hall hearings on the police that begins to challenge the incumbent mayor. All protagonists are frustrated; all are caught up, as the title indicates, in repeating themselves, "time after time." Yet as long as drugs remain illegal, they will sell, and as long as they sell, cops, addicts, dealers, and politicians will keep running in place in what we will eventually see as their "hamster" wheels.

The major difference between *Homicide*'s "Bop Gun" and *The Wire*'s "Time after Time" is that the latter does not overtly seek, as Michael K. Newman states is the case in "typical TV," to "arouse and rearouse our interest."[30] *Homicide* must do this because of its commercial breaks and weak seriality; *The Wire*, however, does not even try, at least not in the usual ways of building suspense to a final outcome. Where a serial offers "clear, ongoing stories about compelling characters facing difficult obstacles" and does so with short beats building to miniclimaxes before commercials, *The Wire* does not parcel out its information quite so evenly, nor does it redundantly repeat information for inattentive viewers. It assumes they are paying attention and even demands that they do if they are to follow the intricacies of story and character even here, at the beginning of a new season. Yet as television critic Ted Nannicelli has noted of this episode, it opens up many narrative threads and story arcs without offering any payoff or closure.[31]

The episode alternates between characters who "keep on doin' the same thing": McNulty and Sydnor's fruitless stakeout, or Herc and Carver's wild-goose chase after corner boys; and those—such as gangster Stringer Bell or councilman Tommy Carcetti—who at least try to initiate change. For Bell, change begins with *Robert's Rules of Order* in a trajectory that will find him aspiring to get out of the drug game and into more "legitimate" business investments. This change, however, will lead to his being "taken in" by the crafty state senator Clay Davis, a bigger crook than Bell precisely because he works inside the law. Carcetti, too, tries to effect change. Though he fails initially, in the first hearing, to investigate the police failure at witness protection, his second hearing, after some manipulation of the press, draws more attention. His movements toward reform, running parallel to Bunny Colvin's more unofficial reform in the creation of the drug zone, Hamsterdam, will occupy the rest of the season.[32]

In this first episode, however, Major Colvin merely registers his disgust at the way things are: his detectives can only bash heads, his superiors can only juke stats, and an ignorant kid in his own district even tries to sell him a "spider bag" of heroin. We are first asked to register the enormity of the dysfunction through the ongoing multisited ethnographies of the three institutions foregrounded in this season: police at all echelons up the chain of command, including Assistant States Attorney Rhonda Pearlman; drug dealers, also at all levels, and including the drug addicts who make their business possible and who are most fully viewed in this season in Hamsterdam's drug zone, and all levels of city government. The rest of the season will then play out how each reformer within each institution does battle with it. This is what seriality with multisited ethnography affords: not only long arcs of characters in different worlds over much time, but comparisons between these worlds. Thus, one of the long-running ironies of the series is that police are almost always less disciplined and less technologically equipped than drug dealers. Another irony is the parallel between Major Colvin's unofficial, but moderately effective, reform in the creation of Hamsterdam and the aspiring mayor Carcetti's platform of reform, as compared to the gangsters' cooperative.

HBO wants us to think its shows are distinct from typical TV; hence the famous tagline "It's Not TV, It's HBO." It is worth asking, then, just how different is this episode from more typical network serial television, apart from its ambitious thematic reach? Each of the twelve units of narrative I have listed above offers a variation on the need for, but the bleak possibilities of, reform taking place in the three major locales of the season: places of policing; places of drug dealing and using; and places of city government.[33] None of these units comes to any conclusion. It seems fair to say that this episode is more richly detailed, thematically and narratively more "complex" (even more "sophisticated," to use Newman's term), than typical TV, but it does not satisfy us, like the end of "Bop Gun," by progressing in a linear fashion toward a single goal. Nowhere is this more evident than in the leisurely cold open's grotesquely backfired gesture at reform by the incumbent mayor. The destruction of the Franklin Terrace Towers, intended to mark progress, immediately makes that space uninhabitable in the process, echoing the greatest public trauma of American history.

Nothing happens in this episode, though the thematics are rich and the narrative and character arcs are long and complex, stretching even beyond the twelve episodes of this particular season and into the next. Nevertheless, the smallest parts, or beats, that compose each episode are surprisingly short. Indeed, they obey the basic rhythmic structure of the typical, short-attention-span televisual beat, only without the little climaxes before commercials.

The summary of "Time after Time" given above describes the main characters and events of the episode but does not convey the rhythm of the beats. If it had, though, we would have found the rhythms to be sometimes surprisingly fast. For example, the narrative arc described in what I called sequence 5 (Bubbles and Johnny crash their shopping cart, lose their pants, sell the metal, buy new pants, and fail to get sufficiently high) is composed of many beats intercut with other beats from

Homicide Season 2, Episode 1 "Bop Gun" 1994	The Wire Season 3, Episode 1 "Time After Time" (9/19/2004)
• 60 second cold open • 45 minutes of drama • 1 minute cold open sets up crime to be solved • 25 beats in 45-minute episode • Average length of beat 1.6 minutes	• 3 minute plus cold open • 59 minutes of drama • 3 minutes 49 seconds cold open sets up theme of reform • 49 beats in 59-minute episode • Average length of beat 1.02 minutes

the other narrative arcs. Between Johnny and Bubbles's first appearance with the shopping cart and their last appearance in their crash pad as they fail to get high are many short beats from four other narrative arcs: Tommy Carcetti's first police hearing; ongoing arcs of surveillance, this time by Kima Greggs, Jimmy McNulty, and Lester Freamon; Avon Barksdale's offer of work to Cutty Wise (with the regular informational rhythm disrupted as this beat takes time to watch how the entire prison ball game stops to respectfully attend to the kingpin gangster's walk across a baseball field to meet Cutty); Police Commissioner Burrell and Daniels jockey over Daniels's promotion, and yet another older arc related to Jimmy's relation to his former wife continues in the scene at the professional baseball game. In sum, going strictly by shifts in spatial location, there are 49 beats in this 59-minute episode, the average length of which is only 1.02 minutes.[34]

A fan of *The Wire* might be tempted here to point out the acute differences between the more popular and more completed episodic serial of *Homicide* and the more complex, less climactic, closure-deferring serial of *The Wire* that manages to compare and contrast so many worlds over time. One might note with praise that *The Wire* has no guest stars. It spreads its narrative evenly in this episode across some twenty-one characters, each of whom matters almost equally. One might thus be tempted to conclude that where *Homicide* is an excellent example of a "typical" television series with some "cumulative" knowledge, and strong enigma but relatively weak seriality, *The Wire* is groundbreaking in its relative lack of enigma (we don't wonder who killed whom in this episode), strong seriality, and deferral of narrative resolution altogether.

If, however, we take what is most "typical" of TV to be fundamentally the quick rhythm of its beats rather than the climactic curtain at the end of each act before a commercial, then *The Wire* is not atypical, but simply a more complex variation of this basic rhythm that drives all scripted television narrative. In other words, if we give less emphasis to the requirements for artificial climaxes before commercials and consider instead the short beat that contrasts, informs, or corresponds to another to be the true backbone of television narrative, then we can also appreciate the surprising formal continuity between *Homicide* and *The Wire* as well as the difference of both from the truly slow *The Corner* or much art cinema.

Consider, for example, that "Bop Gun" sustains the enigma of who killed the white female tourist all the way to the final act. That act "solves" the crime in the manner of a conventional murder mystery, though one with an added moral: gun control would have prevented the crime. However, once the gun is introduced in the first act, we know, according to the rules of conventional drama, that it will be fired.[35] This is an efficient, well-crafted television script that has learned not to editorialize directly. In fact, the need for gun control is never once spoken. We understand that the crime is unnecessary, although this certainly *is* a narrow rifle-shot individual character melodrama pointing to a much larger social problem.

The Wire may be fueled by a similar liberal outrage. But here Simon has learned even better not to preach. Likewise, he has learned to deploy the fuller world and time of serial melodrama. In "Bop Gun" the key enigma is the motive for the crime. The murderer is the "good kid" who, like Gary McCullough of *The Corner*, could have left the neighborhood where such crimes are likely to occur. But Vaughn, like Gary, stayed in the neighborhood, in his case out of allegiance to his drug-addicted mother. There is no righteous good side or bad side to be on in this case, and that is its strength.

Nevertheless, the story of "Bop Gun" is told in such a way that the world of the middle-class tourist and the world of the cops are the only sites the series can access. The world of the restless, ball-playing young black men is purposely left blank, an enigma for Detective Howard to solve—not a "whodunit" but a "whydunit." It is this "other" world of the black underclass, neither vilified nor mystified, for which *The Wire* creates more world and time. It may not be "enough" world and time but compared to the vacant hole of *"Bop Gun"* whose motive simply feeds into the moral of the need for gun control, and compared to most television series and serials, it is a lot. Consider, for example, the sheer amount of overall time—though parceled into short parts—spent in the world of the black underclass, whether in McNulty and Leander's efforts to surveil a corner (1), Herc and Carver's efforts to apprehend penny-ante street-level dealers (2), or the final thread, which is not intercut with anything else, in which Major Colvin simply observes the brazen drug dealing in his district (12).

Even more important than these predominantly black or black and white partnered worlds of professionals, however, is the time spent in the world of the black underclass when it is not being surveilled or chased by cops, when it is this world alone whose operations are observed as closely as those of police and government. Section 5, which I have already discussed, and although it is technically "integrated" by the white Johnny continually trying to become more "brown" through his association with Bubbles, is the underclass world of lumpen metal scavengers—the former "ants" of Simon's "Metal Men" *Baltimore Sun* Series. This world, we have already come to see, has its own labor, its own needs, and its own modest ambitions. Finally, in the 7th thread involving Cutty Wise before and after he gets out of prison, we have the special, slowed down, long beat of the prison ball game and the ball field conversation that operates according to its own sweet (prison) time, highlighted by the oft-repeated phrase of the gangsters who would minimize the time of prison with the mantra: "you don't serve but two days: the day you go in, the day you come out." Cutty, however, does not buy into the mantra, having served fourteen years.

Despite the innovation of bringing these differently raced and classed worlds together so intimately and ingeniously, *The Wire* is not a formal outlier. It *is* TV in the most basic rhythmic sense of the dialectic between flow and segment, part and gap. Indeed, it is precisely the genius of the series to deploy the short televisual beats of all these different sites in counterpoint. Thus, what we attend to in this *Wire* episode is not so much what happens—fall of towers, frustrated surveillance, difficulty going straight, difficulty getting high, police juking stats, a frustrated detective and police major—as the way the beats of everyone's growing frustration compare and contrast, representing small bits of world and time from so many different systems of value. It is this typical rhythm of television now extended to many different but equally important worlds that is so remarkable in the series.

If *The Wire* does not demand a longer-than-usual attention span in its multitude of beats, it does require a more intense one. Its beats are more varied than those of typical TV; they are both longer *and* shorter. In this episode the longer beats consist of 1, the "cold open" fall of the towers (3 minutes and 39 seconds), 2, the fast-paced wild-goose chase after the corner kids (almost 5 minutes, but quick editing makes it seem shorter), and 3, the comical contrast of the sedate funeral parlor meeting (almost 4 minutes). The final beat in which Bunny Colvin observes the drug devastation of his district, culminating in a hopper trying to sell *him* drugs, is almost 3 minutes and holds a long time on his car as it drives away. This beat is uninterrupted.

In contrast to the 49 beats of this episode of *The Wire*, there is an average of 25 beats in a typical network series/serial. If we take into account the fact that the actual running time today is only 43-plus minutes, the rest going to commercials, the average beat length is 1.7 minutes. On average, then, *The Wire*'s beats (1.2 minutes) are shorter than those of network serials, though the beats have a wider range and thus a less regular rhythm. Though it may feel slower than "Bop Gun," owing to the emphasis given to some of these longer beats, the many short beats offset the occasional longer ones. Moreover, to pay close attention is to be richly rewarded, not only by the gradual initiation into the behavior rituals of each of the series' sites, but by the comparisons among them.

The "Bop Gun" season opener for *Homicide* is excellent network television. It sets the tone of the second season by backing off strong seriality and focusing on the A and B stories. "Time after Time," by contrast, eschews all such comforting familiarity. There is no A- and B-level distinction. There is a whole alphabet of important characters occupying different worlds, rubbing up against one another now and then. Lose one of them and the series can still go on. Some, like the Barksdale gang loyalist Wee Bay, might emerge from the background to play an important role, recede, and then emerge again. Others, like D'Angelo Barksdale, emerge powerfully for one season then die. Still others, like detectives McNulty, Freamon, and Moreland, or the addict Bubbles, endure throughout the entire five seasons, but still cannot be said to be "main" characters the way the four main cop characters are in *Homicide* or the way Gary, Fran, and DeAndre are in *The Corner. The Wire* is an ensemble that depends on connections and a rich contrast between different worlds. Each beat moves effortlessly from one site to the next, often in the melodramatic formula of "meanwhile, back at . . ." but without the baggage of overt contrivance. Thus, for example, the instantaneous cuts back and forth between the ongoing police surveillance and the wild-goose chase after low-level drug dealers and longer, slower segments of Stringer Bell's "rules of order" meeting make an implied editorial comment, that never needs to be spoken. This narrative "voice" directs us to see how the "lawless" world is organized and orderly, and how the law itself is disorganized and in a violent rut. Similarly, by cutting back and forth between the newly introduced world of city government—both the ceremonial cold open of the fall of the towers representing the "same old same old," and the new energy of Tommy Carcetti's investigation into the police department—the episode establishes an important connection between their institutionally based efforts at reform.

The Simon editorial voice that we observed in the previous chapter, has been distributed into the voices of characters and can now be seen, through the device of the beat, as part of a rich comparison and contrast of institutionalized efforts at reform at all levels. Here the "outlaws" do not represent an enigma that can be implicitly "blamed" on the presence of guns or drugs; rather, they are part of a social fabric as deeply embedded as police and government. Some of the series's most powerful editorial comments will come from these kinds of beat-driven similarities and contrasts. In the first episode of the next season (4.1, "Boys of Summer"), for example, we find an intricate cross-cut of very short beats comparing a PowerPoint presentation given to teachers with a PowerPoint presentation given to police. Both the teachers and the police are "bad students"; they become restless at the condescension shown them by their superiors in the very form of the PowerPoint. Detective Jimmy McNulty, who suffers like a kid with ADD through the presentation, will toss out the contents of a binder with information, but save the binder itself to give to his kids for school, thus linking the two institutions. Again in 5.7 ("Took"), the season focused on the media, a group of news writers and a group of police are briefed before going out to do their jobs. In this case we see both institutions behaving with adrenalin-fueled efficiency. Nevertheless, at this point we also know that the serial killer they both pursue is a fiction mutually fabricated by an impatient detective and a Pulitzer-seeking reporter; all this efficiency serves no real goal beyond providing resources for each institution. As Christine Borden has shown, the rapid cross-cuts across institutions are Simon's televisual form of editorial critique. Police and reporters are equally "venal" in their avidity for meaningful, melodramatic action; neither checks carefully enough to determine whether their information is true.[36]

Cross-cuts and parallel edits between institutional worlds are certainly not unique to this series, to television, or to movies—they are the bread and butter of much popular, action-packed American moving image culture. Nonetheless, they have never been used to build so many thematically relevant worlds over so much time. This, I believe, is what critics mean when they say *The Wire* is a "visual novel." They do not mean that it has long Balzacian descriptions or that it is grim like Dostoyevsky; actually, it can be quite funny. Rather, what they are reaching to say with this comparison is that the work has the symbolic resonance, complexity, and social critique that television series—even other good ones, like *Homicide*—rarely have and that a discrete episodic drama does not have world enough and time to develop. They are reaching to say that it builds a very large and comprehensive world the same way *Moby-Dick* or *Our Mutual Friend* does. They do not just mean that it is long—many serial television series are longer; and they do not just mean that its plotting is complex—series with convoluted flashbacks and literal multiple worlds such as *Battlestar Galactica* or *Lost* are infinitely more complex. What they are saying, I think, is that world building, as we see it—for example, developed out of the twelve distinct spaces of Baltimore depicted in this episode—are all striving for change. Though at odds with one another, each institution attempts to institute change in its own way.

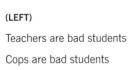

(LEFT)

Teachers are bad students

Cops are bad students

Teachers watch PowerPoint

(RIGHT)

Cops watch PowerPoint

Reporters are avid for action

Cops are avid for action

The movement to reform, growing out of the frustration of doing the same thing "time after time," leads these very different worlds toward oddly similar goals that will end in the creation of Hamsterdam—an experiment in ending the war on drugs, resonant with a larger critique of "the war on terror"—that will ultimately fail. But in the process of trying, and in the brief moment when police, city government, drug addicts, and even dealers recognize the genius of its solution and the real possibility of creating a more just society, the televisual imagination of opposing segmentation and flow, part and gap, combines with the ethnographic imagination of Simon's earlier nonfiction to create an amalgam of ethnography, Dickensian melodrama, and televisual time that is unparalled in American culture.

When Jeffrey Sconce writes that "what television lacks in spectacle and narrative constraints, it makes up for in depth and duration of character relations, diegetic expansion, and audience investment," he is saying that world building needs duration.[37] I would add that diegetic expansion and audience investment are paradoxically the result of what serial novelists like Eugene Sue, Charles Dickens, Honore de Balzac, and Victor Hugo discovered in the nineteenth century and that serial television has furthered in its even shorter beats: that short parts afford more worlds and longer arcs of storytelling. In the epigraph to this chapter, a newspaper editor in the fifth season of *The Wire* tells a cub reporter that great quotes do not necessarily make a great story: "You got a guy telling us how rough it is on the street. . . . That doesn't have much pull; but if you can describe how it really is, *tell his story in moments. . . .*" That editor is giving advice on writing for a newspaper and on writing with authenticity. It is this advice—to build from short moments—applied to television that made *The Wire* authentic and gave it "pull," not as an entirely original form but grounded in the refinement of a tried-and-true serial method of extending world and time.

In this chapter I have described a certain televisual rhythm of *The Wire* as basic to its ability to build complexity and depth. If not typical TV, *The Wire* does not seek to escape what used to be considered television's relative absence of cinematic flourish. With its modest and now outmoded 3:4 aspect ratio and avoidance of what John Caldwell has described as a more slick and stylized visual exhibitionism that he calls "televisuality"—a style that emerged on television in the 1980s.[38] *The Wire* looks neither like a flashy contemporary film, nor like the more "arty" serials like *The Sopranos* or *Breaking Bad*. It possesses few montages, few canted frames, very little slow motion, and only one (miscalculated) flashback in an earlier episode that was never repeated. Its storytelling is exclusively linear; it eschews voice-over narration, and almost all nondiegetic music.[39] Nor does it aspire to the hand-held immediacy of many documentaries, as in the high-speed film and shakiness of *Homicide* or the bravura faux-documentary of *The Corner*.

Rather, as Erlend Lavik has shown in his video essay "Style in *The Wire*," its style is simply plain; it achieves a documentary immediacy but without the guerrilla-style hand-held jerkiness affected in *Homicide* and so many films.[40] By "plain," he means there are simply very few noticeable effects: the camera tends to respectfully follow the action as it happens without anticipating, at least at the beginning of scenes. Simon has claimed that he never wanted to see the camera "fish for" or anticipate the action but preferred to see it arrive on the next speaker late rather than to suggest that the cameraperson had read the script and knew where to go. Nevertheless, the cameraperson *has* read the script well enough to understand the most revealing frames, and there certainly are some characteristic camera gestures, such as horizontal dollies at the beginning of scenes that slowly disclose the scene, and radical shifts to black and white, especially in the first and fifth season to indicate surveillance-style views. So even if the camera does not "go fishing," it does catch what it needs to catch. However, the most overt feature of *The Wire*'s "plain" style is contained in its choice to use the more quadratic and older 4:3 ratio as opposed to the wider and newer 16:9 ratio that was already popular on televisions when the series began. There is a certain retro look and simplicity to this style that coincides with the often behind-the-times technology of the police who are decidedly not part of the CSI school of television genre melodrama. If *The Wire* can sustain very long story arcs and keep us interested, it is not because it is stylistically complex but because the very simplicity of its individual parts allows us to enter into a televisual world that is not about showing that television can be more "cinematic" than television. You might even say that the style of *The Wire* is "classical," but as we shall see in the next two chapters, that word, with its associations to tragedy or, more recently, to what has been called "classical Hollywood," might lead us down the wrong path.

PART II

Justice in *The Wire*

TRAGEDY, REALISM, AND MELODRAMA

3   "Classical" Tragedy, or . . .

> [We have] ripped off the Greeks: Sophocles,
> Aeschylus, Euripides. . . . We've basically taken the idea
> of Greek tragedy, and applied it to the modern city-state. . . .
> What we were trying to do was take the notion of Greek tragedy,
> of fated and doomed people, and instead of these Olympian gods,
> indifferent, venal, selfish, hurling lightning bolts and hitting
> people in the ass for no good reason—instead of those guys
> whipping it on Oedipus or Achilles, it's the postmodern
> institutions. . . . Those are the indifferent gods.
> —David Simon, *New Yorker*, 2007

> Swear to God, it isn't a cop show. Really, it isn't. And
> though there be cops and gangsters aplenty, it isn't actually
> a crime show, though the spine of every season is certain to
> be a police investigation in Baltimore, Maryland.
> —David Simon, *The Wire: Truth Be Told*, 2004

The previous two chapters traced the genesis and genius of *The Wire* from its origins in journalism through its development into an unprecedented form of serial television. We explored the two familiar kinds of imagination—journalistic ethnography and televisual seriality—that fundamentally animate the series. This third chapter further addresses the question of the serial's form in order to challenge both of David Simon's assertions above—that *The Wire* is tragedy and that as such it doesn't partake of the lowly, commercially driven genre of the "cop show." We know what Simon intends by these two statements: *The Wire* is too important and too deeply sad to be considered anything less than tragedy. It is too ambitious and too complex to be considered an ordinary cop show. That was *Homicide*; this is better.

Yet *The Wire* certainly begins as a cop show and keeps that generic thread alive all five seasons through the many procedures of crime investigation: whether ways of breaking down a crime suspect in "the box"; the initial excitement of easy street-level "rips" enjoyed by Herc and Carver; or the more thoughtful long-term wiretaps that offer the hope that "real po-lice" work can reach up to the higher levels of criminal activity by building complex cases that "follow the money."[1] When *The Wire* follows the money it discovers a more systemic understanding of the workings of capital in the multisited city of Baltimore as it shifted from a safety-net Keynesian economic system to more brutal forms of post-Fordist and neoliberal capitalism.

Those who, like Simon, have praised the series as a tragedy have done so because they want to distinguish its exceptional dramatic achievements beyond typical genre television and to stress its importance for our contemporary culture.[2] This is understandable. If the usual fare is the black/white oppositions of certain melodramatic genres, such as cop shows that pit good-guy cops, who solve cases, against bad-guy criminals, who eventually get caught, then Simon is right; it is not a "cop show." However, to deny utterly the generic televisual elements of this serial is to also deny the larger modal qualities of melodrama, which, I argue, come with the territory of narrower genres. Both film and television studies have long been in need of a more flexible understanding of works that exceed the expectations of "typical" genres. Naturally we want to praise such shows. But must our praise leap to grandiose and hallowed terms seemingly beyond the reach of television or its popular genres just because the work is so uncommonly good?

This chapter and the next are about *The Wire*'s ambition to be a realist tragedy and its ironically greater achievement as a modern serial melodrama with generic roots in a cop show. To be sure, it is a great serial melodrama and (much more than) a cop show, and it does aspire to tragedy, but this aspiration takes place in a culture that cannot wholly "do" tragedy. Because so many of the influential appreciations of the serial have come either from those critics who extol its bleak realism or its tragedy (often considered the same thing) and those who pit these qualities against a more popular melodrama, it is important to understand these terms. Consider, for example, the way critic Leigh Claire La Berge describes the serial's realism: "*The Wire* has correctly been labeled unique to the televisual medium for its use of a realist mode. It tends to eschew melodrama, sentimentality, romance, and excessive individualism, and it minimizes their associated techniques of nondiegetic sound, flashback, voice-over, dream sequence, and dialogue-dependent jump cuts [in favor of] long tracking shots, wide-framed environmental shots, and many exterior settings."[3]

This is a fair enough description of the austere realist audiovisual style of the serial, but it is not a fair description of what this style *does*. In a related vein, Fredric Jameson praises the serial's avoidance of typical popular culture tropes, in this case the way it "transcends the usual whodunit formula" by offering a "whole society that must be opened up to representation and tracked down, identified, explored, mapped like a new dimension or a foreign culture."[4] However, Jameson's reference to the work's "Utopian impulse" does not recognize the mass-culture roots of this impulse that are not transcended but beautifully realized as the detection of the cop show and the vow to "follow the money" lead to this larger critique. Moreover, his argument takes an odd turn when he complains of the motives of villains in mass culture, which have shrunk, he argues, to almost pure greed. "This means," he argues, "that the melodramatic plot, the staple of mass culture (along with romance), becomes increasingly unsustainable."[5] To Jameson, the demise of the great villains betokens "an end of melodrama, which threatens to become the end of mass culture itself."[6] Though Jameson aptly recognizes that melodrama is the very engine of mass culture, I confess to a certain bewilderment at this turn of his argument. While nostalgically intimating that great melodrama was aligned with the variable motives of its once-great villains, now reduced to only greedy corporate bosses, terrorists or serial killers "who have become as boring as the villains driven by 'greed'"[7]— he ignores the real achievement of *The Wire* as a systemic melodrama of the evils of unencumbered capital accumulation.

Jameson prefers to identify what is new and remarkable in the series as the "Utopianism" of certain characters who want to restore the past of better employment and functioning neighborhoods: he lists Frank Sobotka's dream in season 2 of dredging the wharf to make more work for unions; Major Colvin's "Hamsterdam" dream in season 3 of restoring neighborhoods; or Roland Pryzbylewski's classroom in season 4. I am perplexed that this great Marxist critic can only recognize what he calls the utopian dimension of *The Wire* in terms of these personalized stories when what becomes much more clearly visible is the less individualized totality of what Jameson himself has previously called "the cultural logic of late capitalism." While the utopian ideals of these characters are in fact what make them prime examples of melodrama's sustained ability to hope for a more democratic justice, Jameson's insistent nostalgia for old-fashioned villainy misses the larger point that he, of all critics, ought to admire: the melodrama of unencumbered, post-Fordist capitalism as itself the arch-villain that foils justice at every turn. With the melodramatization of this entire system played out through mutually connected institutions, personal villains are less important.

This is not to say that there are not also personal villains in the series. Ironically, McNulty himself pretends to be a serial killer to obtain money for his department, and Lester Freamon, whom Jameson oddly designates the "ultimate hero of *The Wire*,"[8] goes along with McNulty's scheme to grab money for his department's misguided quest. At this point in the final season, both cops pervert the notion of following the money by chasing after it themselves—even if it is money in the form of police resources to catch the real serial killer, Marlo Stanfield.

Villains exist at all levels of the social order but the higher up they are, the less we know about them.[9] More proximately in Baltimore, there are many lower-level villains who merely comply with the status quo and enhance or maintain their careers in whatever institution they inhabit. Some of these are pure bureaucrats, like Major Rawls, Commander Burrell, Mayor Royce, or most of the editors at the *Baltimore Sun*, who only want to keep their own institutions well oiled. Some of them, like state senator Clay Davis or the shark defense lawyer Maurice Levy, more actively feed off the misery of others and thus more actively block justice or reform. These villains are the kind we might even enjoy hissing at in the good old melodramatic fashion. None of them, however, can be identified as *the* problem as they once were in the stage melodramas or typical melodramatic movies and television. Rather, they are symptoms of the institutions they inhabit and this, I argue, is what makes *The Wire* a great melodrama of dysfunctional systems and not just a Manichean study of personal villains and victims—or even, as often happens in more contemporary American movies, of villainous, conspiratorial corporations.[10]

Once again, we must return to the question of what the work *does* rather than the realism of how it looks or sounds. Neorealism, for example, was once regarded as the ultimate realist cinema linked to tragic endings. Looked at today, many of its "classics" are unmistakably melodramas with unhappy endings once the realist trappings—city streets, stories of the poor, nonprofessional actors and relatively long takes—are discounted and the central, pity-engendering narratives are examined.[11] As in *The Wire*, the indicator of melodrama is not an *aesthetics* of shining surfaces, multiple mirrors, lush colors, and pounding music, which may govern expectations about certain *genres* of melodrama (American domestic melodrama of the 1950s, for example), but instead certain kinds of pathetic stories about postwar poverty and dislocation that emphasize social critique and dissent. I would even venture to say that there is no set aesthetics of melodrama, not even what Peter Brooks has called the "aesthetics of astonishment" or the "mode of excess."[12] It is pleasurable to recognize melodrama this way, but it is also possible to mistake it by limiting it to mere aesthetic "excess."

There is now an ample bibliography of scholarship that, over the last thirty years, has addressed what Christine Gledhill has called "The Melodramatic Field."[13] Some of this work has sought to rehabilitate the very term "melodrama" from the worst clichés of popular culture that have situated it in opposition to more aesthetically valued forms such as tragedy or realism. Peter Brooks, for example, has refuted the common notion that melodrama is failed tragedy by arguing that when it first appeared on the French stage it was a new and more modern mode of drama reflecting the needs of a social order no longer grounded in the values of religion or those of a recently beheaded king. But Brooks also identifies melodrama as inherently a mode of excess without quite specifying what norms that excess violates. Gledhill adds the very important idea that melodrama and realism are not inherently opposed but mutually reliant modes, neither of which can be confined to a narrow genre. The following chapter will have much more to say about both these notions. For the moment, however, I would like to settle on a simple definition: melodrama always offers the contrast between how things are and how they could be, or should be.[14] This is its fundamental utopianism.

Consider the first, and oft-quoted, cold open of season 1, episode 1, titled "The Target."[15] The sounds of sirens and police radios coincide with the sight of a jagged line of blood mixed with oil on the street caught in the blue light of a police car. We follow this line until it leads to an inert body. A policeman fills out a form, little girls on a front stoop of a row house turn their heads, and in voice-over we hear, "So your boy's name is Snot?" Cut to a rear view of two male figures on a stoop. "Snot Boogie," we learn, is the victim's street name. In a closer side view we see that a white man is casually interrogating a black teenager as they both fix their eyes on the body. The man expresses surprise at the name and immediately weaves a story around it: "One day he forgets his jacket so his nose starts runnin' and some asshole, instead of giving him a Kleenex, he calls him Snot. So he's Snot forever. Doesn't seem fair." Stoically, the kid responds, "Life just be that way, I guess." As we move into a close-up of both their faces, the man finally asks: "So, who shot Snot?" Instantly wary, the kid responds, "I ain't goin' to no court!" Silence follows, but then the kid volunteers: "The motherfucker didn't have to put no cap in him though . . . could of beat him up like we always do." Gradually the man, who is obviously a detective skilled at drawing information out of witnesses, learns what happened: every Friday night the boys in the neighborhood had a craps game, and every time the pot got heavy Snot Boogie would steal it and, if caught, get beat up by the other boys in the game. Finally, the detective has to ask: "Why'd you even let him in the game?" "Got to," the kid responds. "This is America, man!" On this phrase, the reverse field appears. In the foreground the crime scene appears up close to reveal the open-eyed corpse of Snot Boogie.

Even in Baltimore's "dark corner of the American experiment," as Sergeant Jay Landsman calls it in a much later episode,[16] America is both

A jagged line of blood
caught in the blue light
of a police car

Reverse shot reveals
Snot Boogie

a place and an idea. In this place the only opportunity a kid named
Snot will have is to steal the pot. Audiences familiar with any fictional
cop or crime show—*Homicide*, CSI, LA *Law*, NYPD *Blue, Southland*—
recognize these opening procedures of crime scene investigation in an
urban space and the street-smart interrogation of a witness at the scene.
As is conventional also, the detective, Jimmy McNulty, will be a recurring character throughout the series, while victims and witnesses, such
as this one, may only appear briefly. Perhaps the only difference at this
point between an ordinary cop show and this one is the acute raising
of the question of American opportunity, and the fact that the murder
of Snot Boogie does not figure either in this episode or the season as a
whole. (The significant death of a youth in this season will not occur
until Wallace is shot by his friends twelve episodes later.) Nor is the
solution to an individual crime, such as "who shot Snot," the real point

of an episode as it ultimately was in the "Bop Gun" episode of *Homicide*. *The Wire* is on the trail of a much larger crime than street-level homicide. That crime is the failure of American social justice.

The story that Detective McNulty spins around Snot's name and runny nose, which explains his loser status, his compulsion to steal, and then his death, is both realistic and sad, but we should not call it tragic. We try to honor its sadness by calling it tragedy (to offer condolences for a melodramatic death would seem ludicrous but that is only because of the disrespect for a badly understood mode). While I do not mean to split hairs in the use of this term, it seems incontrovertible that tragedy is grounded in fates that we do not even expect to be "fair." Tragic heroes face up to the way things are—to being the "playthings of the gods." The fate of tragic heroes is ultimately accepted. Melodrama, in contrast, compares how things are with how they *ought* to be, and American melodrama does so precisely because "This is America, man!"

If *The Wire* begins as a "police investigation in Baltimore, Maryland," and continues with an investigation as the "spine of every season," then it certainly is a "cop show," but one that uses genre expectation as a way to probe the larger crimes and injustices of the American city. As Carlo Rotella eloquently notes, it is a "superlative piece of genre work distinguished by its sustained success in mating a fresh and sophisticated synthesis of crime show formulas to a humane exploration of how compelling characters lived the consequence of the war on drugs." In short, it is first-class genre fiction that also "advances a coherent analysis."[17] And this analysis begins, but does not end, with the notion that a "war on drugs" or a "war on crime" does not begin to address the American city's real social problems. Such wars waste time, resources, and lives and only make the problems worse. But *The Wire* is also more than a coherent analysis of what is wrong with the American city. It also wants us to imagine what could be right. This is the utopianism of its project, and those critics who point only to its realistic "bleakness" or tragedy miss this aspect.

I take the crucial difference between melodrama and tragedy to be their respective stances toward justice and their different activations of pity. Tragic heroes may be pitied for their great suffering. But pity is typically not deployed in tragedy as a means to alter fate. As we watch Oedipus suffer, we appreciate the tragic irony of how his efforts to escape his fate only ensnare him more deeply in it. There are quite a few ancient tragedies, however, in which the suffering of heroes inspires such pity that the story finds ways to alter the sufferer's condition. These tragedies anticipate the more modern, liberal sensibilities of melodrama. The title character of the *Philoctetes*, for example, in a less well-known play by Sophocles, endures both physical and moral suffering after being left to die on a barren island by fellow Greeks bound for Troy. He suffers there for ten years with an excruciatingly painful pus-filled foot, and no food, water, or shelter, until Odysseus, having been told that he will need Philoctetes to win the war, sends the young Neoptolemus to retrieve him. In a play whose focus on pity anticipates the later workings of melodrama—and not only because it has a happy ending—the tragic hero inspires so much pity that Neoptolemus, who originally planned to trick Philoctetes into sailing to Troy, ceases to obey Odysseus and returns to Philoctetes the bow that is his means of survival. At this point Herakles (former hero, now deity—and thus deus ex machina) appears and promises to cure Philoctetes if he will willingly join the Greeks in Troy.

This play deploys pity in a different way than "typical" tragedy (i.e., a tragedy such as *Oedipus* or *Antigone*, which we usually take as exemplars of the form). Philosopher and legal scholar Martha Nussbaum calls the *Philoctetes* the "pity play par excellence."[18] She adds that "there is something about the sheer vividness of seeing another person's plight that powerfully contributes to forming emotions that motivate appropriate action."[19] In this case, that action is to help the suffering Philoctetes rather than to trick him into going to Troy. Only Herakles, "the god from the machine," can convince him to aid the Greeks in Troy. And this, indeed, is the play's happy ending (though it may leave us a little morally queasy, as many melodramas do, that Odysseus finally manages to get his way).

Of course, it is in the nature of all drama of suffering to generate pity. Aristotle deemed pity essential to tragedy, and the loophole for avoiding too much pity was indeed the deus ex machina—the god who would be machine-lowered onto the stage to save the day. However, Aristotle also seems to frown on such rescues when they are poorly motivated: why, for example, does Herakles suddenly offer at this moment to cure

Philoctetes's painful foot?[20] Perhaps the sympathy shown by the god is also political expediency, since the Greeks want to win the war and fate has it that they do. Today the tragedy that opts for the happy end might be called a melodrama by which critics would also attack its seemingly tacked-on happy ending. Others, like the critics of melodrama before it began to be rehabilitated or, those not fully cognizant of the cultural power of melodrama, might call it simply a "failed tragedy."[21] And the *Philoctetes* does indeed seem melodramatic in its concentration on the sustained and excruciating suffering caused by this hero's pus-filled foot. The hero's injury, caused not by some overweening pride but by his accidental step into a sacred shrine where he was bitten by a snake, proves that unlike Agamemnon or Oedipus, Philoctetes did not *do* anything terribly wrong to warrant his suffering. A tragedy of this sort can open up many questions that do not belong to the realm of classical tragedy. The suffering of innocence can lead to a hope for rescue and an avoidance of catastrophe that is quite untragic: the avoidance of catastrophe, the hope for redemption for the poor innocent who do not deserve to suffer. For although Philoctetes is a hero whose bow will help the Greeks win the Trojan War, at this point in the play he is "great" only in his suffering. In this he resembles the more recent victim-heroes of melodrama, who are put onstage not to be reconciled to a predetermined fate but to either struggle and die, or struggle and win. Whether struggle succeeds or fails, whether the end is happy or sad, the function of such victim-heroes is to demonstrate a virtue proven through the very acts of struggle and suffering. Strict tragedy does not hope for this kind of justice. Melodrama, born in a much later, liberal democratic age, unveils good or evil in order to confront the horrendous failure of justice in a world that has dared to hope for it. Melodrama, in other words, is a mode of feeling that generates outrage against a fate that *could* and *should* be changed. Tragedy, by contrast, does not politically or socially challenge the fate of suffering.[22]

We often misuse the word "tragedy" to refer to any misfortune. The bigger the misfortune, the bigger, so we think, the tragedy. The term has a way of dignifying everything from bad luck to the most calamitous disasters.[23] But as critics of both melodrama and tragedy are frequently at pains to note, tragedy connects to, but is not necessarily caused by, the overweening pride and fatal flaws (or at least momentous mistakes) of its characters. It depicts divided souls who struggle against fate and themselves. Melodrama, in contrast, depicts the most unfortunate victims of avoidable fates who struggle against wrong or simply against misfortune. In the early nineteenth-century stage dramas that gave the mode its name, the absorption of evolving realist practices has often meant that while these plays featured undivided (wholly good or evil) victims and villains, neither the monopathy described by Robert Heilman (1968) nor the Manichean worldview described by Peter Brooks (1976) has fully persisted into more contemporary works of the "melodramatic imagination."

The facile emotional spectacle of the suffering of innocence may be melodrama's most embarrassing cliché, from the stage dramas of Pixérécourt, through Dicken's Little Nell, Stowe's Little Eva and Uncle Tom to all the grand victims of silent cinema, from *The Hazards of Helen* to Rose and Jack on *The Titanic*, or even poor Gary in *The Corner*. But there are also less commercial, more "artistic" forms of melodrama that are often referred to as art cinema, but which are also unmistakably melodrama, from D. W. Griffith's *Broken Blossoms* to Carl Dreyer's *La passion de Jeanne d'Arc* through the contemporary sufferers of, say, Lars von Trier's *Breaking the Waves, Dancer in the Dark*, and *Dogville*.[24] Those who praise *The Wire* as tragedy have done so because they want to elevate its exceptional dramatic achievements beyond the usual televisual fare. But as we saw in the previous chapter, this usual fare has been changing, gaining more complexity with greatly expanded "world and time." If the usual fare is the simplistic black/white oppositions of certain melodramatic genres, such as cop shows that pit good guys (cops) who solve cases against bad guys (usually underclass criminals) who eventually get caught, then we can understand why Simon wants to deny the generic familiarity of "cop show."

Yet if we return to the cold open of the first episode of *The Wire*'s first season and its apparently typical cop-show enigma of "who shot Snot?" we find that the question will never be merely "whodunit?" but why someone like him gets killed—or, more pertinently, why robbing a gambling pot is the only "equal opportunity" presented to a kid like Snot in America. It is not accidental, as critics have noted, that Snot's real name is "Omar Isaiah Betts," echoing the name of another robber of much larger pots who will figure prominently throughout the series.[25] Whereas Omar Little, the daring robber of drug dealers, has a moral code and a personal sense of justice, Omar Betts (Snot) has neither. Both, however, are distorted versions of the ways the equal opportunity promised by the American Dream plays out for young black men in contemporary urban America. Indeed, in season 2, episode 10, Omar Little will sport a T-shirt that ironically reads, "I Am the American Dream."

As we saw in the last chapter, the ability to contextualize larger and larger swaths of urban social reality and to see how they connect is one of the series's great achievements. The connections planted here between two stash robbers, one a bumbler, the other a pro, demonstrate the complexity of the melodrama engaged. Early nineteenth-century stage melodrama relied upon then new deployments of mute victims and cleverly disguised villains—while "typical" genre television such as the multiplying CSI franchises may strictly repeat many of these same formulas with the caveat that they must be more plausibly (realistically) motivated. Because *The Wire* differs from these typical cop melodramas, many critics, bloggers, and viewers have wanted to call the suffering of many of its protagonists tragic.[26] They mean, as does Simon in this chapter's epigraph, that it eschews facile happy endings, that it is "realistic." However, we misunderstand the real achievement of the series if we attribute to tragedy all that is great (and seemingly transcendent) in *The Wire*.

There is such a thing as good, rich, complex, socially relevant, and politically efficacious melodrama, and the case of *The Wire* offers an unusual opportunity to grasp what American genre-driven television culture can be at its best. So, just as melodrama should not be defined as failed tragedy, neither should an ambitious "utopian" melodrama be viewed either as the transcendent achievement of tragedy or alternatively, as Jameson would have it, as "Utopian realism." How, then, might we engage some of the better arguments that have been made for *The Wire*'s aspiration to be tragedy in order to ultimately discover its more fundamental achievement as institutional melodrama?

In one of the earliest and best appreciations of *The Wire*, film and new media critic Marsha Kinder writes that the emotional power of the series depends on tension between many vibrant characters with enormous flaws who find that the "culture is wired" to destroy them. "What results," she writes, "is serial tragedy with a systemic form of suture, which inspires awe and pity week after week."[27] Kinder's judgment that the series is "serial tragedy" is an innovative way of recognizing how its "tragic" effect does not hinge on any one individual tragic hero, and certainly not on one of its most frequently appearing "through" characters, Detective Jimmy McNulty. There is no single main tragic hero in *The Wire*, but there is a fatalist tone and a certain brave acceptance of violent death on the part of many characters that Kinder, like many others, equates with tragedy. For example, she quotes the "hit woman" Felicia "Snoop" Pearson's next to last words, "Deserve got nothin' to do with it," spoken before she composedly accepts her own death at the hands of the young gangster Michael Lee.[28] Kinder takes Snoop's reconcilement with her own abrupt demise as a reflection of the "tragic vision" of the series as a whole.

But the phrase, while stoical, actually describes her attitude toward the character she and Michael are on their way to whack themselves and implicitly Michael himself, whom Snoop believes she is about to kill before Michael gets her first. She does not care if the victim they were about to kill or Michael himself deserves it or not. The phrase is Snoop's way of correcting what she sees as Michael's overly questioning attitude toward the morality of orders from above. Snoop's acceptance of her fate and the decreed fate of others is thus both fatalistic—it is her time, she will not fight—and pathetic. She behaves as what some characters in the serial might call a soldier but as what others (like D'Angelo in the chess lesson) call a pawn. The only dignity she earns in her death is the knowledge that she accepted it calmly, lookin' good. After checking herself in the car mirror she asks, "How's my hair look, Mike?" The answer that precedes the bullet, "You look good, girl!" recognizes an obedient virtue in her acceptance of the rules of "the game." But we cannot call such a death tragic. A tragic hero would have brought this fate more significantly upon him or herself and would then be granted time to rail against the injustice of his or her fate before having to face it. Such a hero would not go "so gently into the good night." That Snoop so gracefully accepts her death may contribute to a tragic tone of bleak despair but not to the tragedy of her own fate.

Tiffany Potter and C. W. Marshall, editors of *The Wire: Urban Decay and American Television*, also make a case for the series as tragedy. In the introduction to their volume, they admit that tragedy's "central preoccupation, the cost and consequences of greatness, sits uncomfortably with the democratizing tendencies coincident with the effects of the Industrial Revolution."[29] They further admit that "the arcs for most of the show's characters are not tragic, but rather merely sad. . . . There are simply too many stories, too many characters whose experience is presented in *The Wire*, for the focus on the individual to assert itself, as would be required by conventional representation of tragedy."[30] Nevertheless, following Arthur Miller's famous insistence that tragedy can still be written in modern America,[31] they enumerate a number of characters whose fates are tragic though lacking in traditional nobility. Some of these characters, they argue, are willing to lay down their lives to secure a "rightful" position and personal dignity and thus might be considered marginally tragic. Others whom they also call tragic—the corner boys Dukie and Bodie, for example—seem far too victimized to be given this status.[32]

However, there are two characters—Frank Sobotka and Stringer Bell—whose fates do seem tragic in the grand tradition of a prolonged and noble struggle against inevitable fate. The second season's focus on Frank Sobotka's attempt to raise money to lobby politicians to dredge the port of Baltimore and create more work for his union offers the clearest example of tragedy—and even explicitly Greek tragedy—in *The Wire*. Sobotka is a flawed but noble leader whose good cause leads inadvertantly to catastrophe: the deaths of thirteen women, the arrest of his nephew, the incarceration of his son for murder, and finally his own death. Unlike Wallace, the innocent scapegoat of season 1, he knowingly tempts fate and brings the tragedy down upon himself. These are tragic qualities of which Aristotle himself would have approved.

Sobotka is the secretary-treasurer of the predominantly Polish International Brotherhood of Stevedores union. In season 2 he makes a Faustian bargain to save his waning union by helping Eastern European gangsters smuggle contraband into the country through his port. We assume, in a story that has so far primarily been about drugs, that this contraband will be narcotics. Sobotka's goal is to pay lobbyists to use their influence to save and expand Baltimore's Inner Harbor. Police discover thirteen Eastern European prostitutes dead in a shipping container. Horrified that the contraband is human, Sobotka attempts to back out of the smuggling deal, but because his son and nephew have become involved in their own small-time smuggling schemes as well, they are ensnared by the police. To assure that the law will go easy with his nephew and son, he makes a deal with the police to turn informant on the head trafficker, known as "the Greek." When the Greek gets word of this, Sobotka is killed. We don't see his death, but we see him walk toward it, and we see its aftermath: the display of Sobotka's multiply stabbed body after it has been dredged from the harbor and lowered by a crane onto the dock. The body displayed after the fact of a violent action, while an audience of citizens (in this case stevedores arriving for work) stand witness in a semicircle, is a self-conscious imitation of one of the most classic aspects of Greek tragedy.[33]

Though this season's twelve episodes far exceed the Aristotelian unities of time and place, the confinement of this tragic fate to the frame of this one season, and the above display of the body, lends it a comparatively tight "classical" form.[34] This is a familial tragedy that sees the ruin of the "house of Sobotka" just as Clytemnestra's murder of Agamemnon ruins the house of Atreus. Like the *Oresteia*, it is also a serial tragedy involving both older and younger generations. Indeed, it is a self-consciously modern tragedy in a rather throwback Arthur Miller style, not unlike *A View from the Bridge*, also about dockworkers. But when it is over in season 2, it is over; it has few narrative tentacles reaching into the other institutions and thus little larger resonance within the series as a whole. The individual tragedy of one man and his family to whom "attention must be paid"[35] is neatly (perhaps even too neatly) contained within this season and it runs against the larger ambition of the series to forge connections between institutions. Although it is certainly part of the story of the urban ruin of Baltimore played against uto-

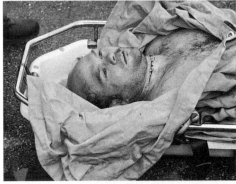

Sobotka's body lowered by crane as in a deus ex machina

Sobotka's body on display

The stevedore-chorus witnesses its fallen hero

pian dreams of revival, the "fall of Sobotka" stands out too much from the tightly woven series as a whole. It does not help that this tragedy is also predominantly about white ethnic workers and that it invites a back-in-the-day mourning for an era in which working-class pride and upward mobility often played out among white ethnics to the exclusion of blacks, Hispanics, and women.[36]

More in keeping with the complex nature of serial television and thus the fabric of the rest of the series is the tragic story of Stringer Bell as it interacts with that of his close friend and partner Avon Barksdale, leader of the Barksdale West Side drug ring. Bell's story is woven into the first three seasons, culminating in his death at the hands of Omar Little and Brother Mouzone, as ordered by Avon. In the first season, Stringer Bell acts as Avon's loyal lieutenant, fending off both Omar and the police to assure the smooth functioning of their corners and towers. But when Avon goes to prison for a year and Stringer must deal with the lack of good product in the second season, his way of doing business diverges from Avon's more feudal model. Stringer makes a deal with the competition, Proposition Joe, who runs the East Side drug ring. Instead of fighting one another for territory, they devise a co-op in which they share the same supply. At first this finance capital model works, and it might seem that a newly enlightened, less violent era of cooperation for mutual profit has dawned—except that Stringer's business model violates Avon's greater respect for family. He has Avon's nephew, D'Angelo, killed in prison because he is at risk to become an informer. In the third season, he also makes an attempted hit on Omar Little and in the process disrespects the traditional Sunday truce that has prevailed "as long as the game itself" (3.9). His hit men miss Omar but offend even longtime Barksdale regulars when they shoot off "the crown" (fancy hat) of Omar's respected grandmother on her way to church.

Stringer Bell's "fatal flaws" come to a head toward the end of the third season when his tendency to ruthlessly eliminate possible informants clashes with his rather naïve belief that he can turn drug profits into a legitimate and less violent capitalist enterprise. Indeed, this hope is his own form of the American Dream's aspiration to middle-class status. His bid for legitimacy is represented by the waterfront condos he is developing under the name B&B (Barksdale and Bell) Enterprises. Thus while his conversion to capitalist strategies represents a relief from the more class-bound, "gangster" violence of his partner Avon—as, for example, his introduction of *Robert's Rules of Order* for the conduct of meetings—his behind-the-scenes manipulations are emblematic of the underlying but hidden violence of capital, which only values the accumulation of wealth.[37] Ironically, then, the man who most advocates the abandonment of unnecessary "gangster" violence has, according to the very logic of his capitalist principles, ordered some of the most unforgivable acts of violence in the series: the deaths of Wallace and D'Angelo.

Two dramatic moments toward the end of the third season reveal this violence and lead inexorably, tragically to Stringer Bell's own death. In the first (3.8, "Moral Midgetry"), Avon, recently out of jail and wounded in a gang fight, challenges Stringer's strategy to lay off fighting for territory. "I bleed red. You bleed green," he observes, meaning that his ties to the street are more important than Stringer's abstract monetary investments. More pointedly, he adds that perhaps Stringer is "not hard enough for this here [the gangster life] and maybe, just maybe, not smart enough for them out there [the business life of finance capital]." Offended, Stringer replies, "Not smart enough because I think before I snatch a life?" Avon sneers, "What life did you snatch?" But as a slow lateral move of the camera shifts from a view of Avon's dismissive back to a rack focus on Stringer's glowering face, he now tells Avon that it was he who had Avon's nephew D'Angelo killed in prison because he thought the young man was about to "flip" and endanger the whole organization. "I knew you couldn't do it. But there go a life that had to be snatched." Furious, the wounded Avon, bleeding red through his bandage, throws himself on Stringer but is overpowered. Holding Avon down on the floor, Stringer explains that he had done what Avon needed to do but could not: "I took that shit off you and put it on me." Thus Stringer confesses to D'Angelo's murder, not out of guilt but from what can accurately be called a tragic fatal flaw that here compels him to prove his ghetto "hardness" linked to his business "smartness." Though Avon cannot argue with the necessity of this crime, things are never the same between them.

Stringer reveals his "hard" side again later in the same season. He has given a quarter million in bribe money to state senator Clay Davis to pave the way for his move into "legitimate" business. But once he learns from his attorney, Maurice Levy, that he has been taken for a ride, he demands a "hit" on the cagey senator. His would-be hit man, the ever-reasonable Slim Charles, correctly perceives that this would be not an ordinary hit but an "assassination," and Avon can only gloat at Stringer's naïveté on both counts—giving the bribe in the first place and thinking he can kill a "downtown" politician with impunity in the second. "They seen your ghetto ass coming from miles away," he crows. In frustration, the usually calculating Stringer breaks protocol and makes a call that allows his phone to be tapped and enables the police to draw closer to their prey. Thus, the business-minded, forward-looking, goal-oriented, and strategic Stinger Bell proves to be naïve; his ghetto ass is not "smart enough or hard enough" to escape the ghetto neighborhood in which he and Avon grew up.

Perhaps the final irony of Stringer Bell's tragic fall is that Avon gets to him before the police do—a source of great regret for Detective Jimmy McNulty. The police, now "up" on Stringer's phone, catch a call he makes to the western district police. In a secret nighttime meeting at Green Mount Cemetery, Stringer divulges Avon's hideout to Major Bunny Colvin, unaware that Avon has already given Stringer up for a hit by Nation of Islam adherent, Brother Mouzone, now working in league with Omar. After each of their betrayals has secretly been set in motion, they share a drink on the balcony of Avon's high-rise condo overlooking the redeveloping Inner Harbor. Like Frank Sobotka in the previous season, Avon is nostalgic for the good old days of their youthful high jinks. The difference, however, is that "back in the day" for them was not a more glorious period of upwardly mobile work and security. The neighborhood below was once the slum where Stringer—ever the upscale aspirant—had once stolen a badminton set from a toy store. Reminiscing at the thrill of their escape from a pursuing security guard, Avon recalls, "I told your ass not to steal the badminton set!" And anyway, what use was such a game when, as both men chime in laughing, "we ain't got no yard!"[38] The former delinquents sigh over the simpler joys of their youth, Stringer adding that he wishes he had been able to buy this property back then. Avon, however, is happy to see how far they have come. "Just dream with me," he enjoins Stringer. But Stringer

"Just dream with me,"
says Avon

doesn't want dreams of glory; he wants "shit you can touch," he wants the material goods that would remove him from his class and his origins, and soon the two friends are warily dancing around each other's plans for the next day. Avon tells Stringer he should relax, in the process ironically echoing Stringer's own words to Major Colvin when he gave up Avon to the police: "It's just business." Their final embrace shows each of them regretful but resolved to carry out their plots.

"Just business" for both turns out to be the mutually assured destruction of the reign of Barksdale and Bell. It is "the gangster as tragic hero" twice over.[39] Although Avon's fall will send him to jail and cause him to suffer the full loss of the family in whose name he has built his empire, it is Stringer whose fall displays the full panoply of tragic catastrophe. The next day he arrives at the condo construction site and chews out his contractor for delays. But when Omar Little and his new ally, Brother Mouzone, arrive and shoot a guard, he runs for his life up the stairs of the unfinished condo. Trapped against a second-floor picture window, with terrified pigeons flying about in the cavernous space that has not yet become the upscale residence he envisions, he faces his pursuers. "I ain't involved in that gangster bullshit no more," he protests, adding, "I could be a better friend to you alive." Omar is disgusted: "You still don't get it, do you? This ain't about your money, bro.' Your boy gave you up, and we didn't have to torture his ass neither." This is the unkindest cut of all: Brandon—Omar's lover in season 1—had never betrayed Omar when tortured by Stringer Bell, but Omar makes sure that Stringer understands that Avon has willingly "given up" Stringer.

Stringer faces his catastrophe

"Coming Soon . . . B&B Enterprises"

With a proper anagnorisis (tragic recognition of fate) registered in close-up, Stringer now faces his catastrophe in the form of the guns of Omar and Mouzone. After a long pause and the quietly spoken recognition that he can't "do nothin' to change your minds," he orders them, "Get on with it, motherf—." Shots ring out from both Omar's shotgun and Mouzone's pistol before Stringer can even finish the epithet. Omar walks into the space against the window where Stringer formerly stood, and when he leaves it, a rack focus reveals that behind him, on the wall across the street, is a yellow sign that reads, "Coming Soon. Residential Opportunities. B&B Enterprises" (3.11, "Middle Ground").

The falls of Sobotka (season 2) and Bell (season 3) are modern, almost textbook examples of classical Greek tragedy. Each man is a larger-than-life leader of his community, equipped with huge ambitions and equally huge flaws. One fate is played out against the failed rejuvenation of the harbor as a place of aspiring middle-class work and the other against the failed transformation of drug money into B&B Enterprises as a "legiti-mate" real estate development on the waterfront. Two visions of the future of Baltimore's waterfront are depicted, both based originally on illegal trafficking, both attempting to launder an original basis in contra-band commodity exchange—smuggling for Sobotka, drug street sales for Bell—into a more pure form of capital accumulation. But where So-botka's investment of capital is to purchase the political influence to buy his union more work with the entry of bigger ships into the harbor, Bell's investment of capital, which also attempts to buy political influ-ence, has as its goal pure finance capital—money with which to make more money, not to preserve a community or provide work beyond pay-ing lieutenants and corner boys. Sobotka's dream is thus *utopian*, part of the fading American Dream; Bell's is "just business" in a telling con-flation of criminality, personal betrayal, and economics. When Detec-tives McNulty and Moreland search Bell's neat, tasteful, cosmopolitan apartment after his death, they not only don't recognize the person they thought was their antagonist, but they are also surprised to find a copy of *The Wealth of Nations*.[40]

Adam Smith's classical liberal vision of economics asserted that the common good would be served if individuals simply followed their own self-interest. Bell's various economic lectures to underlings through-out the series show that he has certainly absorbed this lesson and that he believes his plans for efficiency will be good for all. But it is also clear that in this economic system no "invisible hand" guides the public good and that ultimately Bell is less a representative of Adam Smith's economic vision than he is the neoliberal harbinger of its and his own doom. Stringer Bell may fall, but the economic future of Baltimore that he pursued will certainly prevail as luxury condos beat out real work on the docks. Thus neither the old-fashioned liberalism dreamed by So-botka—the one that will produce middle-class work for self-improving working men and their families—nor the harder one governed by the "iron law of wages" will win. Liberalism, conceived as the universal right to pursue equal opportunity offered by democratic societies ("This is America, man!") is barely an option. Neoliberalism, which only appears to embrace the "rights of man," so strictly adheres to the operation of a "free market" that only the few, already wealthy, already educated, and mostly white have real opportunity. Neither Sobotka, nor Bell can buy this opportunity. In season 4 of *The Wire*, Dukie, the ostracized middle-school kid is given the excellent advice by the streetwise boxing gym coach, Cutty Wise: street life is not the only way to be: the "world is bigger than that." Dukie, who has learned to use a computer and who understands the theory, cannot grasp the practice: "How do you get from here to the rest of the world?" he asks (5.5). Cutty, who has only made it halfway into the rest of the world himself, has no answer. In the neoliberal world there is less and less opportunity, less getting from here to there.

Indeed, this may be the deeper tragedy depicted by *The Wire*—the fall of Smith's very idea of an unfettered market that has the power to benefit many.[41] The true irony of the presence of *The Wealth of Nations* in Bell's apartment would then be that the liberal economic theory that once fueled Bell's aspirations has given way to a world in which a certain quality of life is commodified for the already wealthy (or just lucky) while everyone else's options shrink, including Stringer Bell's as he is dragged down by his gangster past and ghetto origins.[42] Any way you look at it, the future for the increasingly underemployed worker and for the already-unemployed underclass is bleak.

Of course, not all "fates" in *The Wire* are bleak.[43] Even if there is no question that Sobotka and Bell suffer classically tragic falls, their two fates, neither of which extends across the whole narrative, cannot define a serial with some fifty major characters, no discernable levels of A-, B-, or C-level plots, and a relative dearth of personal storyworlds. It is therefore worth attending to how Tiffany Potter and C. W. Marshall, some of the earliest critics of *The Wire* after Marsha Kinder, maintain that even if there are very few actual tragic fates, nevertheless the "show itself . . . functions as tragedy." Their argument sheds light on a common misperception of how tragedy has undergone democratic transformation in the modern age by simply being rendered more "realistic." In a liberal democratic spirit that runs counter to the very spirit of tragedy, they argue that it is the mere fact of "giving a human face to what is usually written off as unavoidable urban blight, criminality, and addiction" that constitutes tragedy in this work.[44] As if the achievement of modern tragedy were simply a matter of lowering the socioeconomic bar on whose fate deserves to be counted as worthy, they argue that the innovation of *The Wire* is, in Arthur Miller's terms, to have "paid attention" to lives formerly regarded as disposable and thus to have advanced the argument "that all of American culture must act with justice."[45]

Justice, however, is itself a highly melodramatic sentiment produced by the same forces that brought about revolution in the name of the "Rights of Man." Even in the exceptionally melodramatic case of Sophocles's tragedy, Philoctetes, the title character who is pitied so much that he is finally given justice, receives that justice, as Martha Nussbaum notes, because he is a "noted hero," "a person of importance." Compassion, she observes, is "in league with hierarchies of heroism and birth. We weep for people whose exploits catch our attention, who are brought before us as fascinating. . . . The ordinary soldier's suffering is boring." This is why, Nussbaum argues, tragedy is an inherently "aristocratic art form."[46] Her failed attempt in this article is to learn from Sophocles's example how tragedy too might become democratic and attend to the suffering of the more "ordinary soldier." However, she rather oddly locates her best example of this more democratic tragedy in the films of Satyajit Ray, which, she argues, make vivid the "ordinary suffering" of "distant Bengalis."[47] This example seems to relocate what was once the importance of aristocratic heroes into the exotic difference of distant Bengalis. To turn to the art films of Ray as examples of tragedy is to avoid a whole history of the mass culture of a democratic age, which has culminated in important ways in a television serial like *The Wire*.

Tragedy, quite frankly, has not adapted well to a mass-culture democratic age because it is not possible to democratically include "ordinary suffering" as tragedy. Nussbaum's inclusion of the suffering of ordinary but "distant Bengalis" into the realm of tragedy almost smacks of its own kind of aristocratic noblesse oblige. Liberal democracy cannot fully *do* tragedy; the mere inclusion of more ordinary (shall we say lower-class?) suffering into tragic plots does not necessarily make the sentiments of tragedy legible when characters have so little distance to fall, when, as in *Pather Panchali*, ordinary life is so frequently subject to catastrophe. What Nussbaum does not seem to recognize is that in the twenty-four centuries since Sophocles wrote both the *Oedipus* and the *Philoctetes*, a form of theater and an evolving form of mass media arose that had already adapted the "morality of pity" to its own ends.[48] Against those critics and theorists of tragedy who would now argue, as Rita Felski has, that it is time to consider the relevance of tragedy to the contemporary moment, I counter that tragedy is mostly *not* relevant to this moment. At the same time, however, I would agree with Felski, as well as Barbara Klinger, that it is time to stop rereading the melodramas of Douglas Sirk and to discover the many kinds of melodramas—good, bad, and indifferent—that have operated before, alongside and since.[49]

Once the "right" to be pitied is asserted, once "an ordinary soldier's suffering" is the substance of a story, once democratic ideals of justice under the law are invoked, and once we are told, as Arthur Miller tells us, that "attention must be paid" even to the likes of the well-named Willy Loman, then we are no longer in the realm of tragedy. When *Wire* critics Potter and Marshall attempt to twist tragedy into what it cannot be—a plea for justice for the lowly and disenfranchised, a protesting "dissent" to the injustice of the world—they inevitably begin to talk about melodrama.[50]

Tragedy is too final, too catastrophic, too inevitable, and too reliant on the exceptional greatness of its victims and our awe of them to make the kinds of claims for justice that *The Wire*, as a whole, makes. Tragedy, in the end, cannot be about outrage at a lack of justice. Quite the contrary, it is an acceptance of fate, even as it seems too terrible to endure.[51] Frank Sobotka and Stringer Bell are the closest *The Wire* gets to tragic protagonists because they are important members of their community who try to make change but when fate overcomes them, they accept it. Stringer Bell accepts his fate when he tries to order his assassins to "get on with it, motherf—," but this order is significantly cut short. The time he is given to contemplate his tragic fate is stunted, not given its full "hour upon the stage," even if the reason for that is Omar and Brother Mouzone's compliance with his wish to "get on with it." In Sobotka's case, though we do not see him heroically greet his fate, we do see his whole community—a veritable chorus—stand in awe of it, registering the significance of his fall. However, if attention is paid to Sobotka, the only person to really mourn the loss of Bell is Detective Jimmy McNulty, who sincerely regrets the lost opportunity to put Bell behind bars.

Melodrama belongs to liberalism's promise of progress, individual self-determination, and the refusal of predetermined fate. The kind of melodrama we encounter in *The Wire* may well represent the discovery of the limits of this liberalism, and it could well be that David Simon turns to tragedy as a way of emphasizing these limits, hence the iconic references to tragedy, especially in Sobotka's case. But the tragic fates of Bell and Sobotka are circumscribed by a larger melodrama that seeks justice and that is governed by the outrage that so little justice exists for the poor and the black. Neither of these heroes fully recognizes, as tragic heroes must, the full significance of his fate. Indeed, in the case of Stringer Bell the problem is not only that he isn't "smart enough" to play with the real finance capital sharks, but also that he himself is a product of the dehumanizing forces of neoliberalism that prioritize entrepreneurship and smooth financial flows at the expense of human relationships and community. In trying to live out the norms of the very system of economic and racial injustice that delimits his possibilities in life, he is trapped by them.

In both cases, though in Bell's case more severely, the full tragedy—the anagnorisis, or transition from ignorance to tragic knowledge—is brutally cut short. Other stories crowd the stage. The very time normally given a tragic hero to contemplate his fate is truncated. Even within a twelve- or thirteen-hour season, the actual wheel of fate turns fast. Sobotka is granted more time than Bell to feel the noose encircling his neck but he is given no time to rail against his fate. You might say that part of the tragedy of the *Wire* is that there is not enough time for tragic recognition in a world with so many pitiable fates. But there is regularly less time for such contemplation in the case of black protagonists like Bell.

Simon is certainly right to claim that it is the postmodern—though the better term is actually "neoliberal"—institutions against which his characters struggle. But these institutions are not the "indifferent gods" of tragedy. Whenever an individual tries to struggle against an institution that fails to serve its citizens—whether it is Bell's attempt to reform the drug trade so that fewer bodies will fall, councilman and future mayor Tommy Carcetti's attempts to make city government responsible to citizen's needs, Major Colvin's attempt to reform the police, or

Young Wallace, season 1

Dukie, season 4

Colvin's later attempt to reform the schools—that reform will usually fail. We habitually call these failures tragic. But there is too much hope for change in *The Wire* and too much pathos for helpless victims like young Wallace of the first season or Dukie of the last two or Bubbles throughout to say that the serial is predominantly tragic. Sad endings do not a tragedy make.

Robert Heilman, in one of the earliest sustained comparisons between tragedy and melodrama, notes that tragedy is not about the plague in Thebes.[52] Oedipus's solution to the riddle of the Sphinx may end that plague, but the play is not about the afflictions of a city that might be set right. It is about conflict and suffering within the great soul of the tragic hero. Melodrama, in contrast, *can* be about the plague in Thebes, Calcutta, or Baltimore. Bad things happen to people in melodrama, but, as we shall see in the next chapter, melodrama enables us to hope for the happier, more just ending. And even if that hope is dashed, melodrama still wants us to know what justice could be—that the plague could be wiped out, that poverty could be alleviated, that burdens such as drug addiction and general human worthlessness could be lifted. This is why David Simon has called his series "dissent." Like it or not, however, it is melodrama, not tragedy, that has the true ability to dissent.[53]

4 Realistic, Modern Serial Melodrama

We have seen that many critics have praised *The Wire* by calling it tragedy but that only a few of its individual story arcs are actually tragic. Often what critics mean by "tragic" is simply that the series is serious and realistic—unafraid of facing the worst aspects of American life. So why do I insist on calling this work melodrama when so many of its advocates, most important its primary authors, resist this term? We bring to the word "melodrama" a great many negative clichés: pounding music, pathetic victims, leering villains, florid acting, and the triumph of virtue in badly motivated happy endings. All of these clichés seem to point to forms of "excess" measured against more "realistic" or more "modern" norms. My goal in this chapter is to show that melodrama need not be recognized by aesthetic or emotional "excess," or any obvious lack of realism—a term whose meaning shifts even more than melodrama. *The Wire* self-consciously avoids most of the clichés of melodrama. Yet both its realism and its contemporaneity qualify it as an exceptionally accomplished serial melodrama, and we can best appreciate it as such.

Most of the negative qualities by which we recognize melodrama are artifacts of the early nineteenth-century stage, when it first became popular, and of the early-twentieth-century film to which it migrated from the stage. In film study the resistance to understanding the ongoing importance of melodrama reflects the belief that something variously called "classical" realism or "classical Hollywood"[1] long ago became the dominant form of mainstream filmic (and televisual) narrative style, while a shamefaced melodrama skulked offstage to be consigned to the repressed lower regions of dramatic narrative, only occasionally resurfacing as the return of the repressed of cinema.[2]

To view melodrama as an archaic excess increasingly banned from a more enlightened and well-motivated "classical" tradition is wrong in several ways. First, it ignores the modernity of melodrama itself by consigning it to a frozen moment in history—the early period of its emergence in high hyperbole on the nineteenth-century French stage. Second, it views all further developments of melodrama as a peculiar atavism rather than as a continuing response to the changing conditions of modernity. It is to ignore, for example, the ways that newer media like film and television have adapted and reinvented it. Third, it is to assume, as does even melodrama's great contemporary rehabilitator, Peter Brooks, that by looking hard under the surface of the great works of realist literature—say a Balzac or a James—we can discern the embedded remnants of an older melodrama. Even among its rehabilitators melodrama is regarded as an embedded "mode of excess."[3] I believe this is the biggest flaw in its theorization.

One has to ask: more excessive than what? We know what this was at the beginning of the nineteenth century: melodrama was excessive in relation to the decorum, unity, and efficiency of the high-culture, neoclassical tragedy and the Greek and Roman models on which neoclassical drama itself was based. This classical tragedy held that characters must declaim their woes with no grand gestures, no startling tableaux— in short, with no *Sturm und Drang*. In relation to ancient and "neoclassical eras," the new upstart melodrama (already intimated by Denis Diderot's earlier call for a new *drame sérieux* that was not tragedy) was radically hyperbolic, the very model of the "bigger than life." Its grand gestures, frozen tableaux, inflated rhetoric, and unprecedented use of music was straining to name ineffables that Brooks claims could no longer be named in language due to the loss of the "myth of Christendom" and a common "sacred."

It is important to recognize the role melodrama once had in shaking up the French neoclassical stage at the turn of the nineteenth century. One of the biggest shake-ups was the use of music, the *melos* from which it received its name. It is easy to forget that the kind of musical accompaniment to drama that we now take for granted in films and television was anathema on the neoclassical stage. At the turn of the nineteenth century "le mélodrame" (drama with music) was both new and modern. As Peter Brooks notes, "music was called upon whenever the dramatist wanted to strike a particular emotional pitch or coloring and lead the audience into a change or heightening of mood."[4] Today such uses of music are the norm for most film and television, while more subdued, understated, or nonexistent music is usually called realistic, as if the melodramatic and the realistic were opposed. We should note, though, that what mattered originally was not so much the apparent excess of the music, but its mere presence at all.

The Minimal Melos *of* The Wire

> When you walk through the garden
> you gotta watch your back
> well I beg your pardon
> walk the straight and narrow track
> if you walk with Jesus
> he's gonna save your soul
> you gotta keep the devil
> way down in the hole

The Wire has one signature piece of music that sets the tone for the entire serial. A version of Tom Waits's song "Way Down in the Hole" (originally recorded in 1987) is performed over the credit sequence of every episode. A different cover of this single song, accompanying a different credit montage that anticipates or recalls what happens in this season, becomes the signature *melos* of the series. In the first season, the song is performed by the Five Blind Boys of Alabama in polyphonic and rhythmic ways that evoke traditional West African roots. This is the song's most gospel-oriented and least bluesy version. In the second season it is performed by Waits himself in its original form, with a more working-class blues emphasis in his trademark gravelly voice. In the third it is performed by the Neville Brothers of New Orleans, who offer a fusion of gospel and blues along with a more syncopated jazz. The fourth version is the most "original" performance, made by a local Baltimore group of teenagers especially for the series. This digitized and synthesized version emphasizes improvised call and response, while the young voices echo the narrative of middle-school boys of the fourth season and contrast with the more traditional "first" version by the much older and more traditional-sounding Five Blind Boys. Finally in season 5, Steve Earle, a musician and recovering drug addict in real life and playing a recovering drug addict in this season of the series, offers a more "country" fusion with all the previous styles.[5]

The song itself is a wailing, raspy mixture of spiritual hope ("if you walk with Jesus / he's gonna save your soul") and haunting blues complaint and warning ("you gotta keep the devil / way down in the hole"). The five different performances of the same song echo, in their very repetition, the way character trajectories in the series are repeated, as when corner boy Michael Lee becomes the "new Omar" and Dukie Weems becomes the "new Bubbles," Marlo becomes the "new Barksdale" and Carcetti becomes the "new Mayor Royce." Like the *melos*, these are all variations on the same theme.[6] Like most songs used with narratives, this one helps cue feelings, in this case about the frustrated cycles of poverty and crime, policing and failure, hope and paranoia that dominate the series. It is an appropriate accompaniment to the weariness experienced by many of *The Wire*'s characters, whether or not they actually believe in Jesus as the hope of redemption or the devil who pulls them down. Of course the stark contrast of good and evil is itself, like all spirituals and most blues songs, inherently melodramatic. It is not necessary that the characters in *The Wire* themselves be in the grip of a struggle between Jesus and the devil, but, as James Braxton Peterson argues, those struggling with addiction (Bubbles and his friends, Jimmy McNulty and sometimes Bunk) translate the original injunction to "keep the devil way down in the hole" into going straight or keeping clean. Indeed, the song itself transmutes into a more insistent and pathetic plea at the end, when instead of "you gotta keep the devil" it becomes "you gotta keep *help me* keep the devil / way down in the hole."

"Way Down in the Hole" is the only unsourced *melos* (extradiegetic, offscreen music) the serial allows itself over five seasons, except for the different music accompanying the five montages that wrap up each season. Other than these highly contained and predictable moments, the only music we hear in *The Wire* are short bursts of blues, jazz, hip-hop, or rock from ambient sources like CDs, radios, cell phones, televisions, jukeboxes, or boom boxes. It is common to describe moving images that eschew music as more realistic than those that utilize it. And indeed, the entire "soundscape" of *The Wire* is deeply realistic in that we hear only what one would be likely to hear on the street, in the bar, on the corner, in the newspaper offices, and so on. Yet what we hear in each place is richly layered—a kind of music of its own. For example, in 3.8, "Moral Midgetry," when the Deacon pays a visit to Hamsterdam, general street noise is mixed with drug touts calling "WMDs," the crunch of grit underfoot, and ambient musical snatches from radio. Much like the effect of more subdued, understated acting, such uses of sound and music are frequently taken as signs of a "realism" that opposes the heightened emotions of melodrama. And indeed, when the Deacon (played by the actual former gangster, Melvin Williams, subject of one of Simon's early *Sun* profiles) registers horror at the sights and sounds of Hamsterdam, the musical texture of these sounds represent a new level of realist content for the portrayal of life on the street.[7] But this realistic sound, along with the visual chaos and intensity of the place where drugs are permitted only enhances the (melo)drama of what the Deacon, who approves of the market, nevertheless, sees as hell. New kinds of realistic contents do not nullify melodrama but innovate it.[8]

It will not do, then, to simply point to a relative absence of music to certify a work as realistic as opposed to melodramatic. In this case, the highly restricted use of music, the repetitive serial nature of the performance of that music, and its inherent conflict between ostensibly good (gospel traditions) and ostensibly bad (secular blues, rock, punk, rap) show that sometimes less can be more: that infrequent music, understated music, and different versions of the same music do not undermine the power of *melos* to make an audience feel, but can even enhance it.

If the innovation of adding *melos* to drama once shook up and enhanced the emotional power of the melodramatic stage in contrast to the neoclassical stage, this does not mean that the addition of music today means melodrama and its relative absence and realist motivation means realism. Rather, melodrama's conventions have continued to grow and change. Within thirty years of its initial shake up, as drama historian Matthew Buckley has shown, when its popularity made it a dominant dramatic form, "melodrama had become Exhibit A in the degenerate decline of the drama."[9] Not surprisingly, then, many who continued to "do" melodrama did not call it by name. For the next century and a half melodrama was viewed, Buckley continues, as a "genre worthy of notice only as the idiotic foil to modern drama's development of a new, legitimate art."[10] This attitude has generally persisted, and many critics of stage, film, and television still use the term "melodrama" as if it adequately described all forms of dramatic excess and manipulation that fail to respect "normal" rules of probability and character motivation. These critics have failed to understand melodrama's ongoing grip on most popular as well as many high forms of cultural narrative. However, ever since Peter Brooks's influential intervention, melodrama has been increasingly approached less as a fly-by-night genre and more as an enduring mode of expression and experience. As Buckley puts it, "no longer exiled from cultural history, melodrama seems now central to it, an essential thread in the warp and weave of global modernity."[11]

Though this may be something of an overstatement considering the derogatory meanings that stubbornly cling to the term, it is true that an increasing number of scholars, myself included, have considered the study of modernity (whether it be defined as the Enlightenment, the "loss of the sacred" brought about by the French Revolution, or the later upheavals of the Industrial Revolution) to be grounded in new conditions and ways of thinking about experience, family, gender, and race that melodrama, not tragedy, affords. The causes proposed for the rise of melodrama are various: Brooks attributes it to the upheavals of the French Revolution and the need for new ways to forge individual and personal forms of "moral legibility" after the "loss of the sacred"; film historian Ben Singer sees melodrama as a product and a reflection of modern experience, itself caused by industrial capitalism, "shifting social demographics and commercial practices."[12] In previous work I have followed Brooks in privileging the moral legibility expressed in alternating forms of pathos and action.[13] Most critics who have tried to comprehend the ongoing importance of melodrama in modern life agree that the morality once evidenced in the tragedy of great heros is reconceived in melodrama in more individual and personal terms. While characters suffer in both tragedy and melodrama, only in melodrama do we find what Friedrich Nietzsche calls the will to power that obtains through the suffering of the weak, or what Nietzsche calls slave morality.[14] In the following, I will isolate the most useful qualities of an evolving melodramatic imagination necessary for appreciating what is unique about *The Wire*.

Melodrama has been defined many ways, but if we are not to fix it at some moment of its previous history, then we must appreciate its protean qualities even as we try to isolate some of them for scrutiny.[15] Neither excessive music nor the defeat of evil by good is essential to melodrama. What is essential, I contend, following Peter Brooks, Christine Gledhill, Robert Bentley, Robert Heilman, Matthew Buckley, Elisabeth Anker, Ben Singer, and many others, is the dramatic *recognition* of good and/or evil and in that recognition the utopian hope that justice might be done.

Consider the clichés of the contemporary blockbuster action film. These films are rarely called melodramas—more frequently they are named by their popular genres: action, adventure, disaster, thriller, and so on—but they are arguably better understood as variants of melodrama than as members of various and sundry genres.[16] It is typical in contemporary blockbuster films for action heroes to be recognized not only by their heroic actions but also, first and foremost, by their suffering of some outrage to which they are not yet able to respond. The hero's suffering seems to earn him (and occasionally her) the moral right to kill the enemy with impunity. Indeed, the pathos of the suffering victim turned righteous-action hero is the curious and often suspect alchemy of contemporary popular melodrama.[17] To suffer, according to a certain Judeo-Christian framework, is to be empowered. The very injury that makes me see the evil in my injurer and the good in myself is the basis of a fundamentally resentful form of moralism—a Nietzschean *ressentiment*—at the heart of much melodrama.[18] We see this in mass-entertainment action melodramas just as much as we see it in the stories we tell ourselves about our righteousness as a nation.[19] Whether it is the oft-told American story of the conquest of the West, or the more recent story of the invasion of Iraq, in our popular melodramatic imagi-

nation we either portray ourselves as suffering at the hands of villainous others or, as became more prevalent in American reports toward
the end of the Vietnam or Iraq wars, we are forced to see ourselves as
the villains. As long as we can see ourselves as victims, then we seem to
morally deserve to conquer and invade—to otherwise occupy the position originally occupied by our injurer. Such is our deeply flawed, and
deeply familiar, melodramatic sense of justice.

If we look for contemporary melodrama only in its most familiar and
clichéd aspects—victims tied to railroad tracks, villains twirling mus-
taches, rescues that happen too late or in the nick of time, or in novel
interpretations of the more static, domestic melodramas of Vincente
Minnelli or Douglas Sirk—then we mistake its contemporary forms and
its protean attributes. Melodrama makes itself up-to-date by confront-
ing new and seemingly intractable social problems to the end of recognizing virtue, or, as I argue in the more ambitious case of *The Wire*,
with the end of recognizing institutional routes to social good.[20] Melodrama is the dramatic convention in which timely social problems and
controversies are addressed. It is not opposed to what we recognize as
realism. Rather, it enlists forms of realism to generate outrage against
realities that could and, according to its creators, should be changed.
Melodrama feeds on the problem of these realities and their forceful depiction to engender outrage against the very injustice of them. To this
extent, much melodrama has been allied with dreams of revolution or at
least the kind of change that might be able to rectify the social injuries
they depict. But even though melodrama has tended to be on the side
of the oppressed, perceptions of justice and injustice will always depend
on where you stand. It might be the injustice of slavery in one melodrama, the injustice of the former slaves to their masters in another, or
the pathetic life of a drug addict and criminal informant in yet another.
Melodrama's commitment to justice is thus not in any way objectively
just.[21] Nevertheless, an audience's ability to recognize good requires the
manifest suffering of an oppressed innocence. Only through the sympathy or empathy extended to those who suffer can moral legibility occur.[22]

This necessary *ressentiment* represents the limits of melodrama: its
preoccupation with injury often leads to self-righteous and addictive
forms of affective conditioning. If I suffer, this self-righteousness con-

tends, I am good and deserve to triumph. The most important question I want to address through the example of *The Wire* is whether melodrama is condemned only to repeat these patterns of personal injury, suffering, and vindication. Is melodrama's hold on our mass consciousness so strong that we have come to require what I have elsewhere called a "melodramatic fix"?[23] Is melodrama itself the problem as greater portions of the modern imagination have been given over to its influence? For example, Buckley asks whether melodrama's affective structures and sensational effects have become by now "a normative form of feeling and thought."[24] And Elisabeth Anker has argued that contemporary "left melodrama"—melodrama that particularly works in the American context toward social justice—is underpinned by a "refusal to acknowledge the loss of left political theory's guarantee that it provides a means to revolutionary freedom, as well as the loss of intrinsic moral virtue implicitly granted to its practitioners."[25] These are penetrating critiques of the dominance of melodrama as a way of reassuring an individual and a group of its inherent virtue, as well as the villainy of those who threaten us. The American "war on terror" is a perfect example of such melodramatic thinking: American freedom was attacked by a villainous other and the response to that attack ironically increased state power and reduced freedom even though it was carried out in the name of freedom and individual sovereignty.

My question is: might it be possible to forge a less self-righteous kind of melodrama, less dependent on wild swings between pathos and action, less a matter of cycles of victimization and retributive violence (whether based on inequities of race, gender, or class), and more a matter of reaching beyond personal good or evil to determinations of better justice?

In a foundational essay on film melodrama, written more than forty years ago, Thomas Elsaesser famously noted that "in the Hollywood melodrama characters made for operettas play out the tragedies of mankind."[26] Elsaesser was writing then about family melodrama of the 1950s considered as a genre, not as a mode as I hope to consider it here. His point was the ironic "mediocrity of the human beings" who tried to live up to an exalted vision of man but instead lived out the "impossible contradictions that have turned the American dream into its proverbial nightmare."[27] Elsaesser's appreciation of melodrama seems to have derived originally from a measurement against the standard of tragedy, as when he writes—again thinking of American melodramas of the 1950s—that they are "not only critical social documents but genuine tragedies."[28] Unfortunately, this standard leaves us with one high-culture, exalted form of tragedy and its ironic and reductive melodramatic degradation.

The viability of the American dream of liberal justice and opportunity for all is still at issue in Elsaesser's formulation, but not because characters fail to play out the "tragedies of mankind." The melodramatic experience is not a degraded, modern version of tragedy; nor is it the failure of inadequate or "mediocre" humans to play out tragedy. Rather, just as there are great tragedies, there are also great melodramas. And seriality means that no single catastrophe (or "happy end") need mark a frequently deferred conclusion, whether happy or sad. The following discussion of *The Wire* argues that we need not examine its melodrama as failed tragedy, nor as drama trapped in the self-righteousness of personal injury. Rather than repeating familiar tropes of the melodramatic imagination, it observes, through the "world enough and time" of seriality, a new dimension of melodrama grounded in social institutions.

The Reimagination of Serial Melodrama

As we have seen, *The Wire* has been considered so good, so "realistic" and so "authentic," that it couldn't possibly be associated with something so contrived and lowly as melodrama. As we saw in the previous chapter, it has even been disassociated from television altogether—not only as in self-advertised "It's Not TV, It's HBO" ads but by many critics as well.[29] Yet if critics were unwilling to call the series melodrama, they often agreed to call it what David Simon rightly regarded as the same thing: "Dickensian."[30]

In the fifth and final season, having heard one too many glowing comparisons of the series to Dickens's novels, Simon created a venal, white, patrician senior editor at the *Baltimore Sun*, James Whiting Jr.—significantly, *not* from Baltimore—who eventually demotes the responsible and hard-working black city editor, Gus Haynes—significantly,

Templeton wins Pulitzer

from Baltimore. This patrician editor also cancels a planned series of (multisited) stories on education and instead urges a junior reporter to develop the "Dickensian aspects" of a story about homelessness. This reporter, Scott Templeton—also *not* from Baltimore—writes a virtuous-victim story about a homeless Iraq War vet suffering from posttraumatic stress disorder that is a model of "surround a simple outrage" rifle-shot journalism (see chapter 1). This story, like many of his others, is fabricated. On the basis of his Dickensian (read: old-fashioned melodramatic) fictions, Templeton eventually wins a Pulitzer Prize.

Much of the fifth season is devoted to the rise of the lying career of Templeton, developed in parallel to the lies told by Detective Jimmy McNulty about a fake serial killer. McNulty lies in order to channel resources to the police in the ongoing investigation of the new drug kingpin Marlo Stanfield. In contrast, Templeton lies out of pure careerism. His venality is contrasted to the virtuous diligence of city editor Gus Haynes and many of the other hard-working younger reporters who are demoted as the paper downsizes while Templeton's star rises. We thus see how the entire profession has been cheapened through the "melodramatization" of decontextualized rifle-shot journalism at the expense of facts and deeper context.

Thus did David Simon have his sweet revenge on the bosses who did not appreciate his brand of contextualized, "multisited" journalism and who only appreciated the rifle-shot journalism that would "surround a single outrage," simplify it, and turn it into crude melodrama. But thus also did Simon melodramatically vilify his former bosses. Not only did he show to what lengths they would go to win Pulitzers, but he also showed how his own serial's contextualized "multisited" institutional storytelling was the virtuous kind that went deeper and further into the problems of the neoliberal city than any newspaper story could ever do. So, although Simon got to vent his spleen on the journalistic requirement to be "Dickensian," the fifth season especially *was* "Dickensian" in its way of deploying uncomplicated victims and villains.

In the fifth season of *The Wire*, then, melodrama is both satirized and performed straight. Some critics who gave accolades to the rest of the serial have criticized this one season.[31] If one of the great pitfalls of the melodramatic imagination is an excess of self-righteousness, then it is possible that the reason some enthusiasm for the series fell off this season is that, in depicting the one institution about which he had no critical distance, Simon could not help but self-righteously grind his ax. We have only to see how the series pats itself on the back for having covered all the multisited stories throughout the city that the paper itself has failed to cover. These include one on education that was planned and then canceled by the paper in order to do a superficial and mendacious one on homelessness instead, when education had already been "covered" deeply by the series itself in season 4's portrait of four middle-school boys. They also include one on Omar Little's death that is canceled in favor of a story about a fire. Indeed, the real melodramatic hero of season 5 might be regarded as the series itself, for it has already told all the important stories the newspaper either ignores, cancels, or garbles: city government's attempted reform, Bunny Colvin's "Hamsterdam" experiment, the succeeding drug dynasties, and so on.

In this fifth season, then, more than any other, we are invited to hiss the patrician villains and root for the downtrodden city editor who is demoted. *The Wire* is too "realistic" to let this city editor triumph in the end. Such a happy ending would indeed be *too* Dickensian. For what Simon really objects to in the epithet "Dickensian" is not the pathos of suffering but the happy ending that produces moral legibility too easily, as in the triumph of virtue caused by a personal change of heart. The "nice old uncle" or guardian, or the transformed Scrooge who comes along in the end to "fix things" is Simon's true objection to Dickens.[32] What gets "fixed" in the typical Dickensian happy ending is only the fate of the few good people who were already born to middle-class or better status anyway. If Dickens could brilliantly display the flawed workings of a single institution—say the Inns of Court in *Bleak House*—he could not show us, as *The Wire* does, the struggles *between* and within the other institutions with which the law works.

Even in its fifth and most recognizably melodramatic season, *The Wire* shows us a way out of the impasse of the nineteenth-century Dickensian melodrama and its repertoire of good uncles and virtuous victims. Its innovation throughout is to reach beyond the good or evil of individuals to play out the melodramatic quest for moral legibility at the personal *and* the institutional levels at once. In this way it also corrects the Dickensian tendency to privilege the virtue of the merely temporarily disadvantaged who turn out, in the end, to be well born and thus deserving. Even if a good-hearted uncle figure comes along to fix what is wrong for the individual, we are acutely aware of how limited a solution this is. Ultimately, *The Wire* is about individuals who grapple with unwieldy institutions and, at best, may claim small victories.

It thus is a matter of great concern whether the police can do more than merely catch bodies or make drug rips, or whether the unions can avoid corruption, or whether the city government can decide whether it is police or schools who need what limited funds are available, or if schools can enable teachers to really teach, or if media can report the truth of what happens in the city. This is where the generic "procedural" element of the series, modeled on the police procedural but extending to these other institutions of the city, becomes crucial.

As we saw in the last chapter, *The Wire* is a police procedural not simply in its observance of the routines of questioning witnesses or gathering evidence, but also in its focus on the moral life of policing as an institution. By the fifth season, when Detective Jimmy McNulty fabricates an attention-getting serial killer in order to receive funding to pursue the real crimes of Marlo Stanfield, and when Lester Freamon follows him down this path, we know that these lies are no more a product of being "good po-lice" than Scott Templeton's fabricated stories are a product of good reporting. In order to solve the case of the many dead bodies walled up in the vacant houses, McNulty invents evidence of a serial killer whose sensational crimes as reported by the *Sun* bring them the overtime and vehicles to work the real case of the bodies found in vacant houses. At this point, both the institution of policing and the institution of journalism have failed the moral test. While there are still good police on the force who refuse to go along with this scheme (especially Kima Greggs and Bunk Moreland), and while there are still good reporters on the beat (especially Mike Fletcher and Alma Gutierrez), the institutions as a whole have failed to perform their most basic functions.

When David Simon insists that *The Wire* is neither a "cop" nor a "crime" show, he associates melodramatic genres of the cop/crime show with the overarching mode of melodrama as a simplistic battle between good and evil: "We are bored with good and evil," he writes. "We renounce the theme."[33] But he has not renounced it; he has simply transposed the theme to a higher level of investigation and that transposition is part of the genius of the series. We may notice that the voice in which Simon supposedly renounces these recognizably generic forms of melodrama is the same one discussed in the first chapter—the royal "we" who speaks resonantly on behalf of society's victims but fails to convey that its voice belongs to them. This is the voice of (yesterday's bad) melodrama, speaking bombastically of the outrage of the persecution of innocence. This is the voice that Simon fortunately lost when he learned to dramatize, rather than editorialize, on behalf of society's victims and against its villains. But the fact that he found a way to suppress the overt righteousness of his own (archaic) melodramatic voice should not blind us to the (better) melodrama of the work created in its stead.

The police procedural frames the series as a whole. But within that frame are many other procedurals, each of which provides a full fabric of moral contexts, each context influencing another. For example, in season 5, because the newly elected Mayor Thomas Carcetti's ambition to run for governor had caused him to refuse to accept a handout for education from the current Republican governor in season 4, he finds himself in this new season without enough funds for both police and schools. He chooses not to fund the police and thus the investigation into the bodies found in the vacant houses is curtailed. This shortage of police funds precipitates Detective Jimmy McNulty's decision to fake evidence of a serial killing by breaking the neck of an already dead homeless man to match the MO of a corpse he recently viewed in the morgue. With such a sensational crime (serial killings of the homeless!), McNulty correctly figures, resources will flow again to the Major Crimes Unit. Something like the same reasoning is employed by Scott Templeton as the *Baltimore Sun* downsizes and reporters, like police, are asked to do "more with less." The "more" that Templeton does is, like McNulty, to completely fabricate local stories.

Thus *The Wire* recalibrates the very meaning of the melodramatic recognition of virtue to an institutional level: the institution of the police either can or can't recognize the "good" of effective community policing (the point at which McNulty fabricates false evidence and begins giving out overtime proves that they can't); the institution of drug dealers either can or can't recognize the good of avoiding the casualties of "dropping bodies" (the point at which Marlo Stanfield begins to kill for the slightest provocation proves that they can't); the unions either can or can't provide work without engaging in corruption (the point at which Sobotka's nephew and son do their own illegal smuggling proves that they can't); the city government either can or can't recognize the good of real reform, not just the appearance of it (the point at which Carcetti chooses his own career over money for schools proves that it can't); the schools themselves either can or can't recognize the good of teaching and learning with the benefit of "soft eyes"[34] (the point at which the special class is canceled proves that they can't); and the city newspaper either can or can't recognize the good of truthful, scrupulous reporting (the point at which Templeton is praised within the paper for his fabricated stories and purple prose proves that it can't).

The fact that in the end none of these institutions can recognize and continue to work for what is just and good (even within its own operation), despite the many individuals who try, is the basis of the series's famous anger and political "dissent." But we must recognize that what this anger and dissent generates is a new kind of melodrama. Except for the tragic cases of Sobotka and Bell (discussed in the last chapter) whose falls do attain a kind of tragic grandeur, the failures of other characters do not form the basis of individual tragedy but the kind of melodramatic pathos that fuels outrage. In the end, Baltimore remains in the grip of self-serving, short-sighted careerist police, ever more ruthless gangsters, a corrupt city government that will always "disappoint," schools where the best an individual teacher can do is control a class and encourage a kid or two, and a media that misses most of the important stories that the multisited ethnographic imaginary of *The Wire* has already told. The point of this form of melodrama is not only to despise the villain and root for the good person struggling for reform, or to just do a decent, self-respecting job. Rather it is to understand how the institutions themselves morally fail.

In the fifth season, for example, we see how Marlo Stanfield is a more "perfected" version of Stringer Bell. We see it in the coldness of his gaze and single-minded devotion to his own power in the drug trade, no matter how many bodies he walls up in the vacant row houses. It is the institution of the illegal drug trade that has made him. This added institutional level of melodrama is the most bravura achievement of *The Wire*. It is the day-to-day workings of these institutions—at the nitty-gritty level of budgets, drug profits, political horse-trading, and editorial practices, all cross-cut for maximum comparison—not private loves, kindly uncles, or personal villains, that determine fates.

In order to fully appreciate the institutional nature of this serial melodrama, consider the way it plays out in relation to two of the most overtly Dickensian characters in the whole series: young Wallace (no apparent last name), who dies in the first season, and Reginald ("Bubbles") Cousins, who endures throughout the entire series. Wallace (Michael B. Jordan), sixteen years old, is the youngest of the hoppers selling drugs for the Barksdale gang in the low-rise housing projects in the first season of the series. He naïvely accepts obviously counterfeit bills in exchange for drugs and has trouble adding up a sale. Over the course of the season, however, we see that he cares for several younger children with whom he lives in a squatter's apartment. He helps them with homework and sends them off to school in the mornings with juice and snacks. When he tries to play checkers with chess pieces with his boss and friend Bodie Broadus, he receives a lesson on the game that resonates with his and Bodie's own limited options as "pawns." He is a good, sensitive young man who, in the course of serving in the Barksdale organization, has the misfortune to recognize Brandon, the partner of stash-robber Omar Little, and to inform his Barksdale superiors of

Brandon's location. The next day he wakes up to the sight of Brandon's horribly tortured body displayed across the hood of a car. Demoralized by his unwitting role in this revenge killing, Wallace begins to brood at home and to take solace in drugs.

When the police question Wallace, he gives up information about the Barksdale organization's role in the torture and killing of Brandon. Though the police send Wallace to the country to live with his grand-mother for protection while they build the case, the shooting of one of their own diverts their attention. Wallace grows bored in the country and returns "home" to ask for his old job back, not comprehending that he is now viewed as a snitch. When Stringer Bell orders Wallace's boss, Bodie Broadus (perhaps only a year or two older), to kill him, Bodie and his friend Poot Carr accompany the unsuspecting Wallace to his crib, where they corner him in a bedroom with a poster of Tupac Sha-kur behind him. Bodie pulls a gun, but then falters; he needs to whip up enough self-justifying anger at Wallace to pull the trigger. When Wallace wets his pants and pleads, Bodie's macho anger is sufficiently stoked. Because Wallace cannot face death "like a man," Bodie circularly argues, he deserves to die. But Bodie's trembling aim only wounds his target, prolonging the boy's suffering until Poot grabs the gun and more firmly finishes the job (1.12, "Cleaning Up").

Nearly everyone who has seen *The Wire* is moved and outraged at the murder of Wallace by his own best friends in the first season. Even David Simon, in the voice-over commentary for this episode, says he can't believe they actually killed him. This death was meant as a signal to viewers that *The Wire* itself would not be soft and sentimental, but hard and seemingly "tragic." But as we have seen, Wallace is too young and too innocent to be a tragic victim. His identification of Brandon was performed without the knowledge of its consequences. Nor was he guilt-ridden for long, as revealed by his blithe return from the coun-try. We feel his suffering as something that could and should have been prevented rather than something "fated and doomed." There is no way of reconciling ourselves to the injustice of such pure pathos. Wallace's death early in the series signals that *The Wire* is serious about the class- and race-based injustices it depicts and that it is not the kind of melodrama that will employ in-the-nick-of-time rescues. But it would be a mistake to consider the senseless death of an innocent "tragic" when it is quintessential melodrama.

Bubbles, too, is an innocent and often pathetic victim. If Wallace is Dickensian in the way of Dickens's more pathetic characters, Bubbles is Dickensian in the way of his more eccentric characters. As a drug addict, he is a regular fixture of the corners; as a criminal informant, he is also familiar with, and to, the police. Indeed, as we have seen, he is crucial to the very ability of the series to connect its many different worlds. As we saw in chapter 1, it was Bubbles who, as an addict, was able to recognize the virtue of Major Bunny Colvin's drug-zone experiment when he agrees that it "was a good thing."

In the introduction to an interview with David Simon, made while *The Wire* was still unfolding on HBO, the novelist Nick Hornby praised it by observing that "the hapless Bubbles, forever dragging behind him his shopping trolley full of stolen goods, is Baltimore's answer to Joe [sic] the Crossing Sweeper."[35] Hornby is referring to Jo, a young vagrant of the slums of Chancery, in Dickens's *Bleak House*. Jo makes his living by sweeping a path through the filthiest intersections for fastidious upper-class pedestrians to pass. Even though Jo is an adolescent boy and Bubbles a mature man, it is easy to understand why Hornby emphasizes their similarities. Both are peripatetic figures of the streets whose very haplessness arouses sympathy. Bubbles's shopping cart is like Jo's broom, a tool that enables bare survival from a street that only wants both of them to, as the constable repeatedly urges Jo, "move on."[36]

However, the differences between Jo and Bubbles also reveal the ways in which *The Wire* diverges from the classical model of Dickensian melodrama. Jo's pathos is Dickens's trump card in his plea for parliamentary reforms that might address the suffering of indigent Londoners. But as a trump card he has a limited role to play beyond generating pity. At one point the poor fellow sits on the doorstep of the "Society for the Propagation of the Gospel in Foreign Parts" to eat a "dirty bit of bread,"[37] wholly in ignorance, since he cannot read, of the irony of what that building is for. There is no institution to help him, only kind benefactors who always come too late because to save Jo would be to present the world with the problem of what to do with an individual who knows "nothink." In addition to being a perfect object of pity, Jo's narrative function is to be a go-between between Lady Dedlock, Esther, and Mr. Snagsby and to give smallpox to Esther so that she might prove her greater virtue by enduring its physical mark.

Jo's pure goodness, and almost equally pure ignorance, allow Dickens to condemn all of those who would pretend not to know him, or to be so callous as not to care about him. The young physician in whose arms Jo dies comforts him with an incomplete Lord's Prayer after which the narrator himself turns self-righteously upon his readers: "The light is come upon the dark benighted way. Dead! Dead, your Majesty. Dead, my lords and gentlemen. Dead, Right Reverends and Wrong Reverends of every order. Dead, men and women, born with Heavenly compassion in your hearts. And dying thus around us every day."[38]

No kind uncle can "fix" things for Jo; there can be no happy ending for the truly "benighted." Dickensian melodrama tends to reserve redemption for the principal characters, like Esther in *Bleak House*, or Oliver Twist, both of whose rightful place in an ascending bourgeois order must be established. In both cases this rightful place turns out to be already assured through previously unrecognized inheritance. The more "benighted" do more social good by dying than by living. Jo is a character who can neither grow nor change, not even over a six-hundred-page novel in twenty originally serialized parts. His virtue is taken seriously, but only because it permits the virtue of the higher-born and more "deserving" to shine in recognizing it.

Bubbles might initially seem Dickensian in this same way—as the poor but good-hearted vagrant with no proper place in society. This is undoubtedly why Hornby reaches for the comparison to Jo. As it turns out, however, if Bubbles is hapless, he is hardly benighted. Indeed, his memory of names, streets, and license plates makes him an invaluable source of information to the police, as when he fingers drug dealers by placing hats on them in an apparent attempt to sell them hats. He is also an irrepressible teacher and mentor to his younger partners in crime, always trying to "school them" with his knowledge of how to make a buck off the detritus of the streets. Deep within this urge to mentor less experienced young men may be buried a homoerotic urge that he himself does not examine.[39] In season 3 Bubbles escalates his economic ac-

Bubbles the entrepreneur

Bubbles with assistant
Sherrod

tivities from scavenging to commodity capital as he invests in goods to
fill his shopping cart, selling used cell phones and T-shirts to the inhabitants of Hamsterdam; later, in response to customers' needs, he stocks
up on condoms, toilet paper, and hoodies. By the fourth season he has
two shopping carts and an assistant (Sherrod) and is on the verge of becoming a full-fledged entrepreneur. And by season 5 he will be clean,
though still on the street, selling the *Baltimore Sun*. Indeed, except for
the fact that his motive until the fifth season is to feed his habit, Bubbles
is the very model of *Homo economicus*, making rational decisions about
his profit margin, asking nothing and getting nothing from the dwin-
dling welfare state.

In the fourth season, however, Bubbles's life takes a different turn.
Unintentionally, he causes the death of Sherrod, his latest partner and
protégé. Devastated, the usually irrepressible Bubbles turns himself in
to the police for murder and tries to hang himself in the interrogation

room. Jay Landsman, the homicide sergeant, known for his obsession with the number of open cases on his watch, pulls him down from his noose and has the decency to send him where he actually needs to go: not to trial and jail (and for Landsman a much-desired closed case) but to a psychiatric unit, where he will get clean and make good use of Walon, his Narcotics Anonymous (NA) sponsor.

The Wire thus dramatically makes the case for the need for state-sponsored care and thus against neoliberal ideology—though without the self-righteous editorializing of Simon's earlier journalism. Indeed, Bubbles's many trials richly illustrate, despite all his industry, the failure of his own neoliberal ethic of self-sufficiency.[40] As political scientist Wendy Brown puts it, in neoliberalism's assumption of the end of liberal democracy, the body politic becomes no more than "a group of individual entrepreneurs and consumers."[41] In making individuals fully responsible for themselves, neoliberalism equates moral responsibility with rational action. But in so doing, she adds, "the rationally calculating individual bears full responsibility for the consequences of his or her action no matter how severe the constraints on this action."[42] Try as Bubbles might, in the fourth season his entrepreneurialism cannot overcome the predations of the more ruthless addict who steals his shopping cart profits and his dope. His former protectors, the police, repeatedly fail to come to his aid. His ingenious but hapless solution to the problem of the predatory addict is to prepare a poisonous shot that he expects the predator to steal but that Sherrod mistakenly takes instead. Here Bubbles becomes a victim of his own scheme of revenge. This unintentional and highly melodramatic murder shatters him, leaving him a twitching mass of grief and guilt.

Though Bubbles does get clean in the state-sponsored psychiatric unit, it is not this care that fully "fixes" him. It merely puts him in the clean and sober place where he can eventually forgive himself. As perhaps the strongest story of redemption in the whole series, it is worth pondering why and how the supposedly anti-Dickensian Simon contrives to have Bubbles's situation "fixed" without resorting to Dickensian kindly uncles. Late in the fifth season we find Bubbles, one year clean, at an NA meeting. He stands against a prominent stained glass window—rather than the usual church basement—and "confesses":

Bubbles "confesses" at NA

both to his lingering desire to get high and to his guilt and grief about Sherrod. In this iconic atmosphere, he receives a nod of approval from Walon, who has been waiting for him to share this burden with others. Bubbles, who always did like attention and was willing to pretend to be earnestly reforming in order to get it, here tells his truth in the approved NA manner. At this point the series seems perilously close to deploying an entirely Dickensian Christian compassion as his rescue (5.9, "Late Editions").

Fortunately, however, *The Wire* has a bigger redemption in mind—not only the personal redemption of Bubbles but also the institutional redemption of the heretofore amply vilified news media. Indeed, it is at the point that these two redemptions come together that the series seems to believe that a happy ending has been adequately earned. To be sure, it is a highly qualified happy ending, and it certainly does not redeem the entire news media as much as it redeems Bubbles. But it leaves us with the hope that justice can, at least sometimes, be done. In this case, the fact that the news media manages to tell one "true" story serves at least as a counterforce to all the lies of the Pulitzer-hungry Scott Templeton and his editors.

As Templeton's star rises at the *Sun* and as city editor Gus Haynes loses clout, Haynes nevertheless continues to do his job by encouraging the young newsman Mike Fletcher to test his wings. Because manipulated publicity has now shifted to the plight of the homeless, Fletcher is now writing about that. But he recognizes and articulates the flaws of such writing: "formula . . . anecdotal lead. . . ." Haynes agrees with this criticism but encourages Fletcher to dig deeper. "Spend some time with these people. Sometimes the weakest shit in a story is the stuff with quotation marks around it. You got a guy telling us how rough it is on the street. . . . That doesn't have much pull; but if you can describe how it really is, *tell his story in moments.* . . . Look, tomorrow, get back to the shelters and the soup kitchens. I mean, just be with folk. . . . If something presents itself as a story, great, but if not, just spend the day being with people. I'm not interested in great quotes, I'm interested in what feels true" (5.7, "Took").[43]

At the same time that Scott Templeton is generating bogus quotes from the homeless and conducts a phone interview with a serial killer whom he thinks is authentic (perfectly enacted by Jimmy McNulty), Haynes tells Fletcher to write what "feels true." In search of this truth, Fletcher finds a guide to this world in the person of Bubbles, who at this point is volunteering in a soup kitchen and selling the *Baltimore Sun* on the street. Bubbles acts as Fletcher's guide to a homeless encampment under the freeway and, encouraged again by Haynes, Fletcher decides to write about Bubbles even though he is not at this point homeless. Compared to Templeton's rifle shots, Fletcher's journalism—the very model of Simon's multisited, contextual reporting at the *Sun*—does indeed take time to build context. However, in the same breath that Haynes grants Fletcher a couple of weeks to write about Bubbles, he chooses to run a story about a fire rather than a story about a thirty-four-year-old black man killed in a convenience store by a juvenile. Thus he misses the "other" most popular personal story in *The Wire*—the death of Omar Little. The *Sun*—even when its "good" editor calls the shots—still misses a lot.

Though we never read what Fletcher writes about Bubbles, we get snatches of it as Bubbles shows the manuscript to Walon, his NA sponsor. Bubbles consults Walon as to the propriety of letting the story be published. Walon does not directly advise, but his judgment about the writing would certainly please Haynes, for to Walon, "it feels true. . . . He's got you. . . . He ain't lettin' you off the hook for shit; he's just putting it all out there: the good, the bad." But here Bubbles interrupts. He doesn't mind the bad, but he does suspect the good. "You skeered of somebody callin' you good?" asks Walon, finally getting Bubbles's number. Bubbles correctly observes that what he is doing is not special. Why should he get special moral credit for simply not getting high? Walon's answer is worth considering, since it is ultimately an answer to the question of the moral value of melodrama itself. He brings out a well-worn quotation passed on to him from an NA meeting, and Bubbles reads it aloud: "You can hold back from the suffering of the world and you are free to do so for it is in accordance with your nature. But perhaps this holding back is the one suffering you could have avoided" (5.10, "30"). In other words, suffering *itself* is good and is here so recognized by a writer whose name Bubbles reads as "Franzie Kafka."

In the end, Bubbles allows the profile to run and we see him read it outside on the street before going home. It is a feature entitled "The Road Home" on the front page of the *Sun*, with a picture of the cleaned-up Bubbles and a caption that reads, "A life at the margins is reclaimed day-by-day in West Baltimore." Bubbles reads, ponders, and seems to approve. He has both allowed his suffering to be recognized and at the same time questioned its automatic moral value, perhaps the best that can be asked of melodrama's alchemical transformation of suffering into virtue. He passes through that process, stands up, puts on dark glasses, and picks up two plastic bags apparently full of food. This is the first time we see him in the role of a consumer (of anything but dope) instead of a scavenger or vendor; it is a sign of his new maturity and citizenship and imminent admission into the upstairs world of his sister and her family. We immediately miss the old Bubbles, for there is no question that once his suffering ends, once his virtue is recognized by the newspaper that is itself partly redeemed in that recognition, his story, and the multi-institutional, multisited one of the serial itself, is over.

We may recognize at this point that this story about Bubbles is *The Wire*'s fictional stand-in for the story about metal men that David Simon claims was "spiked" by editors, but that did in fact run. Its "publication" here is a thoroughly (self-)righteous vindication of Simon's own brand of contextualized journalism and a repudiation of the villainous Templeton's rifle shot. On first sight, then, it might seem that *The Wire* is guilty of doing what Simon most abhors in the whole panoply of Dickensian tricks: the recognition of virtue through suffering leading to a happy end in which Bubbles is finally admitted to the upper re-

Bubbles reads story
about himself

Bubbles ready to
join the world

gions of his sister's house (family and home), thus completing his "road home." Does this happy ending mean that *The Wire* has gone all soft and Dickensian on us? If we simply measure these two works by the standards of the usual clichés about melodrama, it would seem that in the case of street-level virtuous victims, Simon is even more melodramatic than Dickens. For the fact of Jo's death—if not the manner of it—is "realistic," while Bubbles's rescue from abjection could be considered less so. It is, moreover, a rescue that has needed to be repeated many times over before it actually works.[44] To say this, however, would be to fail to understand the key quality of melodrama and the very reason for the existence of the form. For as we have seen, melodrama is not that which opposes realism but that which becomes more modern and relevant by incorporating realism's outward manifestations.

Signs of realism in melodrama are most often in the service of the recognition of virtue or of its opposite, villainy. This is the case for both

Bubbles is finally admitted to the upper regions of his sister's house

Jo and Bubbles, given the different standards of realism of each time. Although Bubbles's attempt at suicide is pathetic, it is also very messy: he pukes all over the sergeant who cuts him down from his noose. This puke offers a more realistic way for us to gauge his suffering and that suffering's tenuous link to the hope for justice. In *Bleak House* there can be no justice for Jo; the recognition of his virtue in pitiable death points out in the most vivid way what needs fixing in social Darwinist industrial Britain. Above all, "the lords and ladies" and "right and wrong" reverends must recognize that Jos are "dying all around us." A society that permits this is unjust, and Dickens shouts, "Shame on you!"[45] Jo's suffering and Dickens's outrage are in the service of establishing the very kinds of liberal institutions that might save other Jos. Rather than dying "benighted," he might one day live and know "somethink."[46]

In *The Wire* young boys are "dying all around us" too, usually from much more violent causes than starvation and smallpox. And there is indeed pity generated for their suffering. Wallace's death, as we have seen, is one of the most pitiable. In season 4 Dukie and Randy do not die, but their suffering in the face of insupportable circumstances is almost as painful to watch.[47] And Randy's subsequent hardening as he goes into the "group home" he has all-along dreaded, is perhaps the most painful of all. Bubbles, Wallace, and Dukie never acquire that hardness and so either suffer or die. Only in the case of Namond, however, could fate be said to be determined by the equivalent of the proverbial kind uncle or guardian. Wallace's death teaches that the serial is serious about unjustified suffering and that the business of drug dealing thinks nothing of killing a Wallace—indeed, it even needs to test the hardness of his friends in their own ability to kill him. On the other hand, the difficult redemption of Bubbles, as well as that of Namond (discussed in the next chapter), teaches that if there is to be a hope for justice, as there must be in melodrama, it must be through an alignment of many complex personal *and* institutional pieces. In the case of Bubbles the good that he ultimately recognizes in his own suffering is earned. And it is earned not only by Bubbles but by a practice of journalism that lends an aura of justice to the story told about him.

We should make no mistake: a *sense* of justice is no substitute for actual justice. But the aspiration to justice matters in melodrama no matter how often it is perverted. What melodrama can offer, at its best, is thus something that tragedy cannot supply. In *The Wire* it is ultimately a vision of a better governmentality, or what Wendy Brown has called "an alternative vision of the good . . . a vision in which justice would not center upon maximizing individual wealth or rights but on developing the capacity of citizens to share power and collaboratively govern themselves."[48] This is the good gained when Bubbles ceases to be a victim and becomes instead what both the police and the outlaw Omar call a "citizen."[49] When Brown argues that we need a "different figuration of human beings, citizenship, economic life and the political—to fashion a more just future," I can think of nothing better than that figuration has in fact been achieved, not in a utopian picture of achieved fairness, and not in a bleak tragedy of the triumph of injustice, but in the mixture of melodrama, and occasional glimpses of the more tragic fates of Sobotka and Bell, that is *The Wire*.

The alternative to Dickensian melodrama is thus not the bleak austerity of Greek tragedy, nor even the more various and entertaining forms of Shakespearean tragedy. The series does not betray its principles by granting a happy ending to a particular individual. Most important to the new type of melodrama that *The Wire* forges are the opportunities offered by the serial's multiplication of worlds and their interaction over time.[50] This sensibility of both "world and time" (see chapter 2) is what cannot be achieved even in a long movie, for it only happens with repetition over time, when the rhythm of certain situations is felt again and again, as for example, happens even in the opening *melos* of the five versions of "Way Down in the Hole." Consider again that moment, discussed in the first chapter, when Major Bunny Colvin stands before the bulldozed ruins of Hamsterdam and asks Bubbles whether it was a "good thing." In this instance it is Bubbles, without even knowing who Colvin is, who recognizes his, and Hamsterdam's, virtue. It is partly because we have known Bubbles since the first season and have come to know the scavenging and pedagogical routines of his life—including the favorite lesson to a new protégé about thinking one is brown (cool) when one is really green (inexperienced)—that we have a strong temporal sense of the trap of repetition in which Bubbles is caught. His own pathos is as evident as Colvin's. However briefly, and without really knowing it, each recognizes the good in the other.

Conclusion

If we can agree that melodrama endures not only as an archaic holdover of the nineteenth-century stage play (and its virtuous victims and leering villains), not only as women's films or chick flicks or Oprah confession, not only in soap operas and disease-of-the-week TV movies, not only as the genre of family melodrama, and not only as blockbuster action and spectacle, then we can recognize it as an evolving mode of storytelling crucial to the establishment of moral good in a secular, liberal age. Melodrama is not old-fashioned, creaky, stage-bound drama; it seeks a justice that is part of the liberal sensibility and it may be proper to say that it endures in *The Wire* but it is also proper to see how with "world enough and time," it moves beyond mere Nietzschean *ressentiment* and beyond the generation of mere pity.

In the last episode of *The Wire*, the gangsters are regrouping. Their former boss, Marlo Stanfield, has left the game. Marlo represented the highest level of ruthlessness, the most extreme devaluation of human life. The gangster Calvin ("Cheese") Wagstaff is the nephew of Proposition Joe—who has recently been killed and whose loss means the end of the kind of sensibility that could make deals and compromise. The basic question before the group in this scene is who shall rule and by what code. Cheese pulls a gun and holds it to the head of another who has spoken up for the old code of cooperation represented by the now deceased Proposition Joe and the previously deceased Stringer Bell. Cheese admonishes the terrified fellow dealer that "there's no back in the day," there "ain't no nostalgia" for Joe or anyone else. Suddenly, however, a quick bullet to Cheese's head saves the man he was about to kill and serves as the answer of an old Barksdale soldier, Slim Charles. Slim Charles explains to all that he has performed this quick justice "for Joe," the reasonable uncle whose memory Cheese failed to respect. At this point in the series, after so many abrupt murders, we are not so shocked by the violence as to miss the fact that according to the morality of the street, a kind of justice has been rendered. Virtue—in this case Joe's ability to propose deals and avoid violence—has been recognized in the violent language of the gangsters themselves. Such is the gangsters' own "sentimental" code of melodrama.

We tend to forgive melodrama for being melodrama if it seems "realistic" and if its politics or sense of justice coincides with our own. We like melodramas in which the good *we* believe in is recognized, as Joe is above, whether that good prevails or fails. The undeniable innovation of *The Wire* is its effort to tell a melodramatic story at the level of the social institutions that have themselves repeatedly failed to serve justice. Seriality enables a new energy and means for the frustration of that justice which in the scene described above is ironically experienced as a felt good even as it contradicts Joe's own sense of how to keep the peace. If Slim Charles's swift justice champions the idea that there *is* a "back in the day," then we should also recognize the trap of such nostalgia. This is a nostalgia that falls victim to what Wendy Brown has called "left melancholy"—an exaggerated mourning for a liberal democracy that may never have actually existed, certainly not for Baltimore's black inhabitants.[51] If we rejoice at the quick justice that kills Cheese, this may be a sign that the justice sought in *The Wire*—the restoration of a nostalgic "back in the day"—is a limited vision of the just. Nevertheless, if the aspirations for liberal democracy are still valid in an era of neoliberalism, and if tragedy cannot stoop to care about the truly powerless, a newly evolved serial melodrama proves to be the primary tool with which mass culture makes the case for some kind of justice.

We should neither laud *The Wire* as exceptional tragedy nor identify it as conventional melodrama. Rather, we should appreciate its deeply felt contemporary reinvention of the mode of melodrama. This mode, as we have seen in the last two chapters, is made possible by a serial melodrama in tension with a self-conscious effort to be tragedy. The quest to recognize a good that is no longer self-evident in a neoliberal era is the dilemma of this series. If melodrama, as Peter Brooks has argued, is a central poetics of modern life and inextricable from popular media, it should be part of our critical vocabulary not only so we can complain about it when its more archaic qualities persist but also so we can appreciate it when, as with *The Wire*, it evolves into something new. The mode of melodrama still holds us in its grip. We should recognize it, even (or especially) when it is "good."

PART III

Surveillance, Schoolin', and Race

5   Hard Eyes / Soft Eyes

SURVEILLANCE AND SCHOOLIN'

Two familiar film and television genres, both ultimately about the acquisition of knowledge, have dominated the popular imagination in
movies and television. Both are fundamentally melodramas in the rifle-
shot way of identifying personal victims and villains in place of the more
institutionally probing melodrama we have seen to be posed by *The
Wire*. The first genre is about intelligence gathering, and its methods are
typically technologies of surveillance—"spy shit," as Kima Greggs puts
it. Its heroes are the smart spies—Jack Bauer of *24* or Carrie Matheson
of *Homeland*—not to mention the more glamorous heroes, like James
Bond, who inhabit big-budget espionage films. These surveillors command the most advanced technologies, work in "the national interest,"
and usually prevail against all odds. The second genre is also about ways
of accumulating knowledge but concentrates on processes of learning
and is usually set in a school. I call these "generic school melodramas."
We know this formula too: a charismatic (often white) teacher enters a
racially mixed or strictly minority classroom and, against all odds, manages to teach at least one or even a group of hardened, often black or
Latino inner-city kids. In both these genres a kind of magic is worked:
the first by technologies of surveillance and the brave, determined, or
debonair hero who wields them; the second by "magical teachers" who
sacrifice, suffer, persevere, and finally "reach" the class. This chapter
explores the ways in which *The Wire* exceeds both these conventional

melodramatic genres to reveal the limits of surveillance and the requirements for real learning.

Up on a Wire: Surveillance and the Lure of Technology

A wire denotes a physical piece of stretched metal whose conductive
properties allow it to carry information over the "wire services" in coded
signals. Today, of course, a wire can also refer to electronic technologies
that no longer need literal wires: wire*less* connectivity. Criminal informants in the series "wear wires," and both wire and advanced wireless
technologies are trotted out frequently throughout the series. They include wiretaps on phones, closed circuit television surveillance cameras
hooked up to wires, and coded data culled from disposable cell phones.

The Wire plays with new wire technologies the way *Mad Men* plays
with martinis—each is the fetish object of its particular storyworld. In
the period serial that is *Mad Men* these objects have a special retro
glamour, a glamour we are meant to see nostalgically but also judgmen-
tally from the greater knowledge of the present (martinis for lunch are
not good for you!). Though not entirely a period drama, and certainly
not glamorous, *The Wire* too has a kind of retro appeal, though mostly
from the point of view of its technologies of communication and surveillance. The serial seems to begin in the present of the series opening (2002), yet this present is purposefully set in what can only be described as a technologically "deprived," anachronistic past in which cell
phones barely exist and police reports are still filled out on typewriters
that must produce lots of "dots"—"the deputy loves dots."[1] The dots of
the typewriter foretell word-processed bullet points, metal wires foretell wireless surveillance, pagers foretell cell phones—a vast panoply of
ever new, but seemingly never new enough, technologies are the holy
grail for police in their quest for the greater knowledge that surveillance yields.

The smart police salivate over ever new surveillance technologies, and
the smart gangsters stay in business only insofar as they foil them. This
is the discipline of the wire—not only the cat and mouse of surveillance
and countersurveillance, but the larger discipline of parallel institutions,
one whose business it is to spy and another that must police itself in case

it is being watched. The surveillance conducted in *The Wire* is the polar opposite of what we see in other television melodramas of surveillance. Fox's *24* (2001–2010) and, more recently and more complexly, Showtime's *Homeland* (2011–) place their audience on the side of the "good guy" surveillors and the panoptic nature of state or institutional power. Our vicarious experience of the technological sublime of ubiquitous surveillance in these works is in the service of a simplistic good-versus-evil scheme: us (the United States) versus them (terrorist others).[2]

However, the primary difference between *The Wire* and these other series is that the figure of surveillance in the former has none of the facility and ease of Jeremy Bentham's over-idealized panopticon, the model of which once served Michel Foucault's wider theory of the surveilled subject's internalization of the apparatus of power. While Bentham described the perfect prison, Foucault described a model of internalized subjection that seemed to produce perfectly docile bodies: "He who is subjected to a field of visibility, and who knows it, assumes responsibility for the constraints of power; he makes them play spontaneously upon himself; he inscribes in himself the power relation in which he simultaneously plays both roles; he becomes the principle of his own subjection."[3] Thus according to Foucault's reading of Bentham's "panoptic machine," the surveilled become "invested by its effects of power."[4] The drug dealers in *The Wire* are not perfectly "docile bodies." They resist the apparatus of surveillance in creative ways. Yet the form their resistance takes is ultimately determined by the powers that would surveil them.[5] Thus even though the panopticon remains a relevant (if no longer the only) figure for the power of surveillance, and even though it often produces the requisite disciplined and docile bodies of Foucault's great study, it does not do so easily in a society where, as Alisdair McMillan puts it, electronic surveillance "pans across the entire social field" and dramatizes the "infiltration of the sphere of 'human value' by a foreign disciplinary logic."[6] In other words, surveillance may not always be all it is cracked up to be.

In the first episode of the first season of *The Wire* (1.1, "The Target"), Detective Jimmy McNulty visits his friend Fitzhugh at the gleaming headquarters of the FBI. "Are you up on a wire?" asks McNulty eagerly. He is impressed by what he presumes to be a "tape" of drug dealers

FBI live surveillance
of drug operation

packaging large quantities of dope viewed on a monitor. Fitzhugh shows him that the operation is no tape. It is live observation made possible through "fiber-optic lensing." McNulty is impressed by the instantaneity of the transmission. He immediately asks about the sound, which we also hear live.

As Fitzhugh explains to McNulty how the scene is miked, a pan to the left shows another monitor that displays the sound waves that transmit the dealers' speech. Another shot then tracks the blue line of the jagged peaks and valleys of these waves as they move across a graph. This is the familiar figure of the wire by which the series is best known: a jagged line, sometimes green, sometimes blue, begins each of the five credit sequences of *The Wire*. Even if we do not immediately recognize these images as the visual registration of sound waves, we perceive the glamour and excitement—the jagged green or blue pulsating light; the abstraction into some kind of visual code—of what would otherwise be seen or heard in actual proximate perception. This is the lure of the wire to the police: learning at a distance, but in real time, the illicit activities of the antagonists they discipline. Flashy, ever new technologies keep the cops tantalized through all five seasons of *The Wire*, making them believe that if only they had *this*, they could catch the bad guys and thereby "win" the war on drugs.

In the same scene in which Detective Jimmy McNulty mistakes instantaneous transmission over fiber optics for tape, his FBI friend informs him that most of the government's good drug cases are shutting down as agents are transferred to the war on terror. "What, the govern-

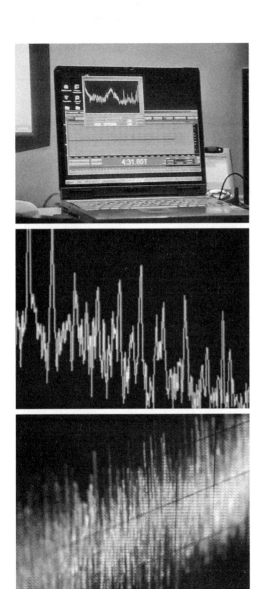

Sound waves that transmit speech

The familiar figure of "the wire"

Variant familiar figure of "the wire"

ment doesn't have enough love for two wars?" replies McNulty. In this exchange we have the first of many comparisons between these two benighted "wars." The old war on drugs, in which the cops can only hope to win a few battles and which succeeds only in incarcerating large numbers of mostly black men, is already perceived as tired and unwinnable. Its futility is telegraphed as early as the first credit sequence by the routinized gestures of faceless bodies handing off drugs under police surveillance. In the meantime, all the really flashy technologies have been shifted to that other war, also unwinnable: the war on terror. Connections between them abound. In season 3, Fitzhugh does McNulty a favor by changing the name of Russell "Stringer" Bell to "Ahmed," in order to permit a high-priority surveillance of Bell.

The allure of ever new surveillance technologies is gradually revealed in *The Wire* as simply a lure. It entraps the police as much as those they would entrap. The road to better policing lies not in the wizardry of any of this technology but in better-built cases and a willingness to "follow the money." The series corresponds to that period in American history when the country itself moved from an era of literal to metaphorical wires in a post-9/11 culture of vastly increased surveillance. *The Wire* first aired on June 2, 2002, just nine months after 9/11. But here, unlike in many other crime or antiterrorist series aired during this period, the devices of faster and more perfect surveillance almost never provide the knowledge the police seek. Thus although some of its criminal informants do wear wires and although the police put their faith in technologically enhanced surveillance, many of the lessons of this series, which is ultimately more about the problem of knowledge/power and the mystery of real learning than the wizardry of technology, will run in a contrary direction.

Yet because we are watching a police series called *The Wire*, we are at first primed to be excited by Jimmy McNulty's enthusiasm to get "up on a wire." Indeed, for *The Wire* to work as melodrama within the genre of the police procedural, we need to participate, at least initially, in the allure of winning a war on drugs with these panoptic technologies. Thus, to the extent that the series *is* a police procedural in which technologies of evidence gathering matter, we naturally begin by rooting for the police as they first pursue the elusive and, to them, faceless Barksdale gang, and later the even more elusive Marlo Stanfield. However, as we are gradually let into the operations of the gangs in parallel to the operations of the police, we come to know much more about them than the police ever do. We thus quickly perceive what legal scholar Susan Bandes calls the "happy symbiosis" between the two institutions. Individual players may fall or lose their jobs, but the institutions of each endure and are determined by each other.[7] The war on drugs is what keeps them both in business. Getting up on a wire becomes the ritual quest of each season. In this first season they do not "get up" until the fifth episode. Though each season's wire is duly obtained and sometimes yields eventual arrests, it never makes a serious dent in the drug trade.

Surveillance devices prove costly, time-consuming, and eminently fallible. First police must get a court order showing probable cause, then they must get the wire if they have the resources and manpower. And even when they do get up on a wire, legally or illegally, it can fail, as when Herc and Carver borrow an expensive audio bug and place it in a tennis ball for eavesdropping, only to see it thrown into the street and crushed by the wheels of a car (season 2). The narrative is built more on the navigation of the laws on surveillance than on an idealized vision of these technological capabilities. Thus *The Wire* is neither a CSI-style celebration of crime-solving technologies, nor designed to inspire confidence in other state or government authorities in a post-9/11 world.[8]

Literal or figural wires can connect and facilitate communication, but they can also just as easily be tangled and crossed. For example, toward the end of the fifth season we see where the lure of the wire has led: Detectives Jimmy McNulty and Lester Freamon find themselves entangled in a mess of blue, green, yellow, and red wires in the wiretap room of the district office. They have intentionally crossed these wires, but that crossing is a sign of the perversion of their pursuit. A legal wiretap on the cell phone of a bogus serial killer, who has been casually warehoused in another town, has been rerouted to permit an illegal wiretap on Marlo Stanfield, the drug kingpin whom Freeman and McNulty have been chasing for two seasons. This, the final season implies, is where the technological fix of the wire finally gets them: faking a wiretap on one, fictive serial killer in order to get information on Stanfield, who is the real one. Like the sick crimes that Jimmy perpetrates on already dead

The tangled wires of
the illegal wiretap

bodies in order to obtain the wire they need to bring down Stanfield, the cops' quest for the technologies of surveillance leads only to their own kind of grotesque imitation of criminality. Nor do they succeed in "catching" Stanfield. In fact, the illegality of the (crossed) wiretap means that most of their evidence against him is thrown out of court.

The neon peaks and valleys of the jagged line that forms the emblematic metaphorical figure of the wire, like the literal wires in which Jimmy and Lester find themselves entangled in the fifth season, perpetually pull the cops away from what we come to recognize as "good police work." Again and again the best policing in the series is that which does not distance itself from the citizens it is designed to protect. When, for example, Major Colvin faces up to the health needs of the citizens of Hamsterdam in season 3, or when McNulty walks the beat of an actual Western District neighborhood in season 4, we recognize a more benign form of proximate surveillance that is genuinely protective of the citizenry as a whole. This, in turn, reminds us of something too often forgotten in critiques of surveillance—that a kindly eye, a soft eye, a proximate eye can be the best thing that can happen to a young person, a dope fiend, or a policed neighborhood: not all surveillance is malign.

As we saw in chapter 1, *The Wire* immediately gains complexity and interest when it ceases to be only a police procedural and lets us in on the activities of the drug dealers whose constant vigilance enables them to elude surveillance. Whether corner boys or kingpins, the drug dealers avoid all forms of communication that might be surveilled. For example, in season 1, drawing on information that Simon had long ago reported

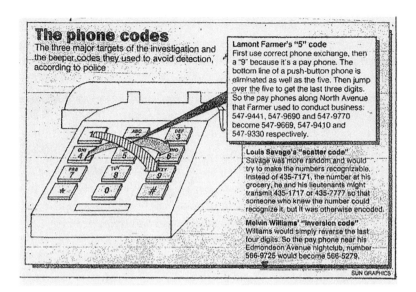

The phone codes

The three major targets of the investigation and the beeper codes they used to avoid detection, according to police

Lamont Farmer's "5" code
First use correct phone exchange, then a "9" because it's a pay phone. The bottom line of a push-button phone is eliminated as well as the five. Then jump over the five to get the last three digits. So the pay phones along North Avenue that Farmer used to conduct business: 547-9441, 547-9690 and 547-9770 become 547-9669, 547-9410 and 547-9330 respectively.

Louis Savage's "scatter code"
Savage was more random and would try to make the numbers recognizable. Instead of 435-7171, the number at his grocery, he and his lieutenants might transmit 435-1717 or 435-7777 so that someone who knew the number could recognize it, but it was otherwise encoded.

Melvin Williams' "inversion code"
Williams would simply reverse the last four digits. So the pay phone near his Edmondson Avenue nightclub, number 566-9725 would become 566-5279.

SUN GRAPHICS

From Simon's "Easy Money" series of articles on "Little Melvin" Williams

in the *Sun* in his five-part series on the career of Little Melvin Williams, model for Avon Barksdale, dealers use older technologies, like pagers and pay phones, in coded and innovative ways. In 1.5 ("The Pager"), the episode in which police finally get up on a wire, surveillance actually takes the form of a clone of D'Angelo Barksdale's low-tech pager. This lowly pager hides its coded messages of drug deals in fabricated phone numbers. For the dealers, then, it is often the most retro technology that has the surprising ability to foil surveillance. Such is the pattern of each season: police finally get a court order to permit some kind of wirelike surveillance and "a little slow, a little late," as this episode's epigraph has it, they gather evidence.[9]

Surveillance Foiled

Just as the figure of the wire is emblematized by repeated neon peaks and valleys standing for the technological lure of surveillance, so there are emblematic images for the gangsters' ability to foil surveillance. Repeated in every version of the credit sequence in every season is a shot of a surveillance camera situated on a pole followed by a view of what the camera sees through its lens: two young men stand below; one of them throws rocks at the lens. Suddenly a rock hits and the lens cracks. Our own eyes, aligned with the view through the lens of the surveilling camera, flinch at the crude but effective violence. The camera drops, and through the cracked lens we stare at the empty pavement below. By the time we reach 1.4 ("Old Cases"), the actual episode from which these credit images are culled, we recognize that it is Bodie Broadus throwing the rocks and D'Angelo Barksdale beside him, telling Bodie he "ain't never gonna hit it"—until, of course, he does. We also recognize the place from which the rocks are thrown: the "pit" or open space between the low-rise housing projects where D'Angelo and Bodie deal.

Some version of this lens shattering, with the sound of breaking glass, is repeated in the credits of each of the five seasons. However much these credit sequences may differ, with images chosen from the already shot thematic events of each season, these two key sequences of images remain in a constant dialectic: the peaks and valleys of the colored line on a monitor, followed by a track along a wire that feeds into a computer, signaling the lure of surveillance, and then, the shattering of the lens and the failure of the camera to see its surveilled subjects, all accompanied by one of the five versions of Tom Waits's "Way Down in the Hole." High-tech surveillance is foiled each time by a simple toss of a rock. As we move through the series, these two repeated images are in constant tension. Panopticism, as Alasdair McMillan writes, has "never quite lived up to its lofty ideals."[10] While it aims to suppress the deviancy of crime, it also produces the very deviants it tries to suppress. The more surveillance there is the more the potential to resist steadily increases. Indeed, the procedures of crime are every bit as disciplined and elaborate as those of the police, and the police are frequently foiled by the discipline of the wary criminals. For example, in the most elaborate and disastrous instance in season 4, detective Herc Hauk "borrows" a police camera to surveil Marlo Stanfield, without obtaining court approval. As soon as Marlo's gang realize they are being filmed, they feed Herc fake information and then steal the camera itself. Surveillance is thus foiled. However, in his efforts to retrieve the lost camera, Herc in-

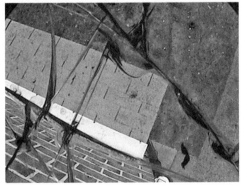

The surveillance camera

What the camera sees as its lens is cracked by a rock

The camera drops and stares at empty pavement

terrogates one of the schoolboys, Randy Wagstaff, and clumsily reveals Randy's inadvertent knowledge of a drug murder to cops and dealers alike. Randy is thereafter stigmatized as a snitch, and his life, and that of his foster mother, is ruined.

Surveillance may be thwarted, but the thwarting leads to catastrophic consequences in the lives of innocent people, not to mention a way of life that is itself shaped by the discipline of the resistance to surveillance. In an era of ever more ubiquitous surveillance, neither Orwell's Big Brother nor Foucault's notion of the internalization of surveillance in Bentham's panopticon is a fully applicable model.[11] Systems of surveillance are only as good as the people who use them. A simple rock, or a "dumb" cop (Herc), can mess them up, but surveillance itself produces consequences in surveillors and surveilled alike. In the end, the attempt to outwit the legal system that requires court orders for wiretaps will cause the master surveillors, McNulty and Freamon, to not only lose their jobs but also to bungle the case against Stanfield they had so carefully built.

We may be more likely to root for the guys who foil surveillance than for those who attempt to enforce it, but the only fair judgment on the discipline exercised by each must be the waste of energy spent in such cat-and-mouse games on both sides of the thin (blue or green) jagged line. For example, in the surveillance-foiled shattering of the lens repeated in the credit sequence, we may note, by the time we see it play out in the narrative (1.4, "Old Cases") that the foilers of surveillance—Bodie who throws the rocks and D'Angelo who eggs him on—are viewed from an unusual angle, no longer from the lens of the surveillance camera, but still from a marked point of view. This new angle is then explained by a reverse shot that shows Detective Lester Freamon sitting in a car holding a notebook and a cell phone. The boys who are in the very act of foiling the optical surveillance of the camera over their drug sales do not realize that they are being watched by Lester and that as soon as Lester calls their nearby pay phone and D'Angelo answers it the police will be up on a wire; they can now tap the pay phone on which business is conducted by number codes in the pit. When D'Angelo answers the phone, Lester's triumphant smile as he clicks his cell phone shows that while one system of (optical) surveillance has just been foiled, another,

D'Angelo answers
the phone and is
caught on a wire

the aural one for which the series is named, has just been inaugurated in this fourth episode of the first season.

Despite the enormous resources devoted to surveillance, the cops never learn much about who they are really chasing. When Jimmy McNulty says, "What, the government doesn't have enough love for two wars?," love equals the resources that allow police and other government agencies to increasingly surveil and curtail the liberties of citizens. In the war on drugs the dumber cops blunder into homes, assault high-rise residential courtyards, and bash heads; the smarter ones, like Freamon and McNulty put their faith in wires and are jealous of the resources (love) given to the FBI after the USA Patriot Act became law in 2001.[12]

In the war on terror just amping up as the series began, there has been a similar blundering interference in the lives of citizens and a similar waste of lives and resources (not to mention wrongly invaded countries based on faulty or downright falsified surveillance). This parallel is drawn acutely in the beginning episode of 1.1 ("The Target") in the Western District office, where detectives Ellis Carver and "Herc" Hauk revel in the attitude of dumb cops who prefer to "fuck the paperwork" and just "collect bodies, split heads." When Detective Kima Greggs accuses them of "fighting the war on drugs, one brutality case at a time," Carver reminds her that "you can't even call this shit a war" because "wars end." The war on drugs, like the war on terror may be fought with surveillance and other remote technologies, but often they do not produce the real knowledge needed to avert either crime or terror. Indeed,

The Wire is intent on showing how often mere gadgets and wires lead primarily to bad justice.

Over and over *The Wire* teaches that the best police work done in the series is not the hard intrusive look of surveillance but the training of human apperception to take in a total situation. For example, in season 4 of *The Wire* the former failed cop and now rookie middle-school teacher Roland "Prez" Pryzbylewski is given a list of rules for classroom management in a teachers' meeting: double-spaced papers, similar headings, windows closed to make students drowsy ("drowsy is good"), and lots of busywork to keep them off guard. An older woman shakes her head either at Prez's inexperience or at the uselessness of these rules aimed at the production of docile bodies. Leaving the meeting she says simply, "You need soft eyes" (4.2, "Soft Eyes"). At first Prez does not know what she means, and neither do we. It will be the goal of this season to teach us, partly through the experiences of this failed cop, what a better way of learning and teaching might be.

As a cop Roland Pryzbylewski was frequently a lost soul. Cockiness covered fear and ineptitude, and both were undeservedly protected by his Polish American father-in-law, District Commander Major Valchek. When we first meet Prez in season 1 he is already infamous for the panicked shooting up of his own squad car, then for falsely reporting the incident. In the first season he loses his cool and shoots his gun again after inciting a riot at the high-rises and pistol-whipping a teenage boy, blinding him in one eye. At the beginning of the first season he is the quintessential example of the "head-bashing" school of policing.

Suspended from street duty, confined to the office of the special detail of other incompetent and unruly officers, Pryzbylewski begins to learn what "good po-lice" do under the tutelage of Detective Lester Freamon. Perceiving the pattern of incomprehensible drug-deal messages passed by pagers in coded numbers, Prez, who has a way with numbers, cracks the code. Under Freamon, he also learns how to research paper trails. With this higher-level familiarity with police work, he gains confidence, finally standing up to his father-in-law in the second season. In the third season, however, he responds to a distress call and fails to properly identify himself, mistakenly shooting a plainclothed fellow officer who is

Pryzbylewski,
lost soul as a cop

black. Accused of racial prejudice, he does not fight the case but simply quits the force, ashamed, disgraced, and sorry.

This is what brings Pryzbylewski to his new career as a math teacher at Edward Tilghman Middle School and thus eventually to learn what is meant by "soft eyes." In this story of a policeman-surveillant who becomes a schoolteacher (as Ed Burns, Simon's coauthor of *The Corner* and cocreator of *The Wire* himself did)[13] the fourth season of the series launches a new level of critique: not only the failure and waste of surveillance, but of how much teaching is, unfortunately, like policing in that both typically aim to produce docile bodies.

Schoolin'

Ignorance abounds in Baltimore; cops, corner kids, dockworkers, and city politicians all desperately need to learn. Sometimes this ignorance is comical, as when a dockworker taken in for questioning by police in season 2 says he "pleads the Fifth Commandment," sometimes it is painful, as when the corner kids in the "special class" go to a fancy restaurant and don't know that the desserts trotted out to be chosen are not also to eat right then, or when Jimmy McNulty, the quintessential smart cop, discovers that his lack of a college education makes him an unsuitable partner for campaign manager Teresa D'Agostino. Thus the series does not really wait until the fourth season for education to emerge as an important theme of the series. It has been fundamental all along, most prominently in the "schoolin'" that Bubbles offers to each of his partner-apprentices in crime, whether the crimes are metal scavenging or con games. "I'm schoolin' you," says Bubbles to his younger white pal Johnny in the first episode of the first season as he takes too big a hit of heroin in a flophouse. Bubbles explains, "I'm trying to give you a little game, man. . . . You green. I'm trying to get you brown, man." "I'm ready. Yo, I'm brown," answers Johnny. "Shit, man," chuckles Bubbles as he nearly nods off, "you ain't even fucking beige" (1.1, "The Target"). Later in the third season, he says nearly the same thing to his black pal, Sherrod, as he teaches him to scavenge metal. "You think you brown, but you green" (3.12, "Mission Accomplished"). This is Bubbles's precious gift of schoolin' to the younger men, black or white, that he befriends on the street: they may think they are brown in the sense of being like himself—a seasoned colored man and addict who knows how to beat the system—but they need schoolin'.

Schoolin' is what Bubbles believes he offers each of the young men he takes under his wing. Indeed, he even insists that Sherrod go back to school in season 4 to learn the math he needs to help him sell goods from his shopping cart. In the end, however, both Johnny and Sherrod will end up dead of overdoses, Sherrod the direct victim of one of Bubbles too-clever schemes. All of Bubbles well-intentioned mentorship based on these proud moments of schoolin' will prove to have been mistaken lessons in survival—bad schoolin' and even more disastrous learning.

Other prominent examples of failed top-down schoolin' occur on the police side of *The Wire* in Major Colvin's pat orientation speeches to his new officers on the force, which begin with the question "Where are you?" The officers are supposed to know whether they are pointing north or south, their exact address, and how the numbers on the streets run. At this stage of his own learning Colvin can only embarrass his officers into learning this basic information. A hands-on sort of teacher, and a man of action not words, he is unable to instill deeper knowledge and resources into his underlings except by example. Hamsterdam will be his best lesson to his community until, like Pryzbelewski, he finds himself off the police force and in a classroom and the narrative funnels into actual schools.

Almost all of the top-down schoolin' lectures offered by police lieutenants or majors to their officers fail similarly. "Good po-lice" rarely respect their commanders because they are too allied with the hierarchy of an institution that is more committed to their own advancement and the acquisition of resources than the prevention or solution of crime. Even Lieutenant (later Major) Cedric Daniels, who *is* both "good po-lice" and a leader, fails to earn the respect of his officers for much of the series because of his former overeagerness for advancement. More often, "good po-lice" recognize and mentor one another horizontally; it is the rogue cops (McNulty, Freamon) who actually want to do the work of solving cases, while the higher-ups want a smooth functioning institution and respectable stats.

Two parallel peer-to-peer lessons stand out in the series, one on the gangster side, the other on the cop side. Together, they illustrate that the possibilities of learning do not prove equal in *The Wire*, nor do opportunities to teach. Consider the famous chess lesson taught by D'Angelo Barksdale to Wallace and Bodie in the pit during the first season (1.3, "The Buys"). D'Angelo finds the two boys playing checkers with chess figures and laughs at their ignorance. "Yo, why you playing checkers on a chess set?" says D'Angelo. "Yo, why you give a shit?" answers a resentful Bodie.

D'Angelo does give a shit: "I'll teach you all, if you all want to learn." He proceeds to explain the power of the "kingpin," whose limited reach on the board means that the other players must watch his back. "Like your uncle," wryly observes Bodie, later adding that the queen—"the go-get-shit-done piece"—is like Stringer Bell. But the "baldheaded bitches" (Bodie's name for pawns) are limited in their movement except when they fight. D'Angelo explains that the pawns are the front lines "out in the field," getting into his lesson on this more complex and thus presumably "better game." But as he explains the kinds of moves each piece can make, he encounters resistance to the inherent feudalism of the game's rules. When Wallace wants to know how you get to be a king, D'Angelo patiently explains that this is not possible: "The king stay the king."

This is a lesson that neither Wallace nor Bodie wants to learn for it teaches them their own expendable role in "the game": that they themselves are mere pawns, the soldiers who fight and die early. Still hoping

"I'll teach you all,
if you all want to learn"

that the game is more like checkers, in which any piece might make it to the other end of the board and become a king, Bodie resists the role of pawn. But D'Angelo again explains, "It ain't like that. Look, the pawns, man, in the game, they get capped quick. They be out the game early." "Unless they some smart-ass pawns," defies Bodie, leaving hope open for his own fate. By season 4, an older and more cynical Bodie recognizes the truth of D'Angelo's lesson. He has been a loyal soldier; he has never "fucked up on a count, never stole off a package." Nevertheless, he complains to Detective McNulty, "This game is rigged, man. We like the little bitches on a chessboard" (4.13, "Final Grades").

But not only are Wallace and Bodie pawns who will never be kings; D'Angelo himself, whom we might think to be at least a knight given his family connections to his uncle, the king of the Barksdale gang, will prove to be a pawn as well. The more D'Angelo plays the game, the more he dislikes the rules he has so helpfully explained in his peer-to-peer lesson. These rules ordain the perfectly unnecessary murders of the witness William Gant, of Wallace himself, and eventually of Bodie. If "the king stay the king," as Avon Barksdale indeed does for a while, before the next king, Marlo, comes along, it is because of the ruthless murders ordered by the "go-get-shit-done-piece," the queen—Stringer Bell. When D'Angelo learns of the murder of Wallace, he hesitates to take the fall for his uncle, and though he finally does take it, he is subsequently murdered in prison because he might betray the family. Unlike in checkers, in this game there is a rigid chain of command that drives every institution, and that hierarchy's main interest is in preserving its own power and resources, not only through the loss of expendable pawns, but up to and including the murder of its own family.[14]

This early chess lesson is an obvious "teaching moment" for the entire series. We perk up and listen to the feudal system of rules, wondering if either Wallace or Bodie will "make it to the end" of the board and the series. But it is also a teaching moment in a wider sense: the teacher, in this case, does something more than school an initiate into the rules of the game. D'Angelo reveals the truth about the nature of the game, more than he even knows. His lesson counters the dream of equal opportunity offered by Snot Boogie's friend in the first episode of this first season: "This is America, man!" When Bodie wants to make it to the other side of the board, D'Angelo's immediate response is "It ain't like that!" What Bubbles teaches is a delusional self-confidence that one can beat the system. What Snot Boogie's friend maintains is the necessity of at least seeming to offer equality. What D'Angelo teaches is a stone-cold reality that he has not quite learned for himself and that his students simply refuse to learn.

In the fourth season, however, we learn about other ways of teaching and learning. The great shame is that these pedagogies are not available to the likes of Bubbles, Snot Boogie's friend, or D'Angelo. These lessons—about soft eyes—are only available to those with a future stake in the culture in which they live, to those more fortunate beings who do not have to harden themselves to merely survive.

Soft Eyes

Not surprisingly, it is in season 4, the season that encounters the world of Tilghman Middle School, that the theme of learning coalesces under the banner of the series's code word for effective learning: soft eyes. As we have seen, the term is introduced in the episode entitled "Soft Eyes" (4.2), by a veteran teacher who simply utters the words to Pryzbylewski. Two episodes later, in our second example of effective peer-to-peer teaching, detectives "Bunk" Moreland and Kima Greggs are at a homicide scene in a vacant lot where Kima, a rookie at homicide, is a little unnerved by the presence of the corpse. Bunk asks her what is needed at a crime scene. Kima answers, "Rubber gloves?" "Soft eyes," corrects

Bunk. "Like I'm suppose to cry and shit?" responds Kima. Bunk finally explains: "If you got soft eyes, you can see the whole thing. If you got hard eyes—you staring at the same tree missing the forest." Kima feigns understanding: "Ah, zen shit." Bunk repeats: "Soft eyes, Grasshopper" (4.4, "Refugees").

Kima's responses to Bunk are the usual police cynicism to what seems like his inflated rhetoric of wisdom. But the lesson is sincere and soft eyes prove not to mean, as Kima first guesses, an emotionally over-wrought kind of softness, the feminized sympathy prone to cry; nor is it mystical "zen shit." Rather, it is genuine advice from a mentor who will end up, at the end of the entire series, her partner. Bunk's lesson is that if you look hard at only one thing you miss the whole. Here it is useful to contrast the difference between the lessons cops and teach-ers can offer each other and the lessons gangsters and drug addicts can offer each other, for D'Angelo's lesson about chess cannot reach for the greater knowledge of the whole the way Bunk's lesson about crime scene investigation does for Kima. Each lesson is adapted to the situation of the learner, and those given no model for future behavior beyond mini-mum wage and gangsterdom cannot afford to have soft eyes. At root, as we subsequently learn, this inability to embrace the "soft" is the basis of the inferior formal education of the underclass.

Bunk introduces the term as he and Kima walk into the vacant lot that holds the corpse. Perhaps if Kima herself had used soft eyes here, she would have noticed when Bunk put the folded piece of paper in the homicide victim's hand. Later, when going through the procedures for a homicide scene, Kima discovers this note in the hand of the victim: "Tater shot me," it says. As a rookie, and without benefit of soft eyes, she failed to observe that the note had been planted by Bunk. Kima learns her lesson and will later demonstrate soft eyes when she solves a crime that has stymied the police and that higher-ups on the force had pre-ferred not to be solved. A state's witness is found murdered in a back alley. Kima is assigned the case by her superiors precisely because she is a rookie deemed incapable of solving it. In a silent, slow scene of in-vestigative perception, she revisits the scene of the crime and tracks the possible trajectories of the bullet from all angles. With soft eyes she stops looking at the same tree and looks instead at the whole configu-

Kima uses soft eyes
to solve a crime

ration, surmising that the fatal bullet could have come from an entirely different direction than originally assumed. Pursuing that hypothesis, she looks around and finds the back of a house where someone had been using bottles for target practice, with potatoes as silencers. The presumed "murder" of a state's witness was thus most likely an accident from a stray bullet, and in a sense, this corpse could also have said, "Tater shot me." When she returns to the homicide office with the bullet slug that matches the one found in the body in the alley she says, simply and enigmatically, "Soft eyes" (4.7, "Unto Others").

Over the course of the thirteen episodes of this fourth season Prez, the former wiretap surveillance officer and failed cop, will also learn to develop soft eyes as he watches over, but no longer surveils with hard penetrative eyes, the problems, interests, and dispositions of his students. We see four of those future students in the first episode of the fourth season trying to catch a homing pigeon in the back alley of their West Baltimore neighborhood (4.1, "Boys of Summer"). Only one of these boys, Duquan "Dukie" Weems, the outcast with addicted parents, even knows how to tell a homing pigeon from an ordinary one. Randy Wagstaff, who is kind to Dukie, has a strict foster mother and is kept on a tight leash. Another boy, Michael Lee, has a crack-addicted mother and a young brother whom he fiercely protects. Yet another, Namond Brice, has an incarcerated father and a mother who pushes him to step up to his rightful position as a dealer on the corner to support the family in his father's place. These boys are desperately in need of schoolin', but most of them will be unable to learn much of what Prez has to teach

Namond, Randy,
Michael, and Dukie

because of their more immediate and necessary apprenticeship to the corners.

In this season we might expect the lesson of soft eyes to be the gift that Prez will pass on to his students, just as Bunk passes it on to Kima and just as the older teacher passes it on to Prez. But this is where the value of soft eyes proves noncommensurate in the otherwise so frequently parallel worlds of police and gangsters. A cop or a schoolteacher can become a better cop or teacher by learning to have soft eyes, as Prez did even as a cop once he learned to take in the totality of the numerical patterns of the gangster codes. And he will become a better teacher as well by standing back to discover the patterns of his students and their different worlds. However, D'Angelo, whose chess lesson to Wallace and Bodie proves him to be every bit as good a teacher as Prez is in his class or as Bunk is at the homicide scene, could not have advised his "students" to have soft eyes. Rather, he had to teach them the hard rules of chess: that pawns get capped early in the game and that it "ain't like" the fair, democratic game they want it to be. The hard lessons that are taught the underclass in *The Wire* are like the hard lesson Marlo Stanfield chooses to teach the convenience store guard in 4.4 ("Refugees"). When he sees Marlo blithely steal a lollipop as if he were not even there, the humiliated guard confronts Marlo and demands that he acknowledge the crime. Sucking the lollipop, Marlo coolly tells him, "You want it to be one way . . . but it's the other way." This cryptic lesson is reinforced later by Marlo's order to murder the guard: this order and its completion are so swift they hardly ripple the surface of the story.

To have soft eyes for those on the street is to comprehend too much. It is to see a whole picture of the matrix of institutions that impede growth and development. Like the multisited ethnography discussed in the first chapter, which attempts to give greater breadth and scope to the discipline in place of the unique, single-sited, perspective of local cultures, soft eyes can take in multiple forms of information about an interconnected whole situation and its contexts of significance.[15] It is not the bird's-eye view of penetrative, isolating surveillance but a situated groundedness.

Though it represents a better, more comprehensive social understanding, the little bit of softness required to observe without reacting with defensive violence is a useless skill in the world of Prez's students. The necessary relaxation, slight passivity, and quietness of this kind of observation betray the ounce of truth in Kima's first understanding of soft eyes as "crying and shit." Softness is feminine; it is associated with the weepy kind of melodrama that generates only sympathy, something that *The Wire* itself—no less than the male-identified Kima, Barksdale gang, Marlo, and the boys on the corner—feels a need to defend against. Indeed, this fear of being perceived as soft may be the deepest reason for *The Wire*'s oft-noted and unmistakable misogyny: women "as" women, as opposed to the women who act "hard" like men, are too "soft" for the series as a whole. Characters like Beadie Russell, the female Port Authority cop who is a mother and whose soft eyes notice a broken customs seal on a container leading to her discovery of a hidden compartment within a container filled with the thirteen dead bodies of young women, are in the minority in the series. It could even be that what some have observed to be the hard dominant masculinity of the series as a whole, which certainly does contain a dearth of women characters, is a defense against the stereotype of melodrama understood as an overly feminized form of soap opera.

Nevertheless the series values soft eyes as a value that is first spoken by a black female teacher. But the difference between Kima and Beadie's exhibition of soft eyes and Snoop and the boys on the corner is that Kima and Beadie can afford to make the gamble of softness (up to a point) that the black underclass cannot make if the corner is the only future they can imagine. As we have seen, when D'Angelo becomes soft enough to care about Wallace, he also becomes vulnerable. Bodie and Poot, who are emotionally much closer to Wallace, must prove their hardness by killing him. And indeed, it is because D'Angelo "goes soft" in his concern for Wallace in a way that Bodie and Poot don't, that D'Angelo is eventually killed. The black street characters get no second chance to play a different game—as Prez does when he leaves the police to become a schoolteacher. Kima can prove herself to her colleagues by acting tough (which her very butchness aids) and can advance up the ladder of her institution with the added benefit of soft eyes, which make her an exemplary cop of the case-building, nonhead-bashing school. D'Angelo, however, has fewer options. He has already missed out on school. His options are dealing, minimum-wage work, or prison. He must either put on blinders to the suffering of others or become a victim himself. Soft eyes demonstrate one's very humanity through the ability to be hurt. But one of the hard lessons of *The Wire* is that this is a luxury the black underclass cannot afford.

This is not to say that soft eyes do not occur among members of the black underclass—whether kingpins, corner boys, or working-class citizens. Dukie Weems demonstrates soft eyes early in season 4 through his understanding of the feelings of a disturbed girl who unleashes a razor-blade attack on another female student in 4.3 ("Home Rooms"). His surreptitious gift to her of a little battery-driven fan comments sympathetically on her need to cool off. It is also Dukie who has the sensitivity to notice the truth of the dead bodies in the vacant houses—that the dead are not zombies, which would give them a certain excitement and glamour, but "just dead" (4.5, "Alliances"). Yet because he has these eyes and can neither delude nor harden himself in the ways of Michael and Randy, he only suffers more, a perpetual victim of his parents and of the other kids. Incapable of the violence necessary to succeed on the street, and too soft to begin high school without the protection of his friends, he has few options.

For a corner kid or a would-be kingpin, soft eyes are a liability; they lead to "crying and shit," which the poignant scene when Dukie and Michael must part shows them both defending against. Casting about for a fond memory of their past as kids, Dukie recalls the time they threw piss balloons at a rival gang of kids and he was caught and beaten. The

Dukie's gift to a girl
who needs to cool off

memory is tender though because afterward Michael bought him "ice cream off the truck. Remember that, Mike?" Although he has been steeling himself against Dukie's sentiments, Michael also seems honestly to not be able to remember this scene of their summer play before middle school, which viewers will fondly remember reaches back to the first episode of this season ("Boys of Summer"). It is clear that Michael cannot allow himself an ounce of nostalgia. That would lead to "crying and shit." Dukie thus manages to feign casualness, saying, "See ya around, Mike" while suppressing tears (5.9, "Late Editions"). This is the real reason they must part: Michael has steeled himself to be hard and has already murdered Snoop. It will be too dangerous for Dukie to be his friend. There is thus no place for Dukie to go but the "Arabers," junk collectors who drive horse-driven carts, who get high and give him a place to sleep. At one point he plaintively asks Cutty, the ex-con gym instructor, who has found his own way out of the game, how you get from this world to the next. Cutty cannot answer. Though Dukie is the one who knows how to distinguish homing pigeons, and who learns the most about computers and math, he cannot parlay his sensitive observational skills into anything but full-time addiction. Soft eyes may make Kima a better cop and Prezbylewski a better teacher, but they cannot save Dukie.

Because soft eyes are not a teachable advantage that can pass from middle-class teacher to underclass student, *The Wire* escapes some of the enduring clichés of the generic school melodrama that indulges in the fantasy of the good of liberal education for all. In this serial melodrama, no magical teacher can utterly turn around students' lives. In the generic school melodrama the enlightened teacher who succeeds at teaching can usually break through defensive hardness and, against the odds, enlighten at least one or two black or Latino inner-city kids.[16] Called "realistic" for the depiction of the dire conditions of the inner city, called "melodramatic" for their happy endings, generic school melodramas depict teachers who persistently break down hard exteriors to transmit their more middle-class, less violent, and hence "soft" outlooks and values. In these films lessons of decency and democracy rule.

Throughout the fourth season, Pryzbylewski works hard to make a difference to his corner boys. The entrepreneurial Randy learns the joy of numbers in Mr. P's math class and beats the odds in a crap game. Dukie receives clean clothes, lunches, and showers at the school, and much-needed attention—all from Mr. P. Yet ultimately the teacher fails with all four of his "homeroom" boys. It is this failure that distinguishes *The Wire* from the generic school melodrama of magical teachers even as it attains a better kind of melodrama. This mold breaking, like the unwillingness to be just a cop show even while it engages us initially in the wiretaps that want to bring down drug dealers, means, once again, that *The Wire* is exceptional melodrama, focused on moral legibility at an institutional level beyond the personal. Pryzbylewski cannot save his students in the manner of the typical school melodrama because personal goodness cannot trump institutional failure. If the kids cannot be "saved," in the still-popular Dickensian fashion, it is because the schools cannot be saved as long as teaching to the test and "juking the stats" are the norm and as long as the uplifting-sounding premise of "no child left behind" ultimately means that all children of the underclass inner city are.

In the end *The Wire* eludes the sentimental fate of many of the most common melodramatic teaching fantasies. Again, this is because it is the kind of melodrama that does not only want to be about "crying and shit" but about the good or bad of institutions and the larger whole in which they function. The best way to save the individuals, this melodrama says, is for the institutions as a whole to work together for justice. And, as we saw in chapter 4, this different kind of melodrama is not simply a matter of a more realistic (and therefore "sad") ending. Indeed, there is a spectacularly happy ending in season 4 for Namond, one of Prez's four students at Tilghman Middle School.

Like Bubbles, Namond is one of the few individuals to be "rescued" in the series. As in the generic school melodrama, his reversal of circumstances is made possible by a teacher. But unlike the ordinary school melodrama, with its generically familiar "stations of the cross" experienced by the good, suffering teacher, the turnaround is not the result of a charismatic teaching or a "tear-jerking moment of redemption as the teach finally reaches the kids."[17] In this case it is not even the result of the efforts of Mr. Pryzbylewski. Rather, what is remarkable and new in the series is how much more deeply it is able to explore—with the soft eyes it inculcates in viewers as well as those demonstrated in some teachers and mentors—the conditions and needs of students over the long haul of their time in the school. These conditions and needs are not met simply because one magical teacher teaches students to emulate himself. Indeed, Pryzbylewski's failures are legion despite his goodwill and developing soft eyes. Like most teachers in ordinary school melodramas, the person he really "saves" is himself, in the conventional way of the naive, white, middle-class teacher. This messed-up former cop becomes a decent person.

Prez is a close mentor to Dukie, who thrives under him. But the one thing Dukie cannot survive is his "social promotion" into high school. Without his protective friends, and without his teacher, Dukie slips into metal salvaging with the junk-collecting Araber, and into addiction in the time-honored tradition of the Gary of *The Corner* (2000), who morphed into the Bubbles of *The Wire*. In a heartbreaking scene, he borrows money from Prez on false pretenses and is last seen shooting up. Similarly, Prez helps Randy calculate the profits of his candy sales. But Randy's delight in math is overtaken by his unwarranted reputation as a snitch, and once again Prez can do nothing to help. Nor can he overcome the directive to teach to the test, at which point his students lose all enthusiasm. Michael, for his part, has been too preoccupied by the need to protect his brother and himself from predatory males who are "too damn friendly" to even pay heed to Prez's teaching. Namond is the one "happy ending" in the group, as judged by his eventual access to middle-class status. But it is not Prez who saves him. In fact, Namond is Prez's greatest pedagogical failure.

Early in the season, when Prez is still a neophyte, Namond repeatedly gets his goat, acting out a police shooting by playing the victim. Later, when Namond mouths off in class, Prez orders him to detention: "Fuck you, Prezbo!" replies Namond as he leaves, perhaps cutting a little close, "Get your police stick out of your desk and beat me. You know you fucking want to" (4.5, "Alliances"). Tossed out of class, suspended from school, Namond ends up in ex-Major Bunny Colvin's experimental special class, invented ad hoc for those students who disrupt the learning in the "gen pop." If Colvin is the proverbial kind uncle who saves the day, and thus a fixture of the melodramatic tradition, it is worth seeing how the construction of this character intelligently reworks the tradition. It is significant, for example, both that Colvin is black and that he has a wife and family of grown kids and thus does not need Namond for his own self-fulfillment or to allay any interracial guilt. In the unspoken racial politics of so many school melodramas, Colvin does not represent the usual savior whose singular success redeems the system. Nor does he ever set out to rescue Namond from the life of the streets or, through teaching, to impose middle-class values on the kids in the experimental class he and sociologist David Parenti establish. Rather, with increasingly soft eyes, he studies them, trying to discover what they need to learn for *their* world, not the one in which cops and teachers live. And contrary to the usual school melodrama, he does not discover a new way to teach math or English. Indeed, he does not initially "give" Namond anything but a place to stay that keeps him from spending a night in "baby booking" (juvenile hall).

This place to stay eventually becomes a permanent guardianship approved by Namond's incarcerated father, Wee-Bey. The removal of Namond from his mother's putative "care" is, of course, a highly Dickensian, not to mention misogynistic and even mother-blaming, outcome. That *The Wire* needs to blame villainous mothers so much for the suffering of their sons is certainly a deeply sexist failure in a series with more than one monstrous mother (Michael Lee's negligent crack mother; D'Angelo Barksdale's cruelly manipulative mother, Briana, and Namond Brice's greedy, self-centered one) and in which the only significant female characters are either lesbian (Kima Greggs), of indeterminate gender (Snoop), or a career-oriented prosecutor (Rhonda Pearlman), leaving only the white Beadie Russell, who loses prominence as the series progresses, as the only nonvillainous mother and simply "good" woman. Nevertheless, in the world of man-to-man relationships that are the chosen melodramatic territory of the series, Colvin's connection to Namond through the special class signifies the further importance of the ex-major's bold willingness to experiment, as he had with Hamsterdam, with modes of policing and teaching that are radically unorthodox, rather than to fall back on sheer sympathy for the underprivileged.

During the time that Namond is in Colvin's special class he is trying to "step up," as his mother puts it, as a corner dealer while his father, Wee-Bey, who had been a chief enforcer in the Barksdale/Bell regime, takes the rap of life imprisonment without parole for the crimes of the Barksdale organization. Unlike his father, Namond fails miserably as a gangster even though he has always been told that this is his rightful position. Like D'Angelo, he has been born into a game that he does not really want to play. Namond is thus no inherently deserving Oliver Twist. He's attracted to the glamour of the streets and hates the routine of school. He has a foul mouth and a sharp wit, but to his own dismay he lacks the necessary hardness to be a drug dealer. Bodie, who hires him to oversee a corner, can only shake his head at Namond's failure to impose discipline. When Namond's pint-sized "lieutenant," Kenard, steals his package, he does not have it in him to beat Kenard as protocol requires. And when Michael does the beating for him, he runs both from the sight of the beaten Kenard and from the brutality of Michael, whom he no longer recognizes.

Namond's very *softness* precipitates the crisis that necessitates his rescue by Colvin. In the premature transition from childhood to manhood required of this particular "boy in the hood" there is, as for Dukie, no saving grace to be found in soft eyes. In a desperate attempt to salvage his "manhood," he turns his pent-up aggression on the misplaced target of the weaker and softer Dukie, at which point a disgusted Michael slaps him like a child. Namond's final humiliation is to break down in tears, proving once again that there is something to Kima's intuition that softness equates to "crying and shit."

In thus crying before former friends and adults, Namond breaks with what sociologist Elijah Anderson calls "the code of the street." This code requires a willingness to commit violence to earn respect.[18]

Namond mouths off
in the special class
Humiliated and defeated,
Namond cries

Bodie obeys it when he beats up Bubbles's sidekick, Johnny, for buying drugs with counterfeit money. He obeys it later when he and Poot kill Wallace. Beatings and murders are de rigueur to maintain the discipline of dealing when there is no possible appeal to the law. D'Angelo's unwillingness to join in this beating and his later outrage at the murder of Wallace signal his own discomfort with this code. During special class Colvin asks the students what makes a good corner boy. The class is at its most cooperative articulating these rules: no stealing is the first rule, and the second is that it is necessary to beat anyone caught stealing, otherwise one looks weak. Namond also points out the hypocrisy of the wider world (of steroids, liquor, cigarettes, and Enron). Another student points out that even Colvin's police salary was paid from working on drugs. Finally Zenobia Dawson explains, "We got our thing, but it's all part of the bigger thing." How can one condemn the code of the street when in fact it is just part of "the bigger thing" (4.8, "Corner Boys")?

Namond's "gift of talk"
exhibited in debate

In the protected space of the special class, the students can teach the teachers about the real world they are training for rather than the fictitious world the teachers want to believe awaits them.

In his public failure to live up to the "code of the street," Namond shows his vulnerability in ways that Cutty Wise, the ex-con gym manager, and Sergeant Ellis Carver recognize. Caught between his mother's willingness to let him go to juvenile hall for a little "hardening" and his deep fear of finding himself in the midst of East and West Baltimore gang wars, where he might be raped, Namond begs Sergeant Carver not to send him there. At the last minute he remembers the name of the teacher of his special class; Colvin is thus his last resort. Like the denizens of Hamsterdam, Namond is neither the sweetest nor the most deserving of the middle-school boys. He lacks soft eyes like Dukie's, even though he himself is soft. However, he is verbally bright and aggressive enough to take advantage when he lands a lucky break. If anything, it is Namond's sharp tongue that impresses Colvin, who has no similar facility. Namond's "gift of talk," demonstrated late in the final season in an "Urban Debate League" public debate, makes the bargain reciprocal.[19]

Conclusion: The Education Season

In a work that contrasts the effectiveness of the hard look of surveillance for purposes of gathering intelligence, to the soft look that takes in and mulls over the whole configuration (trees and forest, single and multisited), we too learn a few things: that the prevailing values of surveillance—what initially seems to be the very premise of a series called *The Wire*—are often quite useless; that soft eyes and multisitedness are better ways to gain knowledge but not available or even advisable to those who must survive on the street.

The institutional equivalent to soft eyes in season 4 is Colvin's special class, a place where one boy who acts out finds it possible to tell his "teacher" that he just found his mama dead on the couch, and where Zenobia can draw connections between the corner kids' "thing" and the larger system. Like Hamsterdam, the special class is a highly illegal temporary haven, a protected place that is, significantly in this most institutional of melodramas, not a loving, private home and often a pretty ugly place. Nevertheless, both soft eyes and the special class hold out some hope for the possibility of institutions that might recognize and better address the more fundamental social problems by ensuring venues where the most damaged students and denizens of the city can explore, under a supervision that maintains order, what they need, if not to function in the world "out there," at least to survive where they are for the moment. In other words, it becomes clear that these are kids who need watching over in the manner of soft eyes, rather than the surveillance of hard eyes.

Neither the lessons of Hamsterdam nor those of the special class offer a magic bullet to better social organization and learning; both are desperate attempts by the same man to triage a wounded population. The special class is repeatedly identified by administrators as "tracking, pure and simple"—"separating students according to expectations of their academic performance" (4.5, "Alliances"), with the less academically prepared kids stigmatized as incapable of much learning. Though Colvin bluntly argues that removing the "corner kids" from the "stoop kids" can only help each group, it is clear that he is stepping on the toes of what are at least hard-won pretenses toward democratic liberal education. His argument is that since the school only pretends to teach the least functional students anyway, why not segregate them according to their ability to learn? Like Hamsterdam, the special class segregates and isolates a problem (drug dealers and addicts in Hamsterdam; corner kids in the middle school). As with Hamsterdam, Colvin has no real plan for how to address the problem, but in both cases he at

Colvin's special class

least ceases to pretend and helps the "gen pop" of those who are functional. The special class, which includes exercises on trust (falling backward while blindfolded), group projects like cooperative construction of model buildings, and endless argument, has no magical effect either, though occasionally it gets the kids talking to each other and with the teachers about their futures. After much too short a time, it is canceled as a form of tracking. Of course, the critique of tracking is based on the false assumption of an otherwise equal society, and therefore is irrelevant in this 100 percent minority inner-city school, which is itself the ultimate tracking.

Like Hamsterdam, the special class is an experiment that works in a limited way and in a way that exposes the hypocrisy of the "bigger thing" of which it is a part. Like Hamsterdam, it is abruptly discontinued as soon as higher-ups discover its "undemocratic" solution of segregating the "troublemakers" from the gen pop. As with Hamsterdam, very few of its students return to the gen pop able to function. Proportionately fewer return from Hamsterdam ready to deal with their addiction— though, as we have seen, one of them is Bubbles. If the "rescue" rates are small, the very fact that, in the midst of institutions that cannot do what they exist to do, someone is able to think up even the most tenuous of solutions to the most intractable of problems suggests that there is some hope for better social justice beyond private forms of virtue.

Two popular Hollywood and television genres—the spy melodrama and the school melodrama—are rewritten by *The Wire*. Both genres are about learning, both offer fairly simplistic good/bad dichotomies. One assumes that surveillance is the key to protecting the good; the other assumes that the value of softness (liberal, democratic values) is a good that can be taught. What *The Wire* teaches instead is that neither genre nor its key methodologies of surveillance and teaching can overcome the intractable problems of class and racial disadvantage. Rather, the series brings the two genres together and explores the limits of each. Surveillance is not the key to better policing. And magical teaching is not the solution to better schools. But it is clear that young people do need watching over and thus some supervision if not surveillance. And it is clear that good policing and good teaching can provide that supervision. Supervision, not surveillance, is what Colvin's Hamsterdam and Colvin's special class provide. In both cases the supervisor-surveillor has a human face.

Sociology departments, film and media departments, even schools of education and health now use *The Wire* as part of their curriculum, and some actors from the series have attempted to use their clout to educate for change.[20] Many academics have readily admitted that *The Wire* teaches what they want students to learn better than they can.[21] The series is good pedagogy in much the same way it is good melodrama. In its fourth season it reinvents the ordinary school melodrama into an extraordinary one through the breadth and depth of the world that it portrays and the time—over one year's narrative, and over thirteen hours of screening time—that it gives the students and teachers to grow and change. School melodramas are a problem so long as they continue to dwell on the exceptional virtues of teachers who go through the stations of the cross to teach. As long as these ideas of teachers and students exist—in our stories about school and in our schools as well—we will still seem to need educational reform with uplifting titles like No Child Left Behind. What we really need, of course, is better opportunity for all.

6 Feeling Race

THE WIRE AND THE AMERICAN MELODRAMA

OF BLACK AND WHITE

BILL SIMMONS: Settle an office debate.
Best *Wire* character of all time?

BARACK OBAMA: It's got to be Omar, right?
I mean, that guy is unbelievable, right?

SIMMONS: We might break this down as like
a March Madness bracket, and I think he's going
to be the no. 1 seed. [*Laughter.*] Everyone is in
on Omar, it seems like.

OBAMA: He's got to be the no. 1 seed. I mean,
what a combination. And that was one of
the best shows of all time.

—Barack Obama, interview by Bill Simmons
on *The B.S. Report*, March 1, 2012

Sociologist George Lipsitz, who is critical of *The Wire* on racial grounds
to be examined below, nevertheless states in a chapter of his probing
book *How Racism Takes Place* that "*The Wire* may well be the best program ever to appear on television."[1] The *Wire* achievements he cata-
logues are grounded in many qualities this book has already detailed: its
eschewal of the usual crime drama's search for the identity of the crimi-

nal, along with its quest instead to "name the crime," its insistence that "social problems are knowledge problems, that social ills persist because we have been encouraged to look at them in the wrong ways," and its ferocious love of Baltimore (to be discussed in the conclusion).[2] Lipsitz also argues that these ills persist primarily because of a war on drugs that has "misallocated resources and misordered priorities."[3] Thus the "true villain is this war" created by "a public policy that produces and perpetuates the very behaviors it purports to prevent."[4]

Yet having granted all of the above, Lipsitz vehemently takes *The Wire* to task for missing the "real crime." This crime, which preexists all the others addressed by the series, is segregation. There is no exposé of blockbusting and white flight in the 1950s and 1960s leading to the failure of school integration in the wake of *Brown v. Board of Education*. In this period segregation became accepted as a natural given for which no one was held responsible.[5] When race as an issue does come up in *The Wire*, Lipsitz claims, it is to portray whites as innocent victims of the city's majority-black population, making it difficult for a white politician to be elected. As he puts it: "*The Wire* cannot tell us how white and Black spaces in the city became separated, how white speculators and blockbusters made money because they were financed by large banks whose officers were unwilling to make loans to credit-worthy Black home seekers . . . how white parents kept their children at home and picketed schools when Black students broke the color barrier in them."[6]

To Lipsitz the failure to understand the differences between white and black "spatial imaginaries," prevents *The Wire* from addressing the true injustices committed by whites against blacks because it does not portray the history of "how things got to this place." Racism, he argues, can only "take place" in particular places. Racialized space gives whites privileged access to social inclusion and upward mobility, while imposing unjust forms of exploitation and exclusion on communities of color. American society, he maintains, is structured by a dominant white spatial imaginary in which the white suburban home is the privileged moral center.[7] If fiction, art, and mass culture are to address "how racism takes place," they must tell the story from slavery forward, of "how things got that way." *The Wire*'s choice to concentrate on the institutions of police, unions, city government, schools, and the press in the post 9/11 period over the more fundamental economic story of banks and housing, thus cannot, according to Lipsitz, get at the root of racial inequities.[8]

Although I agree with many of Lipsitz's judgments about the root causes of racial inequities, I profoundly disagree with his critique of *The Wire*. Consider that if the series had tried to tell the story Lipsitz wants it to have told, it would have become a period piece, deprived of its contemporaneity. Even more important, however, Lipsitz misses the way the series assiduously builds and constantly compares black and white spatial imaginaries. Take, for example, the moment in "Old Cases" (1.4) when Detective Jimmy McNulty, having agreed to drop Bubbles off at "home," takes him on a detour to his son's suburban soccer game. Alarmed at the detour, Bubbles speaks a line originating with Gary McCullough in *The Corner*: "Where in leave-it-to-beaver-land are you taking me?"[9] When McNulty explains that he's late for soccer, Bubbles's rejoinder is "Suck what?" Emerging from the car, blinking at the bright sunshine on the green field, Bubbles extends a hand to McNulty's ex and is snubbed. Preoccupied by an argument with his wife, McNulty misses seeing his son's goal. The ordinary soccer game has been rendered alien by Bubbles's point of view and the insertion of a black spatial imaginary into the white. When McNulty later pulls up to drop Bubbles off in his own neighborhood at the end of this sequence, it is now dark and the contrast could not be more acute. Street lights illuminate a black woman standing while her children run little circles around her. The usual dogs and sirens are heard. "This good for you?" asks McNulty, "Uh huh," answers Bubbles, adding the words we have already seen written in the epigraph: "Thin line 'tween heaven and here." Bubbles, the peripatetic crosser of boundaries between classed and raced spaces notes the difference between the open sunny suburban space where kids play and the dark, fatherless inner-city space where kids still try to play. In this sequence as in so many others the point of view adopted is Bubbles's.

Nor is Bubbles's point of view presented as minoritarian. The suburbs do look alien. Indeed, *The Wire* may be the only dramatic narrative in television or film to proceed from a world in which "integration" itself is not a liberal fantasy of "tolerant" interaction, but a necessary, if uneasy cohabitation in which blacks are already the majority. Of course

Lipsitz is right to note that schools and housing are not integrated, and he is right to note that this is the key problem. However, the fact that the Baltimore depicted in the series is a 65 percent majority-black city, in which Jews, Italians, Poles, and some Latinos also have stakes, means that a dominant black spatial imaginary, if not a black economic domination of space, operates in the series. Even if this dominance is not part of the larger national one, and even if its power is more cultural and linguistic than economic, this is a crucial game changer for the representation of space in the series. Indeed, the fact that *The Wire* is able to generate both sympathy and respect for a wide array of black characters who are *not* portrayed as victims of white villains yet still are victims of the larger, economic and institutional whole is significant. These include two different generations of corner kids—Wallace, Poot, Bodie—and then the younger Michael, Namond, Dukie, and Randy; two generations of cops who, whatever other foibles they may have and despite the inertia of their institutions are in the end "good po-lice"—Bunny Colvin, Bunk Moreland, and the younger Kima Greggs, Ellis Carver, and Leander Sydnor; and two generations of journalists committed to contextual truth, bucking the mainstream of their institution—the older Gus Haynes, the younger Alma Gutierrez and Mike Fletcher. There is also room for a wide variety of black villains on both sides of the law: Deputy Commissioner Ervin Burrell, state senator Clay Davis, and Mayor Clarence Royce, as well as gangsters Marlo, Cheese, and Fruit.

Under these changed conditions of a majority-black culture and a rich array of black male characters (though a paucity of women), the series transmutes into a racially aware, class-aware, and even queer-aware (though oddly gender-unaware) network of interrelated stories. Yet unlike so many stories about race, we are not asked to hiss a white racist villain in order to feel racially just ourselves. Nor need we root for the black macho hero who proves his proper masculinity by beating up "whitey," as in the traditions of blaxploitation through *Django Unchained* (Tarantino, 2012).

Lipsitz argues that *The Wire* "uncritically accepts the neoliberal verdict on the civil rights movement and the war on poverty": that both were dismal failures and that the plight of poor people is incurable unless they are "morally rehabilitated." Lipsitz seems to confuse the series' recognition of the fact of neoliberalism's triumph with an acceptance of its values. Even more seriously, his judgment participates in the very "melodrama of black and white" that may today be the most serious impediment to our culture's ability to envision racial justice. This chapter argues that *The Wire* does not accept neoliberal verdicts on civil rights or the war on poverty but is precisely an important critique of them. For once, however, it is a racial melodrama that does not proceed from the putative position of racially oppressed and victimized minorities. In other words, as I shall endeavor to show, this is one racial melodrama that does not "play the race card."

Playing the Race Card in Melodramas of Black and White

"Playing the race card" is the phrase often used to depict the deployment of past racial injuries in contemporary contexts that presumably no longer apply.[10] One can play the race card as a minority or as a majority race, and Lipsitz is particularly critical of the idea that one thread of *The Wire* narrative shows the difficulty "worthy whites" have becoming police commissioners or mayors.[11] When whites play the race card, they usually do so today to show their own victimization at the hands of affirmative action in a society that by now is supposed to have become "color-blind." A neoliberalism that is no longer willing to take into account past inequities is understandably a problem. But like David Simon, who rails against editors who play up the Dickensian aspect of stories, Lipsitz himself "plays the race card" of the melodrama of black and white when he wants the many stories of *The Wire* to explain Baltimore's past failure to provide fair market housing to blacks, the 1993 protests against existing public housing, or HUD's four-decade violation of the 1968 Fair Housing Act. Housing, he seems to argue, is the race card that this serial should have played to (melo)dramatize the key economic form of racialized injury.[12] But here Lipsitz does not recognize that *The Wire* disdains to join the melodrama of black and white and that this refusal represents a significant game change. It is thus only by understanding something of the history of the melodrama of black and white that we can see how *The Wire* breaks this pernicious cycle.

In *Playing the Race Card: Melodramas of Black and White from Uncle*

Tom to O. J. Simpson I have chronicled the long history of this most galvanizing of melodramatic cycles. Here I will simply summarize some key ideas.[13] Racialized victims and villains abound in the mainstream melodrama of black and white, though never in an equal, tit-for-tat manner. The first racial melodrama that was compelling to a wide American audience emerged as a protest against slavery when a white woman author told the story of a black Christian slave in a way that moved primarily white readers and playgoers to tears for his suffering. This entirely white supremacist yet "negrophilic" serialized novel by Harriet Beecher Stowe, *Uncle Tom's Cabin* (1852), was followed by dozens of other versions of "Tom" plays, many of which could only be described as blackface minstrel musicals. Clichéd and stereotypical as the Tom plays seem to us today, they had real social force in their time. From before the Civil War to the early twentieth century, the Tom show cast the Christian slave as a virtuous sufferer, himself moved to pity for the suffering and untimely death of the white Little Eva. To those who had previously regarded slaves as mere property, the Tom story revolutionized racial feeling, to the extent that Abraham Lincoln regarded it as one of the causes of the Civil War.[14]

After the end of slavery and an incomplete Reconstruction, this hugely influential racial melodrama, while still popular, was "answered" by the negrophobic novels of Thomas S. Dixon, which were also adapted to theater but eventually leapt to an entirely new medium in the filmed version of *The Clansman*, renamed *The Birth of a Nation* (D. W. Griffith, 1915). In this "anti-Tom" cycle, racial sympathy was redirected to the sexually threatened white woman, and racial hatred was engendered toward rapacious, unruly former slaves. With these two "Tom and anti-Tom"—Negro sympathy and Negro antipathy—cycles in place, the initial pattern for melodramatic playings of the "race card" was set. According to the tenor of the times—and sometimes helping to determine those times—one version of this melodrama succeeded another, with a paternalistic negrophilia dominant at one moment, and an equally paternalistic white supremacist negrophobia at another.

Each new entry in this cycle spiraled forward from the point of view of what could be called its different "spatial imaginary," to adopt Lipsitz's term. Initially, though, the black spatial imaginary was produced

by a white-authored sympathetic imagination of black space, specifically the slave cabin of Uncle Tom. I have argued that that cabin was
refunctioned in *The Birth of a Nation* as the log cabin where "former
enemies of North and south" fought to "retain their Aryan birth right"
(as one intertitle from that film puts it). In both cases the "good home"
attempted to explain the enigma of American national identity through
the ongoing crisis of moral legibility precipitated by the presence of a
racial "other" long after slavery ended.[15] Later, under the Hollywood
Production Code,[16] where representations of miscegenation and terms
like "nigger" were taboo, films tended to portray blacks as either background smiling servants or vague threats. More often, films displaced
black/white melodrama into Jewish assimilation, as in *The Jazz Singer*
(1927), or Irish upward mobility, as in *Gone with the Wind* (1939). In both
cases the white ethnic protagonist assimilated and prospered by overtly
or covertly taking on the long-suffering virtues of an aggrieved black
race. It was not until the end of the Code and the trend-setting eight-
episode serial presentation (on consecutive nights) of the television
miniseries *Roots*, in 1977, that a woefully belated entry into this cycle of
racial melodrama finally broke the monopoly of white authorship. Until
Roots, even the sympathetic "Tom" side of the cycles had been authored
by whites. In this new version of the story, black and white American
audiences were encouraged to view black history, from before slavery
to after emancipation, as the "saga of an American family."[17] In other
words, and again in Lipsitz's terms, this new cycle of the Tom racial
melodrama advocated a "black racial imaginary."

It was only at this point (1977) that "an American family" could finally
be imagined as black in the popular, mainstream media. Racial feelings of sympathy for the trials of a diasporic black family ran high with
this work, which stopped American white and black audiences in their
tracks as everyone watched the saga unfold on television.[18] Although
today we tend to deride the overt melodramatic simplicity of this television miniseries, not to mention its disputed "authenticity" regarding
author Alex Haley's specific familial connection to Africa, we do well
to recall that in its time it represented, as we have seen all melodrama
does, a new level of realism meant to counter the original Tom/anti-
Tom depictions of slaves. It thus importantly overcame, again within the

popular mainstream imagination, the previous plantation idealizations of the "peculiar institution" for the new post–civil rights era.[19] Such has been the pattern of black-and-white racial melodrama: if yesterday's outmoded racial melodrama seems hopelessly retrograde, "today's" new racial melodrama in the form of trials, movies, and television shows can prove uncannily gripping.[20]

The melodrama of black and white has continued to hold audiences of all races in its grip because it engages with what can only be considered America's original sin of slavery. Each new entry purports to tell the true story of slavery and its aftermath. The realism perceived in each cycle consists of the conditions that oppress the chosen racial victim: Tom's fatal whipping by Simon Legree in *Uncle Tom's Cabin*; the exciting ride of the clan and the chaotic threat of black rule and miscegenation in the anti-Tom *Birth of a Nation*. In the new kind of "Tom" melodrama offered by *Roots*, the novelty was the portrayal of the idyllic African home from which the young, heroic Kunte Kinte was stolen, the realistic degradations of the Middle Passage, the tortures of slavery, and the separation of families. Thus *Roots* revived and updated the racially sympathetic "Tom" story into a more historically realistic perspective that gave the African slave a home (not previously figured in the mainstream melodramas of black and white) from which he was cruelly stolen. This home, crucial to most family melodrama, restored a certain very welcome patriarchal virility to the emasculated Tom figure. It also provided what Lipsitz would call a "black spatial imaginary," though one that was importantly determined by the need to counter the prior figure of the stereotypical "emasculated" Tom and the hypersexual anti-Tom. *Roots* was also gripping in its innovation of media form, virtually inaugurating American television's experimentation with prime-time seriality.

With each new turn of the screw of the American racial melodrama, there has been a revision of racial feelings regarding who is the proper victim and who is the proper villain of racial injustice. This dynamic occurs in fiction, as outlined above, as well as in the racial feelings generated by real events, most famously in the nearly successive media spectacles surrounding the trials of the police in the beating of Rodney King and the O. J. Simpson murder trial, both of which were so gripping because they could be viewed from a sympathetic Tom (black as oppressed by white villain) or anti-Tom (white as oppressed by black villain) perspective.

And so this melodrama has continued, even (or perhaps especially) when the ideal of a "color-blind" system of justice makes the very mention of race, either for advantage or disadvantage, increasingly taboo. Indeed, the very concept of a color-blind justice has permitted a resurgence of feelings of white injury, feeding an animus against affirmative action as a form of racial bias. It is precisely because of this state of affairs that Lipsitz asserts the importance of delineating the hegemonic white spatial imaginary against which the minoritized black spatial imaginary struggles. In so doing, however, he perpetuates the very melodrama of black and white that he wishes to abolish through more realistic histories—new forms of realism—that cannot be refuted. But notice that instead of seeking the end of this ongoing cycle of injury and retribution, he proposes what amounts to its continuation through yet another spin on the same old melodrama of black and white. His housing/bank story counters a false (racist) white imaginary with the historical truth of black victimization, itself perceived as a true (nonracist) black imaginary.

I accept this "greater truth" of black victimization in the history of how American racism "takes place." And yet it is evident to me that these perpetual playings of the "race card," in which first white, then black derives the moral righteousness of its quest to flourish from victimization are at an impasse. To play the race card now can only contribute to increased racial animosity rather than contribute to solutions for original injury. "Playing the race card" in the usual way—despite the refinement that recognizes different dominant and nondominant white and black spatial imaginaries, and not just black or white people—still encourages forms of racial resentment that only dig deeper trenches of (now often unspoken) animosity. In a neoliberal era no longer inclined to correct social injustices but to blame them on the morally failed character of the disenfranchised, playing the race card can only be regressive.

In his account of "how things got to this place," Lipsitz tells us that blacks perceive themselves as innocent victims of rapacious whites who are never willing to acknowledge the advantages they have at the expense of blacks. Whites in turn try to cast themselves as the "innocent victims of blacks."[21] It galls Lipsitz that in *The Wire* women leaders did not become a major part of its story of the vacant homes and desolate housing projects that dominate the "corner" and that were once places of struggle for grassroots power. And he is entirely right that the important stories of women (except for one state's attorney, one butch cop, and one butch gangster who inhabit entirely male words) find no place in this work.[22]

However, it is worth asking what difference it would have made if *The Wire* had included within its array of institutions and individuals the story of heroic black mothers campaigning for better housing. Though it would have made the series more inclusive of women,[23] it would only have produced yet another entry into the long-running melodrama of black and white. It would not have altered the premise of keeping score of racial injury, the fear and suspicion of the racial "other." No matter how often we remind ourselves that the original injury was slavery and that the cycle of racial melodrama proceeds from that, we remain trapped in what I have called a "melodramatic racial fix."[24] The importance of *The* Wire, I hope to show, is that, while exemplary serial melodrama expanded to the level of institutions and a multisited whole, it does not perpetuate this racial fix. Oddly, however, this is not because the old, overtly racist "anti-Tom" melodrama continues, but because a new kind of (Tom) melodrama has arisen to prove the virtues of blacks. In these melodramas of black and white sympathy for good blacks—especially black men—runs rampant.

No American film or television series today would dare blame blacks as a race for civil misrule the way *Birth of a Nation* did in 1915. Nor would they relegate blacks, as was common during the Production Code, to the entirely background role of servants, whether as a capable Mammy or an incapable Prissy. And of course, today there are, if not an abundance then at least a range of roles for black men and women in American film and television to occupy beyond the Mammy, the Coon, the Sambo, and so on. Yet there is something highly suspicious in the very abundance of racial amity emitted from the white imaginary of our large and small screens, and this is why the seemingly pro-Tom melodrama has become even more insidious.[25] Indeed, if you squint real hard you may see the anti-Tom lurking beneath.

Racial Feeling in the Contemporary "Tom Story"

Mainstream American audiences have great sympathy for black characters, especially if they are poor, uneducated and rural, and even more if they exhibit the qualities of love and devotion to whites that were originally exhibited in the Tom story. As a Christ-like human, Tom was a novel object of sympathy for white readers and playgoers who had not previously considered the humanity of slaves. Eventually, of course, the figure of the patient, suffering Tom would seem as demeaning to blacks as the comic minstrel. Figures like Richard Wright's Bigger Thomas and Alex Haley's Kunte Kinte, and blaxploitation's antiheroes Superfly, Shaft, and Sweetback, were hypermasculine and "bad" precisely to counter the saintliness of the emasculated Tom, even at the risk of playing into the hands of the anti-Tom myth.[26]

In recent years, at least since the late 1990s, the virtuous, suffering black hero who sacrifices himself for whites has endured as a supposedly "positive" racial image with not-so-covert undertones of white racial paternalism in what certainly is a hegemonic white racial imaginary. This endurance gives credence to the ongoing popularity of the melodrama of black and white in its most original Tom form. Perhaps not coincidentally following the racial discord generated by the trials of the police in the beating of Rodney King (a modern Tom story if you thought the beating was excessive) and the trial of O. J. Simpson (a modern anti-Tom story if you thought Simpson was guilty), which so divided the country along racial lines, popular movies in which race is a theme have often retreated to seemingly more inoffensive stories about white men who are aided by Tom-like helpers. Since the immensely popular film of Stephen King's serial novel *The Green Mile* (1999, Frank Darabont) almost seems to have been designed to reestablish racial harmony from a white hegemonic point of view by falling back on the Tom story's tried-and-true expressions of interracial sympathy, it is worth recalling.

A giant black man, John Coffey (Michael Clarke Duncan), is on death row in a Louisiana penitentiary in 1935, waiting to walk "the green mile" to the electric chair. He has been convicted of the murder and rape of two little blond girls found bloodied in his arms. With plenty of his own troubles to worry about, the simple Coffey nevertheless concerns himself with relieving the troubles of his white jailors. Possessing the miraculous ability to suck up into his own body the pain of others through a quite literal "laying on of hands," he absorbs whatever ails them into his own capacious, hypermasculine body and emits it orally in a grand *coup de theatre* as if it were a swarm of insects.

Coffey's method of cure requires intimate contact with the afflicted white bodies he succors and this is where this Tom melodrama seems to intentionally rewrite the errors of the anti-Tom one. For example, he first relieves his jailor and eventual executioner, played by Tom Hanks, of a painful urinary infection by grabbing and holding the afflicted organ.[27] A second cure takes place over the blond, white-nightgowned but cancer-ravaged body of the warden's ailing wife. By kissing her, Coffey sucks up into himself the evil that inhabits her body. In so doing, however, he provocatively reenacts every white racist's worst fear of the black man's sexual threat to white womanhood. Like the "laying on of hands" to his jailor's penis, the kindly gesture disavows the very forbidden desire it enacts, while asserting transcendent purity in a context of lurid, interracial carnality. After this earthshaking cure—and it literally shakes the foundations of the warden's house—the restored warden's wife embraces him and takes minor notice of his own suffering. Racial amity has thus been created through these harrowing near enactments of both homosexual and heterosexual threats to white male hegemony.

What, in turn, do the white jailors do to prove *their* racial virtue and interracial love for John Coffey? Here the interracial love does not flow so freely. As a last wish, Coffey asks to be shown a "flicker show."[28] Rather than escape, which Coffey, like Tom, would not do, his jailors offer him Depression-era "escapism." Beyond that, the best they can offer is a "good"—that is, not botched, as previously witnessed—execution in the electric chair and the removal of the regulation hood to indulge Coffey's childlike fear of the dark. By this time another miracle has allowed the executioner to see that Coffey did not commit the crime for which he is to be executed; again he had merely been trying to "take back" the evil committed by another. We thus must bear witness to the execution, feeling his fear and pain, but also that of his white executioners, who perform their tasks "with love." Outrageously, it is as if the only possible measure of white virtue in the melodrama of black and white, at this point in its development, has become the degree to which the whip or the electricity is applied "with love" rather than hate.

What are we to make of such an interracial act of violence in the name of interracial love? As before we are meant to see that what patently looks like evil—white guards in a Louisiana prison executing an innocent black man is—no less than Coffey's apparently violent embrace of the two raped and murdered white girls, a classic melodramatic misrecognition of virtue. This is not the first time mainstream black-and-white melodrama has posed the spectacle of black punishment by white authority as a disguised form of kindness. In a key moment of the final episode of the 1977 *Roots*, when a kindly and innocuous white friend whips Chicken George's son, he does so only in order to prevent a more brutal whipping from a racist nightrider. With friends like these, black men hardly need enemies. The white racist stereotype exists in these dramas but only to be hated with a vengeance that makes the majority white audience feel good. Either way, however, the black man gets beaten. The lesson for the black onlooker may very well be that white love, no less than white hate, is lethal.

How a still majority-white America is to carry out the incarceration and execution of more and more African American men while still feeling racially virtuous seems to be the deeper issue at stake in the films of this tradition. We can legitimately ask why, in *The Green Mile*, John Coffey is never seen working his miracles for fellow African Americans (even Uncle Tom managed to succor a few of his fellow slaves). We can ask why it is not the justice system itself but only the personal racist villains who are exposed, when surely the pressing issue before the nation today is how to introduce real "moral legitimacy" into a system that seems only to know how to incarcerate more and more black men.

What is perhaps most striking in *The Green Mile* is the remarkable extent to which the establishment of white virtue rests on a paradoxical administration of pain and death to the black man so that "good" white people—personified by Tom Hanks—may bravely hold back their tears.

What was true in the mid-nineteenth century is bizarrely true again today. If the Tom melodrama has always wanted to see the black man's Christian love as the special cure for the white man's hate, this more recent incarnation of the negrophilic melodrama of black and white offers a new twist: it stages the worst fears of anti-Tom race hatred in the guise of the expression of Tom love.

Despite its proven popularity,[29] I would not have cited this particular film in such detail if it were not the tip of the iceberg of a whole class of especially well-loved and popular films centered on what Spike Lee has called "the magical Negro."[30] The list of these films is long, and often the magical Negro occupies merely a supporting role.[31] He exists to save and guide the more troubled and sophisticated white, often as with Coffey, through supernatural powers.[32]

As race scholar Matthew Hughey writes, "When black actors are constantly cast as angels, spirits, gods, and other incarnate supernatural forces, they displace the realities of history into more viewer-friendly narratives of reconciliation and accord."[33] Thus the racism of these representations is obscured by the sheer increase in black roles, the apparent interracial cooperation, the superficial empowerment of historically marginalized subjects, and a general desire to believe that racism is ended.[34] In *Bruce Almighty* (2003), Morgan Freeman, who plays "God," is first introduced as a janitor, mopping floors in an unoccupied building. And although he occupies many different positions throughout the film, by the end, he is returned to this station of sacrificial servant/janitor. As Freeman's character puts it in the sequel, *Evan Almighty* (2007): "You want to know how to change the world, son? One act of random kindness at a time."[35]

"Random acts of kindness" will neither change the world nor alter the basic conditions that have produced greater segregation and incarceration of blacks than was experienced in the 1960s and 1970s. But these mutated "Tom" films, which long ago lost their teeth as radical forms of sympathy for persons once without rights, nevertheless continue the tradition of making whites feel good about their own good feelings toward blacks. "Magical Negro" is an appropriate term for these films, but we should not forget that these throwbacks to an old-fashioned plantation mentality did not arise suddenly out of the blue in the nineties. They exist in conflict with more overtly anti-Tom narratives that, although no one would offer them today as entertainment on film or television, have nevertheless played out in the news: the all-white jury that saw Rodney King as a hulking threat even as he was under the baton and taser of the Los Angeles Police Department, or white Bay Area Rapid Transit policeman Johannes Mehserle, who shot and killed the prostrate and unarmed Oscar Grant on New Year's Day 2009 in Oakland, California, or the white George Zimmerman, acquitted in 2013 of murdering black teenager Trayvon Martin.[36]

Because the anti-Tom lurks beneath the surface of even these overt Tom stories, I prefer to hold on to Leslie Fiedler's older formulation of "Tom" and "anti-Tom" for their longer-term historical understanding of the dialectic of these racial feelings as well as the white hegemony within which they were originally, and still continue to be, generated.[37] The melodrama of black and white is ongoing, and all racially based stories are grist for its mill. To understand the melodrama of black and white, as melodrama, is to see why repeated calls for more accurate, or more "realistic" representations of racially marked characters are powerless to overturn deeply embedded racial stereotypes that seem hopelessly outmoded, yet live on in the culture. It is also to understand why a heartfelt story of black struggle for equal rights and equal housing could do little to break this pattern.

This brief history of the melodrama of black and white suggests that it has become possible, even in mainstream American culture, to present a minority-black perspective, or what Lipsitz calls a "black racial imaginary," in opposition to a villainous majority-white perspective. This is what many racial melodramas, from *Roots* through the cycle of blaxploitation films that celebrated turning the tables on "whitey" through the recent *Django Unchained* (Tarantino, 2012) have delighted in doing. Such works seek either revenge against, or reparations for, previous injury.

Racial Melodrama in The Wire

We have seen that *The Wire* certainly is a melodrama, and a melodrama in which race matters, but it is not a melodrama of black and white in the sense described above: bad racist whites are not pitted against good liberal ones, in the manner of the magical Negro variants, and it is certainly not a series that portrays blacks as a whole as villains, even though there are plenty of individual black villians as well as heroes. Most refreshingly, it does not pretend to exist in a color-blind world. It does not even present the black spatial imaginary as minoritarian. As we have seen, Baltimore is majority black, and not all blacks are in a ghetto. Thus Lipsitz's claim that "no matter how much or how nobly its inhabitants struggle against ghetto conditions, the ghetto remains the seemingly natural habitat of Black people in *The Wire*" does not make sense—nor does the claim that *The Wire* is the "calculated and self-interested creation of white supremacy."[38] The ghetto *is* inhabited by blacks, but there is nothing natural about it. Most working and middle-class jobs are inhabited by blacks, whites, and a smattering of ethnics. As to being a "self-interested creation of white supremacy," it is precisely the melodrama of black and white that, in its swing toward the "anti-Tom" pole, and in its perhaps even more insidious recent swing toward the "Tom" pole, represents versions of white supremacy. Indeed, if the melodrama of black and white begins, as I have argued, in an initial attempt to include blacks within the fold of humanity then it is itself and in its very essence a form of (liberal) white supremacy. Both poles keep white supremacy in place.

I contend that *The Wire* has rewritten the melodrama of black and white in the most progressive way possible. This is the case not because it achieves an actual state of colorblindness, in which race does not matter—race matters enormously in the lives of every character—but because it is no longer part of the black and white, tit-for-tat scorekeeping of racial injury. It ceases to tell the most contemporary version of the Tom story in which racial injury earns the right to be perceived as virtuous—but magically so. *The Wire* is too aware of the neoliberal hollowing out of discourses of rights to follow this trajectory of racialized victims and villains. When aspiring mayor Tommy Carcetti says, "I still wake up white in a city that ain't," he is not portrayed as an innocent victim of the city's majority-black population, as Lipsitz maintains, but as an Italian American cooly judging his odds of getting elected. There is no sense of racial injury in his complaint. Nor does he ride to the rescue of the schools and police as initially promised. What is perhaps most original in the series is that whiteness can no longer represent the norm. The only functioning norm, as Carcetti's very language reveals is the eloquent lingua franca of the streets. Race is acknowledged, spoken, and seen in this language. Neither the liberal ideology of color-blindness, nor the old melodrama of black and white rules. This is what makes George Lipsitz's claim that "the 'otherness' portrayed in *The Wire* remains fully enclosed with a white spatial imaginary"[39] ring so false.

To place a black racial imaginary at the cultural center of *The Wire*'s many worlds also takes the burden off race as the key difference between social groups; class is thus much more visible than it usually is in American television or film. Of course, it also gives the series carte blanche to depict many familiar black stereotypes that have been previously condemned, often by black communities and critics, as too "negative." As long as such stereotypes do not function the way they do in works dominated by a white racial imaginary, this does not prove a problem. Indeed, starting with stereotypes, but not ending with them, may prove the stereotype's most effective antidote in this new institutionally rather than family-based melodrama forged by *The Wire*.

This is not to deny that the demographics of HBO viewership are both predominantly white and middle class. *The Wire* has long been high on the list of "stuff white people like."[40] If the majority viewership of the series is white, as would reflect the majority of the population, there is also no doubt that the series was also popular among black viewers. As Jennifer Fuller argues, blacks watch more cable than whites and subscribe to premium cable in disproportionately high numbers.[41] HBO has appealed to a large African American subscriber base, as Jason Mittell notes, due to its history of sports programing and showcasing of black comics in stand-up specials.[42] *Oz* (HBO 1997–2003) a series with a diverse cast set in a maximum security prison was an earlier series that also appealed to black audiences. It seems that HBO in particular has enjoyed a disproportionately large black audience representing "slightly more than 30 percent of HBO's total viewing pie"[43] Thus white viewers are not necessarily voyeurs of black misery and are not recruited, as Lipsitz puts it, "to inhabit subject positions as analysts and managers of urban life, not as interactive participants in it."[44] It is not accidental, for example, that in 2007, before the series was completed on HBO, *The*

Wire was reedited for commercial interruption and reaired, one episode a night, during primetime on the "basic cable" Black Entertainment Television (BET), with blurred nudity and expletives deleted.[45] It makes a big difference if a majority-white audience is invited into a multisited world that is itself majority black.

It would be fair to say that *The Wire* operates within the cultural context of the Tom tradition of official sympathy for blacks that *The Green Mile* and other magical Negro films express. It may even be fair to say that there is something of the magical Negro in the figure of Omar Little (see below). But one thing that it would *not* be fair to say is that the serial perpetuates the usual cycle of the melodrama of black and white. Indeed, its greatest innovation is to refuse to play the game of "vying to be the victim" of a racialized other. Instead, the serial addresses the very question of the game itself. This may even be what the oft-repeated phrase "It's all in the game" first spoken by Omar, means.

"The Game"

There are many versions of "the game" in *The Wire*. Police, city government, teachers, and the newspaper business all have versions of it. But the game played by those involved in drugs is certainly the most lethal and the most insistently commented upon. The other institutions don't call their game "the game." Because dealers play their game outside the law they have no recourse to it when they themselves are robbed. When Omar Little first utters the phrase as the last line of the first season, he is holding a revolver to the head of a corner drug dealer, doing what he does best: stealing either drugs or money from dealers themselves. He chuckles and says, "All in the game, yo. All in the game" (1.13, "Sentencing"). At this point he probably simply means: "This is fair within the parameters of the outlaw game we both willingly choose to play." And with his facial scar, sawed-off shotgun, and duster Omar looks the part of the western outlaw (with headscarf instead of hat) as he stalks the streets whistling his trademark tune, "The Farmer in the Dell."

Omar appreciates the consequences of the game he plays and he plays it openly, rarely lurking in the shadows. Earlier in the first season he is willing to help the cops acquire evidence on the Barksdale gang because

Omar. "All in the game"

they have tortured and murdered his lover Brandon. But he will help them only up to a point, since "out there it's play or get played." Clearly Omar prefers to play rather than to get played. He does not perceive himself as a victim of any specially racialized villainy. And though he may certainly be a victim of homophobia, Omar never acts the part of the victim. He knows that the only recourse for the murder of Brandon is to seek personal revenge and to play the game as fairly as he can. He thus uses the police in what amounts to a momentary collaboration. When he lands in jail and is in special danger as a known homosexual, his friend Butchie sends two lifers to help him defend himself. They bundle him up in phone books to protect his body and give him a shiv. When he is predictably attacked while in line for breakfast, Omar not only overcomes his attacker but enjoys taunting, even kissing this man before he shoves the shiv up his ass. This too is all in the game: play or be played, kill or be killed (4.7, "Unto Others").

The second time Omar utters "all in the game," he expands the meaning of "game" beyond the world of drug dealers and stash stealers. In the second season, working with police to seek his revenge on the Barksdales, he gives false testimony against a Barksdale operative. On cross-examination, the Barksdale defense attorney Maurice Levy condemns Omar as "a parasite who leeches off the culture of drugs," but Omar interrupts him to draw a comparison between himself and Levy. When Levy registers offense at the comparison, Omar genially explains, "I got the shotgun, you got the briefcase. It's all in the game though, right?" (2.6, "All Prologue"). What's the difference between us, Omar insinu-

Omar in court: "I got the shotgun, you got the briefcase. It's all in the game, though, right?"

ates, since we both profit from the traffic in illegal drugs? The difference, of course, is that Omar's life will be short, while Levy's will be long and prosperous because he operates within and with, rather than outside, the law. Nevertheless, as so often in *The Wire*, the comparison between the actions and motives of disparate institutions cuts deep. Omar *is* like Levy, but as legal scholar Alafair Burke has pointed out, Omar also profits from the drug trade in ways similar to the police, who accumulate overtime in big drug cases.[46]

What is this game, about which so many characters pontificate? Omar is certainly not the only character to invoke its rules. The point of the "game" metaphor as it operates throughout the series is that the rules are not the same to everyone. Gangsters, too, invoke them, especially Avon Barksdale, who has a different, less precise sense of "the game." While serving time in prison in season 3 (3.1, "Time after Time"), Avon recruits Cutty into his organization by noting that while things have changed on the corners—the towers have come down, the Murphy Homes have disappeared—nevertheless, "the game is still the game." He means to say that there is still a need for a good soldier like Cutty to serve as his muscle in the game of illegal drugs. But Barksdale, speaking as the king (as in the chess lesson described in chapter 5) whose reign has been only momentarily interrupted for his stint in jail, does not convince a dubious Cutty who only wants *out* of the game after fourteen years in prison. Nor does he trust what is beginning, by this third season, to sound like an empty tautology.[47]

African American studies scholar Paul Allen Anderson has pointed out that tautologies such as this one make no real claims about reality and are used by authority figures to underwrite their own power.[48] Avon's "the game is the game" asks the person to whom he speaks to assent to its truth without actually knowing what this truth is. Masquerading as reason, all Avon's tautology does is reinforce his supposed mastery of the game through violence. He will repeat this phrase, along with the related "business is business" and "the street is the street" many times over in the series, each time sounding a little more hollow, until he himself loses his kingship and is put away for a long time. But as is clear from the very context of Avon's first utterance of the phrase, times are changing and the game is not immutable; it certainly has, as Slim Charles notes, gotten "more fierce" (3.4 "Hamsterdam).

Stringer Bell had tried to expand the meaning of the game as a way to enter a new level of investment into finance capital, explaining to Avon: "You know, Avon, you gotta think about what we got in this game for, man. . . . Was it so our names could ring out on some fucking ghetto street corner, man? Naw, man. There's games beyond the fucking game" (3.10, "Reformation"). But as we have seen, and as Avon has already noted, Stringer Bell was not smart enough for that (business) game and not hard enough for the (gangster) game.

Finally, Marlo Stanfield, who replaces Avon as the new king—proving that, unlike in the chess game, the king does *not* "stay the king"—never alludes to the game. For Marlo the game is simply his own power, and that power obeys no rules at all. It is significant then that Marlo, who emerges at the end as Omar's major antagonist, is as emotionally cold and dead as Omar is emotionally vibrant and alive. In contrast, Omar's code of "it's all in the game" accepts responsibility for known rules (not to kill or prey on those citizens who try to live within the structure of the law; fierce loyalty to lovers and friends; not even to swear). As he says in the third season to Detective Bunk Moreland, "I ain't never put my gun on nobody that wasn't in the game" (3.7, "One Arrest").

The game only means what any powerful player in it says it means; it does not need to mean anything beyond the acquisition of money and power. At the limit, the game with no rules is pure unbridled capitalism, and if it is explored the most through the lives of the drug dealers, it is because the drug dealers operate, like neoliberal capitalism, outside most conventional systems of constraint. Unlike the earlier Keynesian capitalism and its systems of social guarantees, safety nets, and long-term employment (which poor blacks, women, and other minorities were much less likely to have participated in, back in the day), neoliberal capitalism does not guarantee anything except a comparatively precarious but "flexible" existence of temporary alliances. The very flexibility on which it is built means that it does not guarantee work, economic growth, or stability, at the level it once delivered with systems of social guarantees. What it does guarantee is increased surveillance, intervention into people's lives, and vastly increased incarceration.

In an article on the Deleuzian aspects of *The Wire*, Eric Beck argues that the end of welfare as we know it has not meant a large decrease in money spent on social programs, but their reorganization into different programs "that can more tightly monitor and modify recipients' behavior."[49] If Marlo offers a vision of neoliberal subjectivity at its most ruthless, Omar offers a vision of its more creative, flexible possibilities. The point of the almost universal recognition of Omar as "the best *Wire* character" (Obama) is not to redeem the value of neoliberalism but to recognize that it now reigns: the old economic system "back in the day"—so worshipped by the dockworkers or the cops in their white ethnic pride singing in bars—may never have been all it was cracked up to be, at least not for minorities and women.

"You Feel Me?"

Throughout this book I have steadily argued that there is no single, central protagonist in *The Wire* and that the series' focus on institutions and networks of relations, rather than on unique individuals and their personal will to power is one of its most remarkable features. If Detective Jimmy McNulty initially seems to be the hero even after we have ceased to believe in his moral or professional integrity five seasons later, it is partly because he endures from the very beginning to the very end of the series. His quest to solve crimes rather than juke the stats makes him admirable as "good po-lice." Like all the other sympathetic cop characters

in the series, he is at odds with his institution and we root for him to reform its waste and corruption, though we cannot go along with his willingness to lie and fake crimes in the process. We thus become increasingly disenchanted with McNulty's cocky, self-destructive, alpha-male,
Irish cop character and eventually learn to respect his superior, Lieutenant (and later Major) Cedric Daniels. Daniels at first does not seem to be
"good po-lice," but he later proves to be not only a good leader but also
incorruptible, willing to forgo his career rather than juke the stats once
again. But neither this white nor this black cop is free enough of his institution and its "game" to perform as they should. Both fail in the end.[50]

As for the drug gangsters, some are strikingly heroic, especially the
ones who dissent from gangsterdom, such as D'Angelo Barksdale. But
all of their careers, from the high-level Avon Barksdale to the low-level
Bodie Broadus, are cut short by incarceration or violent death.[51] In all
these cases, and despite considerable respect generated for some of
them, these heroes are too thoroughly cut from the cloth of their institutions and their rules. The same is true of the dockworkers, the teachers,
and the journalists. But as we have seen, there are two black characters
who are present in every season and who are not only loved by all audiences for their intelligence and humor but for their attempt to live with
integrity outside the existing institutions and strata of power: Reginald
"Bubbles" Cousins (Andre Royo) and Omar Devone Little (Michael K.
Williams). From the point of view of the melodrama of black and white
what is unique about them both is that neither presents himself as a
victim-hero, whether of a racist society or of a harsh economic reality.
Each in his own way, as Eric Beck frames it, "plays the middle." The
middle is that small free space in between the other more stratified
organizations. It is not a permanent place but if flexibly balanced, and
if the major institutions can be played off against one another, these
heroes of the neoliberal era can survive by their wits with greater moral
integrity than their institutional counterparts.[52]

Unlike Lipsitz, Beck does not argue that neoliberalism is an absolute
evil that must be fought at every level, rather, he presents it as an economic reality that must be faced. (Recall that Lipsitz had accused *The
Wire* of uncritically accepting the neoliberal verdict on the civil rights
movement and the war on poverty.) Beck does not write in response to

Lipsitz, but his argument that neoliberal capitalism is an already existing reality to which a work like *The Wire* responds, especially in its depiction of characters like Bubbles and Omar, significantly answers Lipsitz. All the other institutions in the series—cops, who seek overtime; drug dealers who embody the senseless greed of unrestrained capitalism; dockworkers who seek work that has disappeared; city government and the media, which themselves can only follow the flows of capital—are stratified entities with no flexibility to maneuver. Those, like Omar and Bubbles, who only temporarily affiliate with any one institution from the place of the "middle" can maneuver, and can also keep a modicum of moral integrity.

We have already seen how Bubbles, despite his addiction, persists throughout the series as a flawed moral beacon, working as a confidential informant (CI) for the police in the first season, delivering an important message from them to Omar in the second, working as an entrepreneur in "Hamsterdam" in the third, attempting to "school" Sherrod in the fourth, volunteering in a soup kitchen and selling the *Sun* toward the end of the fifth. As Beck notes, Bubbles "finds a way to inhabit the space of the slums without being completely subjected to the command of the drug gangs."[53] Like Omar, he works middle areas between the larger institutional strata. Unlike Omar, however, he remains a slave to his addiction until the last season and thus often becomes a victim of the gangs who prey on him. Bubbles is a compelling and much-loved figure, and he served in chapter 4 as my exemplar of a melodramatic victim-hero, though significantly not the victim-hero of any racialized villain or racial ideology. We have also seen how Bubbles is able to exist in the place between institutions as a connector between them all—a border crosser—but not fully a member of any. We have even seen how Marsha Kinder, in an early article on *The Wire* judged Bubbles to be gay, presumably because of his frequent attachment to young men whom he mentors, whether in the art of scams, scavenging, or itinerant sales via his shopping cart "Depot." There is very little actual evidence that Bubbles is gay in the sense of a fixed identity, beyond his friendships, whether with Kima or his younger friends, but there is considerable reason to think of him as queer in the larger sense of a person who does not fit into any preexisting strata of society.

However, when it comes to electing the most truly exciting and most novel hero of this melodrama—the one who seems to be everybody's favorite character, no less an authority than Obama has said the obvious: "It's got to be Omar, right? I mean, that guy is unbelievable, right?" Omar is a special kind of hero, one who, contra the druglords, the police, the judiciary, or even the Nation of Islam as represented by Brother Mouzone, can more adeptly maneuver the middle ground between all the institutions while holding on to his independence. He is a slave to no one, least of all to an identity as a victim. As the "gay stick-up man who robs drug dealers" in Baltimore, Omar is quite literally, as Barak Obama puts it, "unbelievable": an outsized superhero who at one point leaps from a fourth-story window and magically disappears (5.5, "React Quotes").[54] Though we might at first think that this disappearance— which Marlo Stanfied refers to as "Spiderman shit" could place Omar in the lineage of "magical Negroes," it is worth noting that Omar's magic does not serve a down-on-his-luck-beleaguered white man, but his own escape that allows him to continue his own pursuits.

What, then, does Obama mean by "unbelievable"? I think this claim has to do with the fact that Omar is a kind of hero who has not previously been seen in popular media, even though his almost unused last name echoes that of a very real African American hero, Malcolm X (né Malcolm Little). Already a folk hero by the time we meet him in the first season, Omar is affiliated with no institution and moves freely throughout the projects and hollowed out neighborhoods, his presence usually announced before him either by kids and hoppers calling out, "Omar coming! Omar coming!" or by his own whistling. He has only to stand near a building with a stash in it to have it magically dropped at his feet. Robbing the currency of the realm (drugs) from the one group that, if any, deserves to be robbed, Omar readily gives it back to the drug-dependent community, or sells it over again to the same people he stole it from. Like Bubbles, he makes it clear that he is not a drug dealer and late in the game he even tosses drugs down a sewer drain. Omar belongs to none of the institutions profiled in the series, though he forms temporary associations with various groups and even his own ad hoc gangs from whom he demands, unlike the feudal Barksdales, no fealty. Unlike Bubbles, he is free of addiction and walks tall. He is not after money;

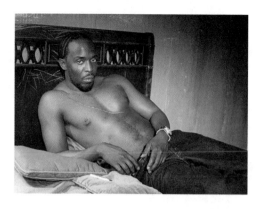

The kind of hero not previously viewed in popular media

he "plays" for the excitement and skill of the game, and until nearly the end, he obeys the rules of "the game." He is in every way a "free spirit" whose heists are carried out creatively and with panache.[55] He defies all laws, written and unwritten. He especially defies that most important code of the black male underclass: to be hard and macho.

This is where Omar differs from every previous black hero of folklore, film, or television. He is not "bad" in the grand tradition of Stagger Lee's outlaw "bad nigger" who kills for a Stetson hat, or any of the cool pimps or macho Sweetbacks or Shaft figures of blaxploitation lore who prove their masculine hardness (always measured, however distantly, against the feminine softness of the loyal Tom) through violence against whites or blacks.[56] Omar differs from these legendary figures not simply because his interpretation of the "code" of the game is to only rob dope dealers who are already robbers. He adheres to this code not simply because he has a Robin Hood ethic, and not simply because he has a finely honed sense of justice, but primarily because he "feels" and shows his feelings in a way that the traditional "baadasssss nigger" does not. Indeed, he sometimes even flaunts his feelings.

Apart from "all in the game," Omar's most emblematic phrase is the question posed repeatedly to any and sundry characters: "You feel me?" Though it most strictly means "Do you understand me?" or "Do you think the same way I do?," more carefully examined it is not just a matter of thinking or understanding, but quite literally an assent to feeling— "Do you feel my feeling" as much as "Do you *feel* the way I do?" In asking this question, Omar exposes his raw feelings, both to those whose will he wants to influence—as when looking down the barrel of a gun—but also in simple conversations with lovers.[57] The question "Do you feel me?" cannot be separated from his position as a queer man of color in a black community that is especially homophobic.

When Avon Barksdale learns that Omar is gay, he doubles the bounty placed on his head and that of his gang (1.4, "Old Cases"). We first see Omar display gay affection publicly after his gang's raid on the Barksdale stash. While sitting casually on a stoop with his small gang of three, selling off Barksdale drugs, Omar fondly strokes the face of the baby of an addicted mother, who is no more than a baby herself, and indulges her in a free fix. He then shifts his attention to Brandon, sitting on the stoop below him. He strokes his cheek, kisses his forehead, and plays with his chin. At the same time, he is making plans with Bailey, the third member of his team. When Omar extends a familial affection to Bailey, by touching his shoulder in a nonsexual way, we can see Bailey's conflict between his respect for Omar's leadership and his reflexive homophobia.

In this same first season (1.6, "The Wire"), after Avon tortures Brandon and displays his mutilated body like a deer on the hood of a car, there is no question that this is a special message to Omar, not just as a queer man but as one who has been willing to show his affection for another man in public. Omar accompanies McNulty to the medical examiner's office to identify Brandon's body. This scene is masterfully presented both to reveal and to turn away from Omar's pain at his most extreme moment of feeling.

The scene begins through the impassive black and white eye of a high-angle surveillance camera as McNulty and Omar enter the hallway, accompanied by McNulty's two sons, one of whom holds a soccer ball (once again McNulty, ever the negligent father, drags his childcare into his work). A normal angle shot, now in color reveals the same hallway as the two sons settle on a bench, one with a video game making *ping* noises, the other holding a soccer ball. Farther down the hall a guard listens to an Orioles game. We hold on this scene a few moments until a cut reveals another seemingly black-and-white, high-angle shot of a white sheet as it is pulled off an upside-down head. This is the corpse-reveal, so familiar in a crime show, and already familiar, including the

(LEFT)

Omar divides the loot

Omar strokes baby's cheek

Omar strokes Brandon's cheek

(ABOVE)

Omar touches Bailey

upside-down view of the head, from *The Wire*'s second episode (1.2, "The Detail"). What is not familiar is the momentary shift to black and white, recalling the many previous moments of black-and-white surveillance and the cold institutional eye that impassively sees the unveiled face—the same face that Omar had lovingly stroked two episodes previously, now a face with several wounds and a gouged-out eye (shot 3). A reverse shot shows Omar's grief-stricken reaction. But instead of recoiling in horror, he leans down toward the face (shot 4). Another angle reveals Omar still leaning in the foreground, but now we see McNulty gaze at Omar as Omar's still leaning body leaves that space. Thus we do not actually see what we presume to be Omar's kiss on Brandon's once lovely face. McNulty, ashamed to witness so private a moment, soon looks away (shot 5). An extremely long shot shows Omar leaning over the body and the medical examiner and McNulty standing awkwardly as the sound of the baseball game and the hum of freezers continues (shot 6). We return to a close view of Omar as he rises from the corpse, openly weeping, and turns away from the camera beating his head with his fists (shot 7). While a normal grief scene might end there, this one continues as we cut back to McNulty's two boys in the outside hallway, now kicking the soccer ball between them. A heart-wrenching scream that is also a roar of rage stops them in their tracks (shot 8); it continues as the now unattended soccer ball wanders down the hall, now seen from the original point of view of the black-and-white surveillance camera (shot 9). The scene thus ends on the surveillance point of view with which it began.

This scene is a small masterpiece of alternating impassivity, as signaled by the surveillance point of view, and raw emotion, registered first in Omar's reaction to Brandon and then in the reaction of others to Omar. It displays a mutilated body and Omar's grief. But it does not just display them. Like Omar's repeated question "Do you feel me?," it checks in with the responses of others to his overwhelming pain and loss, registered initially by McNulty as he first looks, and then looks away. When McNulty looks away, it is not out of homophobic panic but out of respect for Omar's grief and perhaps out of sympathy for the fact that Omar will never have a proper occasion to mourn the loss of his loved one. Omar's feeling is so vivid that it will finally even register

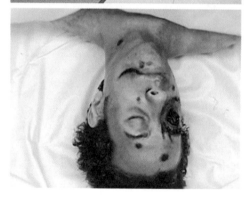

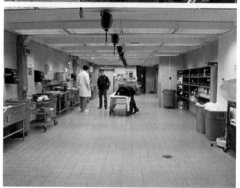

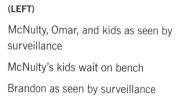

(LEFT)

McNulty, Omar, and kids as seen by surveillance

McNulty's kids wait on bench

Brandon as seen by surveillance

(RIGHT)

Omar leans in toward Brandon

McNulty looks away

Omar still leans over the body

Omar pulls away from Brandon

McNulty's kids startled by scream

Back to the surveillance view

aurally with McNulty's startled kids in the hall; uncomprehendingly, they too will "feel" Omar. Yet we do not really see (though we do hear) this scream that is a roar, nor do we actually see the kiss that precedes it. And in the return to the point of view of the surveillance camera as the reverberating roar echoes and then fades, we are reminded by this episode, whose very title is "The Wire," that this story is part of a larger story of surveillance to which Omar's grief is incidental.

If we consider all the deaths that take place in this series—and all the wakes that follow—it is striking to compare the elaborate rituals of mourning afforded the cops and dockworkers to the absence of mourning afforded Omar and other major black characters. In the third season, one of Omar's new gang members, Tosha, partner to Kimmy, is shot down in the street after a botched stash robbery (3.3, "Dead Soldiers"). Omar not only takes responsibility for this death, but extinguishes one of his Newports in his palm in self-punishment. But perhaps his greatest pain is, as with Brandon, not to be able publicly to mourn another loved one. Tosha's body lies in a funeral home, but because it is watched over by callous members of the Barksdale gang in case Omar or what's left of his gang should show up, Omar can only lurk behind a tree in pained silence. Yet only one scene earlier the raucous wake at Kavenaugh's, the Irish bar, for "Ol' King Cole"—the actual *Wire* producer, Ray Colesberry, who played the minor role of the cop Ray Cole—has gone on long into the night. When the real Colesberry died suddenly, the writers awarded his character a funeral out of proportion to the importance of his role, in obvious contrast to Omar's silent wake in the shadows. This is the only mourning Tosha receives as the episode ends.

At the end of the series another wake, this one "fake," is given at Kavanaugh's Pub, for Jimmy McNulty's symbolic death as a cop, while Omar's death, when he is unexpectedly shot down in a convenience store by the young hopper Kenard, will go not only unmourned but also unnoticed. Almost as an afterthought, a coroner notices that the wrong identification tag has been placed on his toe. Neither the police nor the *Baltimore Sun* will note the significance of his passing (5.8, "Clarifications"). Like all of the other blacks who die in this series, from Wallace to D'Angelo Barksdale, from Stringer Bell to Bodie Broadus, Omar dies abruptly and violently. While whites have the luxury of mourning their friends, and

Loud, public mourning
by cops

Silent, hidden mourning
by Omar

often, as in the case of the dockworkers, seem to be mourning their lost privileges "back in the day" of Keynesian liberal democracy, blacks die with no warning and with no possibility of public mourning, and no occasion to "be felt." This does not mean that *Wire* audiences do not mourn Omar—we do, like that of no other character in the series. But his sudden death at the hand of the little Hopper, Kenard, who is as surprised as anyone by his deed, seems utterly random and unappreciated by any other character in the series. Omar's death is neither tragic nor melodramatic in the manner of melodramas of black and white. He dies neither a racial victim in a melodrama of black and white nor does he turn the tables on "whitey" in a melodrama of black revenge.

If whites mourn too much and blacks not enough in *The Wire*, these differentials of expressible feeling may indicate the deepest lesson of a racial melodrama that has moved beyond measuring racial injury as a zero-sum game in antagonisms between black and white. Political scientist Wendy Brown has argued that liberalism as a political doctrine has long functioned as "a modest ethical gap between economy and polity."[58] Melodrama has worked that ethical gap. The end of liberal democracy, to the extent that it has ended, has also meant the closing of this gap: "There is nothing," she writes, "in liberal democracy's basic institutions or values—from free elections, representative democracy, and individual liberties equally distributed to modest power-sharing, or even more substantive political participation—that inherently meets the test of serving economic competitiveness or inherently withstands a cost-benefit analysis."[59] Neoliberal rationality has not caused but has merely hastened the dismantling of liberal democracy in the post-9/11 period. When America fights wars against terror to defend "our way of life," Brown argues, this way of life is less and less understood as classical liberal democracy and more and more as the ability of the "entrepreneurial subject and state to rationally plot means and ends." In other words, what we increasingly expect from government is simply for it to secure the "rationality" of the market at home and abroad."[60] Democracy, to Brown, no longer signifies a set of independent political institutions and civic practices comprising equality, freedom, autonomy, and the principle of popular sovereignty. Rather, it indicates a state and subjects organized by market rationality. Thus neoliberalism, as Brown puts it, "openly weds the state to capital and resignifies democracy as ubiquitous entrepreneurialism."[61] Could this really be what Snot Boogie's friend meant when he said, in the cold open to season 1, episode 1: "It's America, man"? If so, *The Wire* was prescient. The America of equal opportunity has been reduced to the opportunity to steal. As early as 2002, it saw the hollowness of the American Dream, especially for disenfranchised blacks.

Brown argues further that for leftists to hold on to the tenets of liberal democracy in the face of their erosion by neoliberalism, is a hopeless exercise of melancholic dependency on a "lost object." This dependency only enshrines and fixes the lost object—equal opportunity, guaranteed work, the welfare state—as if it were the key. This dependency overidealizes—indeed, fetishizes—the imperfect democratic institutions and values. This is what the white ethnic cops and dockworkers mourn in their long wakes and bar sings. Their "back in the day" is the American Dream that was never realized for many minorities and women, although the ideology lives on in small ways. Instead of mourning the loss of liberal democracy, Brown maintains, there is a need for an alternative vision of the good, "one that rejects *homo economicus* as the norm of the human *and* rejects this norm's correlative formations of economy, society, state, and (non)morality."[62] This alternative vision would rest not on maximizing individual wealth or rights, but on a "modestly egalitarian distribution of wealth and access to institutions" and "human flourishing."

This, I believe, is what the two most stateless, strategically disconnected heroes of *The Wire* represent. Unlike their white counterparts in the institutions, they have no nostalgia for "back in the day." One is a scavenger who becomes a modest entrepreneur, the other is a robber of robbers. Neither Bubbles nor Omar has any liberal democratic illusions, but they are not, like Stringer Bell, driven by the pure rationality of *Homo economicus*. Each has a vision of justice that runs counter to the neoliberal ideology of the worlds they inhabit, and they do not rely on racial injury, or any other kind of injury, to define themselves. They have access to institutions, but they are not represented by or vested in them. To that extent they are freer than anyone else in the series. These outsiders working the middle forge what Brown has called a "left vision of justice." They may be the products of a neoliberal rationality that has placed them outside all existing strata of power, but it is that very place outside, yet also in between, that gives them the ability to invent themselves. The fact that these are black heroes within a predominantly black spatial imaginary is what gives them a fresh moral authority, but for once not because we perceive them or they perceive themselves as racial victims, but rather because they have the imagination to challenge or maneuver around the existing institutions of power.

The Wire is certainly a racial melodrama; race matters in the lives of every character and in the opportunities afforded them. The series does not ignore racially based advantages or disadvantages. It is an advantage, for example, for Lieutenant (and then Major) Cedric Daniels to be black, educated, and good-looking in a city with a majority-black population. Daniels can eventually advance over his white counterparts, such as the white ethnic Major Valchek or the cagey but white Major Rawls. Within the hierarchy of the city government and the police, it is also a political disadvantage to be white. Tommy Carcetti does not complain about that disadvantage though he notes it as an obstacle he must overcome. Importantly, and pace Lipsitz, the series does not try to engender any special racial sympathy toward him. Jimmy McNulty is also white, but unlike Carcetti or Daniels, he is not educated (thus his perennial need to prove how smart he is). Race is not his problem, but class is, and he is easily humiliated when he learns that political consultant Teresa D'Agostino is bored by his mind but not his body. Class matters and the very proliferation of characters allows it to matter almost as much as race.

For example, it is a disadvantage for the corner boys to be born into all-black neighborhoods where drugs are the main source of income, and the way out is not clear. But within the ranks of these boys, class makes an important difference. Namond Brice, who is born into a relatively well-to-do family of drug dealers, is much more advantaged than Dukie Weems, whose mother is an addict. Namond, as we have seen, will eventually thrive once removed from the drug culture, while Dukie will succumb.

Race matters in *The Wire* and consequently does not go unmentioned in the prescribed "color-blind" way. Yet the series does not play off one racial advantage or disadvantage against another in the tit-for-tat way of the melodrama of black and white. We might note that in the "white cop, black cop" duo of Herc and Carver, it is the black cop who learns to be "good police" and the white one who goes over to the "dark side" to work for the corrupt Jewish gang lawyer Maurice Levy. But we also realize that it could equally be the other way around. Indeed, if season 5 has been criticized for being too melodramatic, it is not because it is actually so, since melodrama is pervasive in the series, but because it too obviously reminds us of the schemas of the melodrama of black and white in its reliance in the newsroom part of its story upon a clichéd "Tom" scenario of good (that is, victimized) reporters of color (Gus, Alma, Fletcher) and bad white villains (the patrician James Whiting Jr. and Thomas Klebanow).[63]

Finally, *The Wire* is not afraid to show how interracial desire can play a part in the kind of love and career choices operating in the affair between Rhonda Pearlman and Cedric Daniels. Pearlman clearly desires Daniels not only as a person but as a tall, good-looking black man who "dresses right." And Daniels finally loosens up and enjoys himself, sexually and socially, in her company. Race figures into both of their ambitions, but not in a way that invites us to blame them for it. If this were a melodrama pitting black injury against white, such desire would certainly be blameworthy in one or the other of these partners. Here it is part of real life in a racially mixed Baltimore. No wonder President Obama seeded the show, and Omar, as number 1.

Conclusion

HOME SWEET BALTIMORE

In the final episode of the final season of the series, ex-detective Jimmy McNulty has retrieved a catatonic homeless man from a halfway house in Philadelphia. The man had been hidden out of the way while McNulty pretended he was dead—the victim of a serial killer preying on the homeless. On the drive back, McNulty stops his car at a vantage point overlooking the skyline of Baltimore. A final montage accompanied by one last version of "Way Down in the Hole" plays out. As McNulty looks out over the city we revisit the (multi)sites we have become familiar with over the course of the serial: cops, corners, docks, city government prison, courts. All continue in the manner we might expect except that an indeterminate amount of time has passed—the gap between that makes seriality possible: a new group of corner boys carries on business against a mural with the names of some of the fallen dealers on it; Lester Freamon, retired, continues to make miniature furniture under the admiring eye of Charlene; Herc (now working for Levy and equipped with an expense account) buys drinks for cops in a bar; Dozier, one of the worst of the cops is prominent among them; Templeton feigns modesty as he receives his Pulitzer at Columbia University; Slim Charles confers with the "Greek"; Carcetti, ever the ambitious politician, runs for governor; Fletcher carries on reporting for the *Sun* under the watchful eye of a demoted Gus; Valchek is promoted by the new mayor, Nerese Cambell, to police commissioner; Dukie shoots up at the Arabers; Rhonda's first act as a judge is to recuse herself from a case Daniels, now a public defender, would have argued before her—they exchange smiles from their different positions in the courtroom; Wee Bay and Chris Paltrow both serving life terms for the bigger crimes of their former bosses, Avon Barksdale and Marlow Stanfield, meet at the same fence in the prison where Cutty, Wee Bay, and Barksdale once met; Carcetti is elected governor and, Rawls, as he has been promised, is promoted to state police superintendent; Bubbles ascends the stairs, finally welcomed into his sister's family; tiny Kenard is placed in a police car (a cop puts a hand on his head in the typical gesture that prevents the suspect from hitting a head, but for Kenard, who does not even reach the roof of the car while standing, this is unnecessary; a gang of corner boys throw rocks at a surveillance camera, but this camera, though hit, is more sturdy than the old one, and its lens does not shatter; a homeless man eats directly out of the garbage while a man in a suit grabs a newspaper; finally a white girl we have seen many times before once again buys drugs on the corner in a business-as-usual fashion. Very little has changed; white characters go on working, the song ends with the same final line "way down in the hole" after an increasingly fast montage paints a portrait of ordinary Baltimoreans, mostly black, going about their daily lives.

This final montage—in contrast to each season's final montage and to the credit montages that begin each episode—resembles the opening montages in the rare deployment of unsourced music, and in this one case by using the same song that we have come to identify with *The Wire*. The difference is that while the opening credit montages are thematic and not narrative, engaged with the repetitive and typical gestures of each site—indeed, we do not even recognize key characters in these brief gestures—the closing montages of each season tie up as many plot threads as possible in an ongoing serial. Voices are sometimes heard under the music. Frequently the cops will box up the files on a case, or the basement space of the special detail will be emptied of furniture, sentencing will occur, or new leadership will be seen to emerge among the gangsters.

In this final montage of the whole series, then, the final chords sounded are particularly resonant. But it is not possible to portray this ending as either happy or unhappy, or even, for that matter, as much of an ending at all, if by that we mean something that does not continue.

If Bubbles is admitted to the upper world of light and family, Dukie is condemned to the same limbo of addiction that Bubbles recently left. If Rhonda Pearlman and Cedric Daniels as well as Lester Freamon and Charlene form unmistakably happy couples, their coupledom does not matter to the greater good of the city, though at least we know Daniels will be a good public defender. And if Nerese Campbell, Carcetti, Rawls, and Valchek are promoted, that is par for the course in a city that cannot honor those who would do it the most good. Carcetti's "white" rule has made no more difference to the city than Campbell's return to "black" rule will probably mean. Valchek represents pure mediocrity, and Rawls, the greatest hypocrite of all, will continue to frequent gay bars while acting the role of the homophobic tyrant. Herc's appearance in the bar treating former colleagues only tells us that cops are more in league with the gangsters than before: the symbiosis continues.

Threads are tied up, but nothing has really ended; it all continues. Most of the black underclass characters are dead or addicted. A new generation rises and it all continues. The port police, both patrol car and the "boat" keep on patrolling. Disproportionately rich and poor citizens continue to coexist and drugs are still for sale. After this vision of the future plays out before McNulty's eyes in the last montage, he gets back in the car and proposes to the hapless man he has retrieved that they now "go home." This gesture toward a home that this man does not possess, and that we have reason to wonder if McNulty himself still possesses, is the series's final homage to Baltimore, a city that is fiercely loved by all its born-into-it denizens and disdained by the elite snobs who come from, and aspire to be, elsewhere (e.g., Templeton, Whiting, Rawls, even Brother Mouzone). After McNulty and the homeless man drive off, the camera holds for a long time on the unimposing cityscape of Baltimore, the home to which McNulty and his passenger return.

What does this home mean? Why is it that this single word, rather than all the story threads that either tie up or continue, sound the most satisfying note of finality? Why does this wholly disfunctional home still seem the place to be? Love of Baltimore can only be irrational. And often it manifests as simple ignorance (as when Wallace grows uneasy at the sound of crickets in the country and so returns to the city of his doom, or when Old Face Andre thinks he can escape the wrath of Marlo by moving from the East Side of Baltimore to the West Side rather than leaving town altogether, or when Bodie Broadus loses his local radio station, unaware that "radio in Philly is different").[1] For these denizens it is hard to imagine any other home. Sometimes, however, characters with more life options show the same loyalty, as if there really were no other place to be, as do Daniels, Omar, and McNulty. Thus, despite the graffiti that accurately nominates the city as "Bodymore Murdaland" in the opening credits of the first season and the graffiti that marks the demise of so many "soldiers" at the beginning of the final montage, despite the many miscarriages of justice, despite the trash and rubble and corpse-filled "vacants," the affection for "home sweet Baltimore" is both palpable and infectious. One "makes it" here, not, as in so many "Boyz in the Hood" stories, by a one-way ticket out, but by staying, by finding a niche. What, then, does Jimmy McNulty mean by this "let's go home" in this most undomestic of melodramas?

Certainly, there is irony in this statement. Home itself is not only absent in *The Wire*; it is actively eschewed. Most of the homes we do glimpse are broken or worse. Cops, gangsters, dope fiends, dockworkers, politicians, teachers, and reporters are most often seen in masculine places of work and play (bars, shooting galleries, sports events, restaurants, cars, streets, etc.)—almost anyplace but home. Yet Baltimore itself, writ large serves as the home "where the heart is." This affection for the city derives in part from the over-familiar rhetoric of "back in the day," even though we realize that that day could never have been all it is cracked up to be. Nevertheless, if we only invoke our own memory over five seasons of viewing, it is true that by the time we get to the end we may ourselves fondly remember a time before the fall of Sobotka when unions still had some clout, a time when gangsters like Avon Barksdale still gave to charity (e.g., Cutty's gym), a time when Bodie Broadus still thought he could be a "smart-ass pawn," a time when Bubbles still thought he could scheme his way to his next high, and a time when McNulty still thought he was the smartest detective on the beat. If *The Wire* covers enough ground to make its viewers fondly remember the hope of its multisited storyworld's beginnings, even in the face of constant disappointment and traps of repetition, this nostalgia still does not explain this strange affection exhibited by so many. It seems there is more to this "home sweet Baltimore" than sheer nostalgia.

Home has often been viewed as the key ingredient in melodrama. In "women's films" and soap operas, home is the primary scene, original scene. In classic stage and film melodrama home is the good place from which one comes, what Peter Brooks calls "the space of innocence" crucial to the melodramatic mode.[2] On the nineteenth-century French stage it might be a garden surrounded by a high wall into which a villain intrudes or from which a victim is expelled. But in American melodrama I have argued, and especially in the melodramas of black and white discussed in the last chapter, it is more often the space of the humble home, ideally a simple cabin, belonging to the "time before it is too late."[3] In America, such homes are often situated in the "old" South as the "space of safety and mooring for whatever we imagine we have lost"[4] and thus as a means to figure the good. But, of course, this space is also, as Grace Elizabeth Hale has argued, a space of horror (the Gothic South, the plantation, slavery). Uncle Tom's cabin, which is problematically both his loved "Old Kentucky Home" and the space of slavery where bodies are sold, bought and used up, becomes an object of nostalgic affection for Tom after he himself has been sold to a worse place "down the river." When melodrama ends happily, some aspect of the "home space of innocence" is retrieved; when it ends sadly, the inherent goodness of home is lost. This tendency to look to the past rather than the future for the model of the good has often been viewed as melodrama's most regressive feature.[5]

Once again, however, *The Wire* breaks the mold of conventional melodrama without ever ceasing to be melodrama. It reinvents serial, television melodrama by channeling automatic feelings about the goodness of home into more ambivalent feelings about its simultaneous horror. For home is where Dukie, Michael, and Namond suffer, where Kima and Jimmy grow restless and where Cedric Daniels only pretends to live. The only time I ever visited Baltimore I walked around the West Baltimore neighborhoods where "Little Melvin" Williams, the model for Avon Barksdale, once ruled. I absorbed the sheer devastation of the neighborhood and I stuck out like a sore thumb. More than once I was di-

The familiar orange couch
of the first season

rected by kindly denizens to the Poe House on Amity Street, which was deemed my only possible touristic interest in the neighborhood. The Poe House was closed, and it wasn't why I was there anyway, but it was a good excuse, so while exploring I pretended to be lost and kept getting directed back to it. One of the better jokes in *The Wire* begins with a young black man working at a Barksdale stash house explaining to another that a white tourist had asked him for directions to the Poe House, and without knowing what that was, he had answered, "Look around you, every house here is a po' house!" (3.2, "All Due Respect"). Poe's house not only exists in a neighborhood of po' houses; it was already a po' house when he himself lived in it. Poe did not own the house, which is a small, narrow unremarkable Baltimore row house, now sitting amid a housing project called the Poe Houses. The pun on Poe is especially apt given the theme of Poe's own Gothic stories of haunted houses, his own poverty and addiction as well as the lore that this house itself is haunted as it sits adjacent to so many boarded-up vacants—vacants which in *The Wire* become the mausoleums of Marlo Stanfield's victims.

Home in *The Wire* is like the Poe/po' house: an ambivalent symbol of a maternal comfort, safety, and warmth that has been longed for more than felt. It is most famously evoked by one highly condensed and evocative image on which I would like to conclude this book: the familiar all-weather orange couch of the first season.

To trace the life of this orange couch in this first season is to understand many things about melodrama's "home space of innocence" in a neoliberal era when neither good nor evil can be as simple as it once seemed. The couch is first glimpsed 35 minutes into the first episode (1.1, "The Target"). It is seen from above. Bodie Broadus is already seated on it when D'Angelo Barksdale comes to take over this perch at the center of the "pit"—the outdoor drug market in the low-rise projects. The couch will subsequently be sat on, lounged on, stood on, and slept on. It serves for all intents and purposes as home to the gang of boys who deal there. It is even where they entertain both cops and bosses when they come visiting. Surreally displaced from the usual focal point of private family life, it becomes the communal home where D'Angelo, Bodie, Poot, and Wallace work, play, philosophize, and argue in all seasons. In its minimal representation of comfort, it is an eloquent figure. Originally retrieved from a dumpster by the series's art director,[6] it encapsulates the essential homelessness of these boys as well as their inventive ability to make themselves at home, even when at work. At one point in 1.7 ("One Arrest"), the boys arrange it the way they would a living room and stand back to admire, saying offscreen, "Let's leave the couch right there. . . . It's nice" while the camera simply admires it.[7] In many ways the couch comes to embody D'Angelo's desire to treat addict-customers with more respect and to dispense avuncular advice to his younger workers. When the couch turns up later in the series, with only Poot on it and now black rather than orange, we miss the orange one much the way Uncle Tom missed his "Old Kentucky Home."

However, the couch is not only a symbol of a (failed but still wanted) home. Very often it is also the panoptic point of observation at the center of the pit from which the director of the operation (D'Angelo most of the time, Bodie and Poot occasionally) directs his minions to make sales without direct evidence of the exchange of money for drugs. At the panoptical center of the operation, and without ever touching the merchandise, one of them can oversee the proper protocol of the deals without becoming directly involved. Indeed, if the law-*enforcing* panopticon aims to surveil docile bodies in schools, prisons, and other institutions, then it is remarkable the extent to which this law-*breaking* panopticon produces similarly docile bodies of its often zombielike addicts and its more disciplined administrators.[8] But if the perch on the couch echoes the panopticon, it is also, as we saw with regard to surveillance in chapter 5, an imperfect echo. Unlike in the invisible and

(LEFT)

Bodie, first seen on the couch

Home to the gang of boys

In all seasons

(ABOVE)

"Leave the couch there . . . it's nice"

D'Angelo gives advice to Wallace

The panoptic center
of "the pit"

"Look at me!"

elevated observation tower of Bentham and Foucault's apparatus, in the pit the director-observer is so low down that he is also surveillable himself—by cops, by criminal informant Bubbles, and by his own superiors, who occasionally visit to check on the operation. When in episode 1.8 ("Lessons") Poot is delighted to be given momentary authority over the operation and the central position on the couch, he rejoices with a little dance, saying, "Shit! Look at me!" But *looking* at the observer-director (in this case Poot) is the one thing that should not be possible within the panopticon, and Poot's "Look at me!" only calls attention to this flaw in the system. An imperfect instrument of panoptic observation, doubling as substitute home, the orange couch is like so many "solutions" in *The Wire*, from Hamsterdam to the "special class," both utopian and dystopian at the same time.

There is no sense in which these boys, in arranging and using their couch, are attempting to return to a lost good home. To this degree, *The*

Home Sweet Baltimore

Wire rejects the atavism so familiar in the melodramas of home where characters seek to return to the good, but cruelly interrupted, home. Instead, in this more forward-looking melodrama, they are like Colvin, trying to fix a problem and accommodate themselves to the materials at hand. But we are never asked to believe that any past home represented a golden age. No one is trying to "get back to the garden."[9] What is most forward-looking in *The Wire*, then, is actually its ability to project into the future a feeling about the illusory "good home" of the past. *The Wire* does not seek to refind the good home that never was; rather, it seeks to forge a future with the utopian ability to imagine it out of the ruins of the past. None of the series utopias are realized, but the very fact that each one (except Jimmy's) contains a hope for less violence, honest work, better justice, and the betterment of the community indicates to Fredric Jameson the exceptional ability of *The Wire*'s utopianism to occasionally break through, "before reality and the present again close it down."[10] But what shall we call this utopianism-within-realism if not melodrama?

Jameson is happy to glimpse a utopianism amid the grim realism of *The Wire*, and he praises the series as exceptional for this reason. But in doing so he claims that melodrama is dead (or at least, for him, without interest). He does not see that melodrama rises like a phoenix in the very work he praises as exceptional utopian realism.[11] The kind of journalism that David Simon wanted to escape—the "surround a simple outrage" rifle shot—was the bad melodrama whose constraints he labored against at the *Sun*: the five-part series with simple villains (the criminals) and simple victims (the houses stripped of their metal). As we have seen, Simon's ambition was to get inside the workings of a much larger outrage of a whole society—an outrage (should we say evil?) that could not be surrounded, an outrage he mistakenly thought was best expressed as tragedy. By including media as part of the problem rather than as the "exposing" solution, by turning to serial television to unfold the interconnections of the unsurroundable outrage, by permitting glimpses of a (lowercase!) utopian good, Simon and his team of remarkable writers refashioned the melodrama of social good and evil into a masterpiece of serial television whose most potent symbol is a tattered orange couch.

Notes

Introduction

1. In the last minute of a podcast interview conducted by Bill Simmons on March 1, 2012, an interview otherwise devoted to basketball, President Obama was asked to "settle an office debate" by naming the "Best *Wire* character of all time." His answer—"It's got to be Omar, right?" was backed up by the statement "And that was one of the best shows of all time." Simmons, "B.S. Report Transcript: Barack Obama."

2. Indeed, at one point he even goes so far as to compare his achievement to *Moby-Dick*, with police procedural substituting for whale procedural. Simon, "Introduction," 25.

3. Michaels calls it "the most serious and ambitious fictional narrative of the twenty-first century so far." Walter Benn Michaels, "Going Boom."

4. Chaddha and Wilson, "'Way Down in the Hole,'" 163.

5. Jameson, "Realism and Utopia," 368.

6. As Jason Mittell has passionately argued, "Television at its best shouldn't be understood simply as emulating another older and more culturally valued medium. *The Wire* is a masterpiece of television . . . and thus should be understood, analyzed, and celebrated on its own medium's terms." Mittell, "All in the Game," 429.

7. Talbot, "Stealing Life."

8. See Williams, *Playing the Race Card*.

Chapter 1: Ethnographic Imagination

1. Falzon, *Multi-Sited Ethnography*, 1.

2. Lanahan, "Secrets of the City," 24.

3. Williams would later play the Deacon in this series.

4. Simon, *Homicide: A Year on the Killing Streets* (New York: Henry Holt and Company, 1991, 2006).

5. Ibid., 624.

6. Already, as his first editor at the *Sun* notes, Simon "was writing about the sociology of the city through the prism of the cop beat and the criminal-justice system. . . . He fairly uniquely looked at the people who we tend to view just as victims or bad guys, and looked at these neighborhoods as real places that we had better understand." Lanahan, "Secrets of the City," 2.

7. Ibid., 538.

8. Daily interactions over a long time constitute the qualitative social research that is the "lifeblood of the data produced." Falzon, *Multi-Sited Ethnography*, 1.

9. Simon, *Homicide*, 638.

10. Marcus, *Ethnography through Thick and Thin*, 33.

11. Ibid., 333.

12. Ibid., 98.

13. Ibid., 100.

14. Ibid., 13.

15. Ibid., 14. Marvell's poem, "To His Coy Mistress," begins, "Had we but world enough, and time, / This coyness, lady, were no crime. / We would sit down and think which way / To walk, and pass our long love's day." However, for the ethnographer as much as for the poet who would woo slowly, there is neither world enough nor time. I am arguing that it is this imaginary "world enough and time" that *The Wire* forges.

16. See Sconce, "What If?," 95.

17. Wolfe, "The New Journalism," 18.

18. Boynton, *The New New Journalism*, xvi.

19. Simon, "The Metal Men."

20. Ibid.

21. Ibid.

22. According to Lanahan, who interviewed Carroll years later, Carroll killed the story because he objected to Simon's contextualized reporting and because the material in *The Corner* was too much like the material in the article. I interpreted this to mean that they objected to the redundant presence of Gary in both "The Metal Men" and in the work that became *The Corner*. Simon has corrected me, stating that Carroll raised the issue of redundancy in the two works long after the fact.

23. The piece ran in the *Baltimore Sun Magazine* on Sunday, September 3, 1995, pp. 6–18. It was prominently displayed on the front of the magazine. Lanahan, "Secrets of the City," 29.

24. Ibid., 30.

25. Ibid., 27.

26. Ibid., 26.

27. Ibid., 30.

28. Lawrence Lanahan's story on Simon's quarrel with his bosses occasioned by the airing of *The Wire*'s fifth season on the media, shows Lanahan struggling with the right or wrong of these two sides, unable to perform rifle-shot journalism himself.

29. Quoted in Lanahan, "Secrets of the City," 30.

30. Moore, "In the Life of *The Wire*."

31. See Michaels, "Going Boom." See also, Marvell, "To His Coy Mistress," 183–184.

32. Lanahan, "Secrets of the City," 31. Many of the ideas about the form of *The Wire* and the form of journalism are taken from Christine Borden's excellent unpublished paper "Cross Cutting in *The Wire*. I am deeply indebted to Borden's insights and to Irene Chien's research on "The Metal Men."

33. Simon and Burns, *The Corner*, 57–58.

34. Ibid., 159–160.

35. Ibid., 223.

36. Ibid., 283.

37. Ibid., 478–479.

38. This problem is not entirely solved; see chapter 6.

39. Linda Williams, *Playing the Race Card* and "Melodrama Revised."

Chapter 2: Serial Television's World and Time

1. Simon had been asked to write the first episode but did not then feel he knew enough about writing for television.

2. The producing team, Robert Colesberry, David Mills, David Simon, and Nina Noble, was formed for the making of this series. Simon and Mills worked together again as writers, and Clarke Peters, Lance Reddick, and Delaney Williams, all future *Wire* performers, played roles.

3. Gallo, "HBO Puts Straight Dope," 37.

4. In this letter Simon argued that although it was a "significant victory" for HBO to counterprogram "standard network fare" (as in the above shows), it would be a "more profound victory for HBO to take the essence of network fare and smartly turn it on its head, so that no one who sees HBO's take on the culture of crime and crime fighting can watch anything like CSI, or NYPD *Blue*, or *Law & Order* again without knowing that every punch was pulled on those shows." Quoted in Alvarez, *The Wire: Truth Be Told*, 34.

5. Long ago, television scholar Horace Newcomb wrote that except for the daytime soap operas, television had not exploited the one resource it had in abundance: time. Newcomb, TV: *The Most Popular Art*. Serials like *The*

Sopranos, The Wire, and *Mad Men* show that television has finally learned to harness that time.

6. Sconce, "What If?," 98 (italics mine).

7. Ibid., 99.

8. Brett Martin, *Difficult Men,* 10.

9. Premium cable has no commercials; AMC, a less premium cable station that carried *Breaking Bad* and *Mad Men* does have commercials but is frequently viewed on DVR, On Demand, or DVD. The point is that network television not only invariably has commercials but is perfectly tailored to the rhythm of those commercials. The question, however, is: how much does cable serial also follow familiar televisual rhythms?

10. Of course, this line between the two has begun to blur, as some network series, such as *Lost* (ABC, 2004–2010), are highly serialized and rarely resolve anything, even at the end of the season, while some cable series can still be episodic.

11. Jason Mittell has argued that *The Wire*'s internal storyworld is "arguably the most complex ever to appear on American television, providing a rich experience that encourages—or even demands—multiple viewings." Mittell, "*The Wire* in the Context of American Television," 26. Mittell also offers a comprehensive discussion of "complex TV" in his remarkable compendium *Complex TV: The Poetics of Contemporary Television Storytelling.* In this work he discusses all forms of complexity, not just serial ones, describing episodic shows as "classical." See the section "Complexity in Context," released March 24, 2012.

12. "To His Coy Mistress," in *Andrew Marvell: The Complete Poems,* 50. The poet then imagines what he would do if he had this world and time to woo.

13. I should add that some cable channels, the less premium ones, do have commercials and that it is not necessarily the premium cable serials without commercials that compel the kind of attention I am describing. Network television has proven itself capable of doing much the same. ABC's *Lost* (2004–20010) and NBC's *Battlestar Galactica* (2004–2009) operating within the strictures of network television's much longer seasons and the punctuation of five commercial breaks per episode have come close to compelling comparable attention. However, the overall impact of these network serials, while among the best of commercial television since the millennium, is diminished perhaps by the sheer number of episodes per season. What is striking, as we shall see, is that the pace and rhythm of what can only be called the televisual hour of drama is surprisingly the same across both network and cable television.

14. Such, at least, is the tradition of American television, which still operates, to an important degree, in rhythms born out of commercials, as we shall see below. BBC and other nationalized forms of television seem to proceed in larger parts.

15. Gendelman, "Zero-Degree Seriality," 73.

16. Lorrie Moore notes that *The Wire* is "not entirely sui generis but it is beautifully evolved. Nor is the force of the conventional medium entirely absent. Although there are no breaks for commercials, one feels *the pressure and shape of an hour imposing itself on each episode*, even if the plot of each remains unresolved and the pacing broodingly languorous despite sharp-edged cutting." Moore, "In the Life of *The Wire*," 24.

17. Raymond Williams has famously discussed the importance of "flow" as a feature of broadcast television. Jane Feuer, however, has qualified the importance of flow by pointing to the fact that television is based on program segments, ad segments, and trailer segments—that segmentation without closure is actually the very definition of flow. See Williams, *Television*; See Feuer, "The Concept of Live Television," 15; See O'Sullivan, "Broken on Purpose: Poetry, Serial Television and the Season, 62."

18. Many creators of theater, dance, and film also use this vocabulary, but in television it is most overt.

19. Newman, "From Beats to Arcs," 17.

20. Ibid.

21. Crary, "Suspensions of Perception," 71.

22. Ibid.

23. Ibid., 18.

24. Ibid., 21.

25. Ibid.

26. On DVD it has been repositioned where it was originally intended to be: at the end.

27. There were fewer commercials in those days!

28. This razing of the "towers" alludes to the actual 1996 razing of the Lexington Terrace Housing Project—significantly not called "towers"—in which there was apparently no blowback, but from which no improvement in low-income housing came. Renaming them "towers" and adding the blowback added a powerful reference to 9/11. See Alff, "Yesterday's Tomorrow," 23–24.

29. Nannicelli, "It's All Connected," 192.

30. Newman, "From Beats to Arcs," 20.

31. See Marshall and Potter's discussion of the first episode in "'I Am the American Dream,'" 3. See Nannicelli's discussion of this episode in "It's All Connected," 192.

32. Colvin will be fired for his reform, which actually does reduce violent crime in the city. In contrast, Carcetti will shake up all of city hall as he runs for and wins the office of mayor. His personal career will prosper as he rises to the position of governor, but at the expense of his original issues of police and school reform.

33. Ted Nannicelli proposes that "Time after Time" offers thematic closure in place of narrative closure. Nannicelli, "It's All Connected," 193. Though thematic closure might not be the exact word for what happens at the end of this episode—nothing really closes—it is certainly true that there is thematic richness and resonance, and not just in the four last major scenes, as Nannicelli points out, but throughout the entire episode, which opens up a theme of the whole season: how to stop repeating oneself.

34. Another way of counting that does not, for example, count the spatial shifts in the first scene in which we go back and forth between the surveillance site and the district office would yield forty beats per episode, but either way the average beat rate is quite short.

35. "One must not put a loaded rifle on the stage if no one is thinking of firing it." Anton Chekhov, letter to Aleksandr Semenovich Lazarev (pseudonym of A. S. Gruzinsky), November 1, 1889.

36. These examples are all Borden's. Christine Borden, "Cross Cutting in *The Wire*: The Journalist's Editorial Comment," unpublished paper.

37. Sconce, "What If?," 95.

38. Caldwell, *Televisuality*, 352–353.

39. Music without a "source" in the story is avoided except in end-of-season markers.

40. Lavik, "Style in *The Wire*." Lavik finds many exceptions to the plainness of the style, but the squarer frame does indicate a resistance to what Caldwell calls "televisuality" and to what many others might call cinematic flourish.

Chapter 3: "Classical" Tragedy, or . . .

1. As Lester Freamon puts it, "If you follow the drugs you get drug addicts and drug dealers" but if you "follow the money . . . you don't know where the fuck it's gonna take you" (1.9, "Game Day").

2. Simon has done so in almost every interview on *The Wire* and in many of his voice-over commentaries on individual episodes. Many other creators have followed suit, such as producer Karen Thorson and Joe Chappelle, director of the episode in season 2 in which Frank Sobotka's body is pulled from the harbor: "You know it's a street drama but also has the elements of a Greek tragedy" ("Middle Ground"). But all arguments to this effect, especially Chris Love's "Greek Gods in Baltimore: Greek Tragedy and *The Wire*," have dwelled on a certain self-conscious "theatricality" that would seem to be at odds with the also much-noted realism of the serials. My discussion here attempts to reconcile this apparent contradiction.

3. La Berge, "Capitalist Realism," 550.

4. Jameson, "Realism and Utopia," 362.

5. Ibid., 367.

6. Ibid., 368.

7. Ibid.

8. Ibid., 363.

9. At the top is undoubtedly "the Greek," the details of whose international drug trade are merely glimpsed, leaving him a shadowy figure. The only thing we really know about him is that he is not Greek!

10. Jameson's lament for the loss of grand and idiosyncratic villains would seem to contradict his own influential essay on "cognitive mapping," which called conspiracy "a degraded figure of the total logic of late capital, a desperate attempt to represent the latter's system, whose failure is marked by its slippage into sheer theme and content." Jameson, "Cognitive Mapping," 365. Marxism itself, as Wylie Sypher and Jane Gaines have well noted, is a kind of melodrama, one tending toward happy endings. See Sypher, "Aesthetic of Revolution," and Gaines, "The 'Melos' in Marxist Theory."

11. For example: a poor old man loses his dog (*Umberto D*); a man's bicycle is stolen and he cannot earn a living without it, he and his son search the city for it to no avail (*Bicycle Thieves*); shoeshine boys dream of owning a horse, get involved in stolen goods, and betray one another (*Shoeshine*).

12. Brooks, *Melodramatic Imagination*, 24–55.

13. Before melodrama became a key—though shifting—term in cinema studies, and before it became attached to domestic women's films, it had a long history of scholarship in literary and dramatic studies where it has had a more stable meaning: usually called sentimental fiction in literary studies, regularly called melodrama on the stage, it was rarely confused with tragedy because it was understood to be the form that replaced tragedy with more appeal to popular audiences. For American stage melodrama see Gerould (1982), Mason (1993), and McConachie (1992). For British melodrama see Michael Booth (1991). Robert Heilman's (1968) elaborate comparison between tragedy and melodrama argues for the modernity of melodrama even as he traces elements of both in contemporary life. Tomkins (1985) offers the classic explanation of the generation of tears in nineteenth-century literature by women. In film, Christine Gledhill (1987) "mapped" the "melodramatic field" in the wake of both Peter Brooks's (1976) theatrical and literary study of the mode of melodrama and Thomas Elsaesser's (1972) influential treatise on films called American family melodrama in the 1950s. In the wake of Brooks and Gledhill, melodrama has increasingly come to be understood as a mode of modern culture rather than only a genre. In Ben Singer's (2001) melodrama is the sensational expression of industrial modernity in silent cinema and stage; in

my work (2001) it is the mode through which American anxieties about inequities between the black and white races find expression. Melodrama far exceeds any special address to women, and is simply one of the most enduringly popular forms of moving-image drama. Its uniquely modern function is the quest for moral legibility in an era where moral, let alone religious, certainties are no longer self-evident; it is what we mostly see at the movies and in most forms of television drama.

14. Gledhill, "Christine Gledhill on *Stella Dallas*," 45.

15. Many commentators on the serial have cited this cold open as key to the series as a whole. See, for example, Marshall and Potter, "'I Am the American Dream,'" the introduction to their 2009 anthology *The Wire: Urban Decay and American Television*, 1–3, 14. See also Kraniauskas, "Elasticity of Demand."

16. Season 3, episode 3, "Dead Soldiers."

17. Rotella, "The Case against Kojak Liberalism," 115.

18. Nussbaum, "The Morality of Pity," 149.

19. Ibid., 162.

20. Iphigenia, for example, is whisked away by Artemis in some versions of her story and never sacrificed by her father. The conventional judgment has been that tragedies relying on such devices are less successful as tragedies than those that do not opt to avert disaster. See Halliwell, *Poetics of Aristotle*, 48.

21. Thomas Elsaesser's essay on film melodrama, identified melodrama's emphasis on powerless characters as exemplified in 1950s domestic melodramas. Elsaesser noted that in the "Hollywood melodrama characters made for operettas play out the tragedies of mankind" ("Tales of Sound and Fury," 67). With this essay, Elsaesser ignited a whole generation of budding film scholars, myself included, who discovered in melodrama all the condensations, displacements, and sublimations of powerful emotions. Elsaesser also saw more in melodrama than the usual showdown of good and evil generated out of mere "incompetence or cynicism" (ibid., 74). Indeed, he identified a fundamental *"mode of experience"* (ibid., 74) in the writings of Dickens, Balzac, and Hugo that was not simply a matter of manipulation or excess but the turning of a body of techniques into a stylistic principle that could express spiritual, economic, and ideological crises (ibid., 74). However, Elsaesser's treatment of all other film melodrama except the ironic and distanced ones of Sirk, Minnelli, Ray, etc., was haunted by the vision of melodrama as a "tragedy that doesn't quite come off," either because of its over-self-consciousness in straining to be tragedy or because, as Elsaesser put it, "the predicament is too evidently fabricated on the level of plot and dramaturgy to carry the kind of conviction normally termed 'inner necessity'" (ibid., 87). For this reason

Elsaesser finds all but the most ironic of film melodramas "unaccomplished" or "unsophisticated."

22. The plays of Euripedes, which often emphasize the sheer pathos of intolerable fate might thus be considered protomelodramas, not only when they deploy the deus ex machine, but also when they don't and the Trojan Women just suffer.

23. Heilman, *Tragedy and Melodrama*, pp. 74–75.

24. Doxtater, "Figuring Danish Melodrama."

25. Marshall and Potter, "'I Am the American Dream,'" 2.

26. See, for example, ibid. Among blogs see *What's Alan Watching*: "There are many great tragedies throughout the run of *The Wire*, but the death of Wallace is the first and still the one that probably cuts deepest." sepinwall .blogspot.com/2008/08/wire-season-1-episode-12-cleaning-up.html.

27. Kinder, "Re-Wiring Baltimore," 52.

28. Snoop is unwittingly quoting a line spoken by Clint Eastwood's Bill Munny in the western, *The Unforgiven* (Clint Eastwood, 1992) before he kills in cold blood an antagonist who claims he does not deserve his fate.

29. Marshall and Potter, "'I Am the American Dream,'" 5.

30. Ibid., 5–6.

31. Also cited by Nussbaum, "The Morality of Pity," 165.

32. Potter and Marshal try to follow Arthur Miller's defense of American tragedy and even go so far as to equate the passive drug addiction of Dukie at the end of the serial to the suicide of Willy Loman. The differences, however, are obvious. Dukie's self-destructive addiction is a sad acquiescence to his pathetic lot: Loman's self-destruction is equally sad but it is at least an act of will. However, the idea they seize upon—that the possibility of victory must be there—is an attribute of melodrama's greater belief in justice, not an attribute of tragedy. In the end, neither this argument, nor the idea that the series blurs the lines between fact and fiction, makes a convincing argument for the series as tragedy.

33. See Love, "Greek Gods."

34. Aristotle, "Poetics."

35. Miller, "Tragedy and the Common Man," 3–7.

36. Liam Kennedy and Steven Shapiro argue, though not specifically about this season, that "back in the day" is both a plaintive "slogan of social erasure and an incomplete mechanism of explanation." I add, however, that there is much more "back-in-the-day" lament in the second season than all the rest of the series. Kennedy and Shapiro, 162.

37. See Read, "Stringer Bell's Lament."

38. See Clandfield, "'We ain't got no yard.'"

39. See Warshow's foundational essay, "The Gangster as Tragic Hero."

40. Smith, *An Inquiry into the Nature and Causes of the Wealth of Nations*. They are amazed to discover, in addition to the Smith volume, a modern, sleek, but almost characterless, decor. McNulty comments, "Who the fuck was I chasing?" as the camera tilts down to reveal the title of the book.

41. On neoliberalism, see Harvey, *A Brief History of Neoliberalism*, and Brown, "Neoliberalism and the End of Liberal Democracy."

42. Freamon: "From the looks of things Stringer Bell's worse than a drug dealer . . ." Prez: "He's a developer!"

43. Marshall and Potter say this themselves, even as they attempt to argue for *The Wire* as tragedy. "'I am the American Dream,'" 8.

44. Ibid., 7.

45. Ibid., 8.

46. Nussbaum, "The Morality of Pity," 165.

47. Ibid., 166. Nussbaum concludes: "The task of cultivating a truly balanced and equal pity is a daunting one. . . . But Sophocles' drama helps us get started by reminding us that the body's needs for food, drink, shelter, and release from pain, and the bodily human being's needs for friendship, talk, and political voice are both universal and of central significance for all." Ibid., 167.

48. However, I do think Nussbaum is correct when she argues that although pity can be valuable in prompting appropriate action, it is "fickle and in league with hierarchy." We tend to pity those we know and love over those who are "distant" to us. The question is what to do about that. Serial melodrama, if it takes an institutional as well as a personal approach that makes us intimate with the day-to-day lives of the lives it narrates, can overcome this problem of distance by making the day-to-day life of individuals and the larger institutions they inhabit matter.

49. This is something that even Elsaesser, whose 1972 essay on melodrama in film has been foundational, did not truly do. He ultimately labeled these films failed tragedies.

50. This confusion is compounded by the fact that while the editors Potter and Marshall unconvincingly maintain that *The Wire* is tragedy, a contributor to the volume, Amanda Klein, argues that it is the "melodrama . . . of the socially conscious text." Klein, "'Dickensian Aspect,'" 178.

51. Robert Bentley, for example, cites Rainer Maria Rilke to assert that tragedy is a kind of consent to "the terrible in life." He writes, "If suffering alone does not make a tragic hero, and there has to be resistance to suffering, so in us, the audience, it is not enough to shrink from terror *in* terror, we have to grasp terror by the hand. Paradoxically, as we accept terror more, we shall

be terrified less—another possible meaning for the word Catharsis." Bentley, *Life of the Drama*, 281.

52. Heilman, *Tragedy and Melodrama*, 97.

53. Melodrama is the "principal vehicle of protest and dissent, of polemic." Ibid., 96.

Chapter 4: Realistic, Modern Serial Melodrama

1. One of the most unexamined premises of film and media studies has been the assumption that, after evolving out of the archaism of a "primitive" early cinema, cinema became "classical" by suppressing the excessive qualities of its obvious inheritance from earlier stage melodrama, which nevertheless survived as a genre of excess. Though I will not delve deeply into this problem here (see my forthcoming essay "Tales of Sound and Fury Signifying Something"), I will briefly summarize the dilemma this assumption of a dominant "classical" style of cinema has created for the understanding of popular film and television. Originally deployed by André Bazin (*What Is Cinema?*, 29–30) as a way of describing a maturity of film art reached in the 1930s in Hollywood genre films, the idea of the classicality of cinema transvalues, as Miriam Hansen ("Mass Production of the Senses") has aptly put it, from aspirational maturity into a rather villainous ideological hegemony—in the work of Christian Metz and many others in the 1970s. In 1985 it transvalued again into David Bordwell, Kristen Thompson, and Janet Staiger's notion of an objectively observed fact: "The principles which Hollywood claims as its own rely on notions of decorum, proportion, formal harmony, respect for tradition, mimesis, self-effacing craftsmanship and cool control of the perceiver's response—which critics in any medium usually call 'classical'" (*Classical Hollywood Cinema*, 3). The classical, in other words, is posited by this theory as the reigning dominant of cinema since 1917 through 1960, but extended by Bordwell in later work (*The Way Hollywood Tells It*) into the present.

2. In other words, and to put it melodramatically, melodrama has been wrongly treated—rather like the Furies at the end of Aeschylus's *Oresteia*. In that great serial tragedy, the Furies represent an ancient form of blood lust appeased by the new justice of trial by jury that ended the cycle of intrafamilial violence. My point, however, is that melodrama is not ancient, like the female Furies, but itself the product of a more modern ethos of democratic justice, of which the Greek trilogy's final "happy ending" is an anticipation.

3. This notion was located prominently in the subtitle of Brooks's great book *The Melodramatic Imagination: Balzac, Henry James, Melodrama, and the Mode of Excess.*

4. Ibid., 49. Brooks also notes that monologues punctuated by music were on their way to becoming operatic arias, and thus "melodrama finds one possible logical outcome in grand opera, where melody and harmony, as much as the words, are charged with conveying meaning" (ibid.).

5. Peterson, "The Depth of the Hole."

6. Ibid., 464.

7. An interesting comparison can be drawn between the feature film *The Soloist* (Joe Wright, 2009) about a homeless person, and *The Wire*, which in its final season portrays a homeless encampment. Although *The Soloist* is about a musician who lives on the streets, its much more constant use of music blocks out most of the sounds of the street and leaves the street very uncharacterized as a place. Thanks to Mark Berger for this comparison.

8. I have argued this point, drawing on the foundational work of Christine Gledhill ("The Melodramatic Field") at length, in *Playing the Race Card: Melodramas of Black and White from Uncle Tom to O. J. Simpson*. In that work I mention five axioms of melodrama. Here I want to focus on the most central and limited ones: "victim heroes" or the fact that suffering renders a protagonist good and thus leads to the dialectic of pathos and action; and the way new "realist content" makes melodrama seem modern.

9. Buckley, "Refugee Theatre," 176.

10. Ibid.

11. Ibid.

12. Brooks, *Melodramatic Imagination*, 16; Singer, *Melodrama and Modernity*, 1.

13. Linda Williams, *Playing the Race Card*.

14. Brooks, *Melodramatic Imagination*, 16; Singer, *Melodrama and Modernity*; Linda Williams, *Playing the Race Card*; Nietzsche, *On the Genealogy of Morals*.

15. Henry James referred to *Uncle Tom's Cabin*—the most influential American melodrama of the nineteenth century—as a "wonderful 'leaping' fish" alighting first in one medium and then in another. It had become a more general "state of vision, of feeling and consciousness" rather than a novel, a play, a circus, or even an association of songs. See Linda Williams, *Playing the Race Card*, 13.

16. The Russian formalist Sergei Balukhatyi's "Poetics of Melodrama" (1926) argued that melodrama exists in many types of drama in which a "melodramatic skeleton" has been "covered with the solid flesh" of realistic, psychological, ethical, social, or philosophical content. In such cases we "lose the feeling of melodramatic style and accept the play [or film or television series] as a 'higher' genre" (129). Although Balukhatyi was not using the term "genre" the

way film and media scholars do, the central idea that melodrama is not just a matter of style but a way of making audiences appreciate a felt good, often through more complex forms of realism, psychology, or social or philosophical content, is crucial to a more sophisticated understanding of melodrama. Indeed, it is precisely this idea of melodrama as a mode, or larger skeleton, and of different genres as particular embodiments of that mode that I would like to adapt here. This chapter argues that *The Wire* is an amalgam of gangster and cop genre but that if we only look at the genres we miss the larger skeleton of the melodramatic mode. Balukhatyi's metaphor of the skeleton and the flesh is an apt way of describing the way classical theatrical melodrama has evolved in the direction of more inherently realist media. See also Doxtater, "Figuring Danish Melodrama."

17. *First Blood* (Ted Kotcheff, 1982); *Die Hard* (John McTiernan, 1988); *Air Force One* (Wolfgang Petersen, 1997); *Avatar* (James Cameron, 2009).

18. Nietzsche, *On the Genealogy of Morals.*

19. Linda Williams, *Playing the Race Card*, 296–310.

20. Christine Gledhill and Thomas Postlewait have both convincingly argued this point. Gledhill writes that melodrama seizes upon the timely social problems of everyday reality. Yet it differs from realism in its will to force the status quo to yields signs of moral legibility within the limits of the "ideologically permissible," even as it builds on genuine social concerns ("The Melodramatic Field," 38). Postlewait, for his part, argues against the simple dichotomies: "Melodrama distorts, realism reports; melodrama offers escapism, realism offers life; melodrama is conservative, realism is radical; melodrama delivers ideologies. . . . In fact, both melodrama and realism distort and report, conserve and criticize. And both articulate and challenge the ideologies of the time" ("From Melodrama to Realism," 56).

21. Melodrama is not necessarily for the truly just cause; it is for whomever can be construed as the underdog victim and is thus, at least ostensibly, on the side of the oppressed and powerless. However, the powerless could be slaves in one melodrama, Reconstruction Era former slave owners in another; Jews in one, the Germans they "infect" in another.

22. See Brooks (*Melodramatic Imagination*), who mostly uses the term "moral occult" but sometimes calls it "moral legibility," a term I find more legible as long as we recognize that good is not easily made legible in a modern, or what Brooks calls "post-sacred," world. Brooks's point is that melodrama reaches for the "domain of spiritual forces and imperatives that is not clearly visible within reality" but that operates and "demands to be uncovered, registered, articulated" (ibid., 21). Thus melodrama is "not only a moralistic drama but the drama of morality: it strives . . . to 'prove' the existence of a

moral universe which, though put into question, masked by villainy and perversions of judgment, does exist and can be made to assert its presence and its categorical force among men" (ibid., 20).

23. Linda Williams, *Playing the Race Card*, 296–310.

24. Buckley, "Refugee Theatre," 188.

25. Anker, "Left Melodrama," 131.

26. Elsaesser, "Tales of Sound and Fury," 67.

27. Ibid.

28. Ibid., 89.

29. For example, in an otherwise insightful article, Alberto Toscano and Jeff Kinkle deny the work's very televisuality: "*The Wire* is barely a television series. . . . We literally know of no one . . . who watched it on television when broadcast" ("Baltimore as World and Representation"). Simon, on the other hand, gets angry at those who did not watch and thus support the series while it was on television.

30. This descriptor, which has often been used to point to the novelistic and realistic qualities of the work (see Chaddha and Wilson, "'Way Down in the Hole,'" 166) and is thus interpreted as praise, can also be taken to point to a gripping narrative with a rich array of social types. It is clear, however, both from evidence in the serial and from Simon himself, that it can also mean cheap melodrama. See his interview in *Vice* magazine; see also Klein, "'The Dickensian Aspect.'"

31. Those who found it wanting pointed to a lack of realism. Indeed, one of the more critical reviews comes from the television critic at the *Baltimore Sun*, David Zurawik, who accuses the final season of "blurring fact and fiction and ignoring any sense of proportionality. . . . Newsroom villains are patterned on editors and a reporter long gone from Baltimore. But Simon presents his story as if it is taking place at *The Sun* today." Another criticism is that season 5 offers a "simplistic critique of media": "The first seven episodes of [season 5 of] *The Wire* have almost nothing to say about the biggest story in newspapers: the vast technological change sweeping through media today. And that is most surprising given how up-to-the-second—even prescient—the series has been about the use of the latest technology by criminals" ("*The Wire* Loses Spark").

32. Simon admits that Dickens was a great writer who "exposed the fault lines of industrial England . . . where money and power route themselves away from the poor." However, "in the end, the guy [Dickens] would punk out. . . . *The Wire* was actually making a different argument than Dickens, and the comparison, while flattering, sort of fell badly on us." The invocation of "Dickensian" was "a little bit of tongue-in-cheek satire on the show directed at people who were using Dickens to praise us." But he adds a more personal

motive: "When I was coming back off of the reporting for *The Corner* and preparing to go back to the newspaper, this editor and I talked about writing columns about life on the streets in West Baltimore. That, to me, would have been the narrative equivalent of telling some stories that you ultimately saw on *The Wire*, but using real people. The first one that I tried to tell . . . he spiked. It was about a guy very much like *The Wire* character Bubbles who was harvesting metal—two guys harvesting metal, actually. . . . He came to me and said, 'I want to do the stories that are about the Dickensian lives of children growing up in West Baltimore.' What he was saying was, 'If you give me a nice, cute eight-, nine-year-old kid who doesn't have a pencil, who doesn't have a schoolbook, who lives in poverty, who's big eyed and sweet and who I can make the reader fall in love with, I can win a fuckin' prize with that. Write me that shit. . . . Don't give me a guy who's, like, trying to get high but maintain his dignity. Don't give me anything complicated.' And he really used the word 'Dickensian'" (Interview, *Vice*).

33. Alvarez, *The Wire: Truth Be Told*, 4.

34. Soft eyes are a way of teaching and detecting that can take in the whole scene without looking hard at any one thing and that can intuit the whole. See chapter 5.

35. Hornby, interview with David Simon. No doubt influenced by the Dickensian model, Hornby writes that Bubbles pulls his cart rather than pushing it.

36. Dickens, *Bleak House*, 168.

37. Ibid., chap. 16.

38. Ibid., 439–440.

39. Kinder ("Re-Wiring Baltimore") calls him gay but does not explain. All attention goes to Omar on this score. But Bubbles's less overt, less examined desire may certainly contribute to his deep sense of guilt and responsibility both for Johnny Weeks and for Sherrod.

40. Neoliberalism can be briefly defined as a "theory of political economic practices that proposes that human well-being can best be advanced by liberating individual entrepreneurial freedoms and skills within an institutional framework characterized by strong private property rights, free markets, and free trade. The role of the state is to create and preserve an institutional framework appropriate to such practices" (Harvey, *A Brief History of Neoliberalism*, 2). Harvey's succinct book traces the emergence of this ideology in the late 1970s as deregulation and the withdrawal of the state—in China, the United States, and Britain—from the role of social provider has left an ideology that "seeks to bring all human action into the domain of the market" (ibid., 2–3). Neoliberalism holds, counter to much evidence to the contrary, that "social good will be maximized by maximizing the reach and frequency

of market transactions" (ibid., 3). The underlying argument of this chapter is that as neoliberalism has transmuted to a self-evident "common sense," it has become the role of a new kind of melodrama to counter these assumptions by revealing not only their human but also their larger institutional cost.

41. Brown, "Neoliberalism and the End of Liberal Democracy," 43.

42. Ibid., 42.

43. See chapter 2.

44. It represents the combined efforts of Jay Landsman, the state's psychiatric clinic, Walon's volunteer work as Bubbles's NA sponsor, the young reporter Mike Fletcher, and Gus Haynes, Fletcher's mentor at the *Baltimore Sun*.

45. Much as David Simon once did in "Metal Men" and *The Corner*.

46. Jo can only intuit the good; he does not know it.

47. Though there is some hint that the career of Dukie might head in the direction of Bubbles.

48. Brown, "Neoliberalism and the End of Liberal Democracy," 41.

49. "Citizen" is *The Wire*'s term for a person not involved in crime.

50. See Linda Williams, "Mega-Melodrama!"

51. Brown, "Resisting Left Melancholy." See also Anker, "Left Melodrama."

Chapter 5: Hard Eyes / Soft Eyes

1. Bullet points before they were so called, in a coming age of computers and PowerPoints. McNulty proudly shows his report to his sergeant: "It's got dots. The deputy loves dots."

2. Of course the more recent *Homeland* renders this good-vs.-evil scheme more ambiguous by introducing the ever constant possibility that Carrie Matheson's investments might be more pathological than professional.

3. Foucault, *Discipline*, 202–203.

4. Ibid., 217.

5. See Ericson and Haggerty, *The New Politics of Surveillance and Visibility*. In the introduction Haggerty writes, "An important political dimension of resistance concerns how it can foster a dynamic back and forth of evasion and official response that tends to ratchet up the overall level of surveillance and control," 21.

6. McMillan, "Dramatizing Individuation," 42. See also Schaub, "*The Wire*: Big Brother Is Not Watching You."

7. Bandes, "And All the Pieces Matter," 440.

8. For example, *Law and Order* (1990–2010), *Without a Trace* (2002–2009), CSI-*Miami* (2002–2012), and so on.

9. These are Avon Barksdale's words.

10. McMillan, "Dramatizing Individuation," 43.

11. See Lyon, "The Search for Surveillance Theories," and Haggerty, "Tear Down the Walls."

12. The USA Patriot Act stands for Uniting (and) Strengthening America (by) Providing Appropriate Tools Required (to) Intercept (and) Obstruct Terrorism Act of 2001. One of its provisions, not eliminated in Barack Obama's extension of some of its parts, was roving wiretaps.

13. Burns worked in the Baltimore Police Department for twenty years. Upon retirement he taught seventh grade in the Baltimore public schools. In this case as with Pryzbylewski, the schools were not too particular about teacher training.

14. Bandes, "And All the Pieces Matter," 437–440.

15. See Marcus, "Ethnography in/of the World System," 98. Marcus seeks to bring the multiple sites of ethnography "into the same frame of study and to posit their relationships on the basis of first-hand ethnographic research" (100).

16. The mold was cast with *Blackboard Jungle* (Richard Brooks, 1955)—a new English teacher at a violent, unruly inner-city school does his job, overcoming resistance from both students and faculty. It continued with the novel and then film *Up the Down Staircase* (1965, 1967) about a female teacher of English in a Harlem school. (At one point in episode 3, the vice principal, Ms. Donnelly, yells at the kids on the first day of school, "Don't go up the down staircase!") *To Sir, with Love* (James Clavell, 1967) reverses the conventional racial dynamic with a black teacher and white students in London's tough East End. In a more comic vein the school melodrama was revived with the American television sitcom *Welcome Back, Kotter* (ABC, 1975–1979). It enjoyed a major comeback in 1989 with *Lean on Me* (John Avildsen), *Stand and Deliver* (Ramon Menendez), and *Dead Poets Society* (Peter Weir). The genre was reinvented for female teachers (Michelle Pfeiffer, Meryl Streep) with *Dangerous Minds* (John N. Smith, 1995) and *Music of the Heart* (Wes Craven, 1999). A slightly different version—from the student's point of view, but otherwise quite similar—is *Precious* (Lee Daniels, 2009).

17. See Hynes, "Educational TV." Hynes coins the apt term "stations of the cross."

18. Elijah Anderson, *Code of the Street*, 120.

19. Colvin tells his friend the Deacon that if he had had "that boy's gift of talk, I would have really made a stir" (5.9, "Late Editions").

20. See, for example, Drake Bennett's 2010 report in *Slate* about college courses on the series. Observing that professors at Harvard, UC Berkeley, Duke, and Middlebury are now offering courses on the show, Bennett also notes that "the classes aren't just in film studies or media studies departments;

they're turning up in social science disciplines as well, places where the preferred method of inquiry is the field study or the survey, not the HBO series, even one that is routinely called the best television show ever. Some sociologists and social anthropologists, it turns out, believe *The Wire* has something to teach their students about poverty, class, bureaucracy, and the social ramifications of economic change" (Bennett, "This Will Be on the Mid-Term. You Feel Me?"). See also Brown and Krahe, "Sociocultural Knowledge and Visual Re(-)presentations of Black Masculinity and Community." See also Sonja Sohn's use of episodes from the series as a basis for conversations about life chances for Baltimore youth. Her program, Rewired for Change (see website) has been lauded for community activisim. See also Terry Gross, March 15, 2012, "*Sonja Sohn: Changing Baltimore Long After 'The Wire,'*" *Fresh Air*, NPR, retrieved April 17, 2012. Finally, see Peter L. Beilenson and Patrick A. McGuire's *Tapping into The Wire: The Real Urban Crisis*, a book that uses *The Wire* "as a road map for exploring connections between inner-city poverty and drug-related violence." In this book a past Baltimore health commissioner joins forces with a former *Sun* reporter to examine urban policy and public health issues that affect cities across the nation.

21. "Asked why he was teaching a class around a TV drama, [Harvard sociology professor William Julius] Wilson said the show makes the concerns of sociologists immediate in a way no work of sociology he knows of ever has. 'Although *The Wire* is fiction, not a documentary, its depiction of [the] systemic urban inequality that constrains the lives of the urban poor is more poignant and compelling [than] that of any published study, including my own,' he wrote in an e-mail" (Bennett, "This Will Be on the Mid-Term. You Feel Me?").

Chapter 6: Feeling Race

1. Lipsitz, *How Racism Takes Place*, 95.

2. Ibid., 97–98.

3. Ibid., 98.

4. Ibid., 100. Lipsitz also praises the social programs spawned by the series, such as the nonprofit Rewired for Change, organized by Sonja Sohn (Kima Greggs), which uses episodes from the series as the basis for conversations about life chances and choices for Baltimore youth, or Moving Mountains, organized by Jamie Hector (Marlo) and Felicia "Snoop" Pearson (herself), to teach performing arts to former gang members.

5. Ibid., 104.

6. Ibid., 105. Lipsitz pursues a long litany of the economically based crimes of segregation that *The Wire* "will not tell us about," all the way up to Wells

Fargo's recent crime of foreclosing on homes in black neighborhoods at a rate four times greater than in white.

7. Ibid., 6, 12–13.

8. As the second half of Lipsitz's book seeks to prove, it is only those works that have come directly from the black spatial imaginary that can address the "real" problems of race (ibid., 122–123).

9. In *The Corner* Gary calls the place he must go for a court hearing with "the sentinels of suburban justice" "Leave It to Beaverland"—for although some of the new judges at the western county courthouses are black, "Gary can't help thinking of the other side of the city line as the kinescope stomping ground of Eddie Haskell, Wally, and the Beaver. All the desperation and foolishness that counted for something in a city courtroom only serve to make you a nigger in Catonsville or Owings Mills or Towson" (311–312).

10. The term was popularized during the 1995 O. J. Simpson double-murder trial, whose verdict of not guilty sparked unprecedented white resentment. The black prosecutor, Christopher Darden, accused black defense attorney Johnny Cochran's team of playing the race card when they introduced evidence of a detective's prior use of the word "nigger." The prosecutor, who lost the case against Simpson, said in court, "If you allow Mr. Cochran to use the word and play this race card [then] the entire complexion of the case changes. It's a race case then. It's white versus black" (Bugliosi 1996, *Outrage*, 66). Behind this statement is the belief that within American jurisprudence, race should be unmentionable. As this trial made it possible to say that one privileged African American male may have "gotten away with murder" by deploying the usual disadvantage of being raced to encourage the jury to see him as a racial victim, it also became possible to say that affirmative action and other ways of rectifying past grievances no longer deserved priority. In effect, one race card of racial grievance seemed to be used to trump another.

11. And this is because a certain conception of black linguistic power, aligned with a Bald'more-ese dialect, not only has a modicum of political power, but also has cultural power. Variants of black vernacular are the lingua franca of the series, as the majority of the epigraphs that begin each episode indicate ("The king stay the king"; "Be a little slow, a little late"; "You come at the king you best not miss"; "This is me, yo, right here," etc.). Other vernaculars are, of course, important: police, drugs, newspapers. However, whenever a character of any race, class, or ethnicity reaches for eloquence, it is most effectively said in some form of black vernacular. Thus mayoral aspirant Tommy Carcetti says, "I still wake up white in a city that ain't," and thus Bunk Moreland says to Omar, "Makes me sick, motherfucker, how far we done fell." As we have seen, perhaps the most telling of these phrases is Omar's question "Do you feel me?"

12. Lipsitz, *How Racism Takes Place*, 105.

13. Linda Williams, *Playing the Race Card*. This summary is drawn from chapters 1, 2, 6, 7, and the conclusion.

14. Ibid., 47.

15. Ibid., 3–9.

16. The Code was developed in 1930 and adopted with some "teeth" in 1934. It ended in 1968 when it was replaced by an earlier version of today's ratings system.

17. See my discussion of this series as racial melodrama in *Playing the Race Card*, 220–221.

18. Ibid., 220–251.

19. If we consider *Gone with the Wind* (1939) to have been the previous mainstream depiction of slavery, then Haley's book and television serial *Roots* represented an important change: the first black spatial imaginary, though one that was importantly determined by reactions to the "emasculated" Tom figure.

20. Ibid., 296–310.

21. Lipsitz, *How Racism Takes Place*, 110.

22. See the discussion in chapter 5 for speculation as to why this is so.

23. Movies such as *The Long Walk Home* (1990) or *The Help* (2011) skirt around such issues from white points of view.

24. Linda Williams, *Playing the Race Card*, 296–310.

25. Mathew Hughey has introduced the term "cinethetic racism" by which he attempts to describe a cinematic synthesis between the reproduction of stereotypical and racist representations and the normalization of white (especially male) representations," 551. The more useful term, not introduced by Hughey, is "magical Negro" discussed below, though I believe the whole tradition of racial virtue and villainy needs to be understood.

26. See Richard Wright's *Native Son* (1942) and blaxpoitation films *Super Fly* (1972), *Shaft* (1971), and *Sweet Sweetback's Baadasssss Song* (1971).

27. As a side benefit, Coffey also restores potency to his jailor, who makes a point of telling him the next day that the "missus" was pleased by his cure "several times."

28. It is Fred Astaire and Ginger Rogers singing "Heaven, I'm in heaven" in the "Cheek to Cheek" number from *Top Hat* (1935). Watching them dance, he appreciatively murmurs, "Angels, just like up in heaven."

29. In addition to the many awards it won at the time of release, one might cite the populist IMDB (Internet Movie Database) "Top 250 Films" of all time, which is established by vote, where *The Green Mile* occupies number 69. It also received an Academy Award for the performance of Michael Clarke Duncan

as John Coffey and has, perhaps perversely, become something of a children's classic, occupying much the same position that *Uncle Tom's Cabin* occupied in the early twentieth century, as the popular story designed to "prove" the goodness of the Negro—although now, in an age of equal rights, this goodness should no longer need to be proven.

30. In 2001 Spike Lee introduced the term, at first to describe the *Legend of Bagger Vance* (2000), about a washed-up white golfer (Matt Damon) and his magical, wise sharecropper caddy. He soon after extended the epithet to *The Green Mile*, saying, "Michael Clarke Duncan tongue-kisses cancer out of a white woman and cures her. And in the end Tom Hanks offers to set him free, but guess what? He refuses to leave Death Row. He'd rather die with Hanks looking on. Get the fuck outta here! That's old grateful slave shit" (Lee, "Thinking about the Power of Images," 211).

31. A more complete list of these films includes *Meet Joe Black* (1999), *Unbreakable* (2000), *O Brother, Where Art Thou?* (2000), *Pirates of the Caribbean: Dead Man's Chest* (2006), *Pirates of the Caribbean: At World's End* (2007), *Blade I* (1998), *Blade II* (2002), *Blade III* (2004), *The Matrix I* (1999), *The Matrix II* (2003), *The Matrix III* (2003), *The Time Machine* (2002), *The Punisher* (2004), *Happy Gilmore*, (1996) *Holy Man* (1998), *Dogma* (1999), *Bedazzled* (2000), *Down to Earth* (2001), *Bruce Almighty* (2003), and *Evan Almighty* (2007). It is interesting to note that an attempt to reverse the interracial "helping" in *The Blind Side* (2009), where a middle-class housewife played by Sandra Bullock helps a giant young high school football player win a scholarship to college, is just as cloying as the reverse process.

32. Rarely a woman, though; see the important precurser, *Ghost* (1990), in which the female magical Negro's primary aim in life is to selflessly offer wisdom or aid to the white female protagonist.

33. Hughey, "Cinethetic Racism," 551.

34. To Hughey, however, racism has merely changed its form to demonstrate overt support for racial equality underlain by a "covert and/or social-psychological discomfort with and even hate of nonwhites" (ibid., 551).

35. Ibid., 562.

36. The unarmed Grant was fatally shot by BART police officer Johannes Mehserle, who claimed to have mistaken his gun for a taser. Police had detained Oscar Grant and several other passengers who allegedly resisted arrest. The shooting was captured on many cell phone cameras. Mehserle was ultimately found guilty of involuntary manslaughter. See also, *Fruitvale Station* (Coogler, 2013), starring Michael B. Jordan, who played Wallace in *The Wire*.

37. See Fiedler, *The Inadvertent Epic*.

38. Lipsitz, *How Racism Takes Place*, 119.

39. Ibid., 119.

40. See, for example, the clever blog *Stuff White People Like* (*The Wire* is number 85 on its list; stuffwhitepeoplelike.com/2008/03/09/85-the-wire/), which treats white people as if they were the minority to be studied by blacks. This very inversion of the usually dominant racial imaginary is, I argue, what *The Wire* itself successfully does, making the series more immune to the joke than many other examples.

41. Fuller, "Branding Blackness," 291. See also Farhi, "A Television Trend."

42. Mittell in Kennedy and Shapiro, 17.

43. Richmond, "Black Fare Makes $ense for HBO."

44. Lipsitz, *How Racism Takes Place*, 120.

45. HBO does not release the demographics of its viewership, if indeed this is known. However, the demographics for pay TV more generally indicate that its viewers are concentrated in the $35,000–100,000 annual income range, and only 22 percent of black viewers subscribe, compared to 65 percent white. To the degree that one can extrapolate from this information, it seems fair to assume a predominantly white, middle-class viewership. See "Pay TV Industry Demographic Profile," Valassis, www.valassis.com/by-industry/telecom-pay -tv/consumer-demographics.aspx?r=1. Nevertheless, its representation on the more affordable "basic cable" BET does suggest an important appeal to more exclusively black audiences. Moreover, the unpopularity of the second season to these viewers, which ran in an abbreviated format of only sixty minutes with commercials, compared to the ninety minutes with commercials for all the other seasons, further argues for its great popularity as a "black" show. The cuts in the second season meant that large sections of the narrative about a feud between police major Valchek and union leader Frank Sobotka were deleted, to the point of making large parts of the story incomprehensible.

46. Burke ("I Got the Shotgun," 451) quotes a detective who notes that cases go from "'red to black' (meaning open to closed, as noted by the color of ink used to list a case on the whiteboard) 'by way of green' (meaning overtime paid to officers). Police departments also skim money from the drug trade through asset forfeiture, frequently evading local mandates that forbid the use of such assets for non-law enforcement purposes by funneling the cases to federal prosecutors through 'adoption' procedures."

47. See Paul Allen Anderson, "'The Game Is the Game,'" 386–389.

48. Anderson uses Roland Barthes's notion, augmented by Theodor Adorno, that such a tautology only gives the impression of factual necessity, because that is the way things are. However, the impersonality of the utterance only masks the exercise of the will of a superior (ibid., 387).

49. Beck, "Respecting the Middle."

50. Lipsitz would say this is because the real crimes can't be named. But the real crimes are not fundamentally the racial ones that Lipsitz identifies. Those are the crimes liberal democracy committed "back in the day," when it failed to live up to the promise of the American Dream.

51. Though we admire D'Angelo Barksdale for his attempt to separate from his institutional-familial ties and his unwillingness to be a party to beatings and murders, he himself is murdered in prison in the second season. Though we may have sympathy for Stringer Bell's attempt to run the drug operation with less violence, we recognize that he fails abysmally when he murders first Wallace, then D'Angelo, and then attempts to kill Omar and shoots off Omar's grandmother's crown in the process.

52. Beck, "Respecting the Middle."

53. Ibid.

54. In the next episode we see that he has found his way into the basement of the building with a painfully broken leg. The usually unflappable Marlo, when he sees the distance Omar jumped, exclaims, "That's some Spider-Man shit."

55. Cormier, "Bringing Omar Back to Life," 212.

56. It is telling that Herc, the dumbest of the dumb white cops, tries to imitate the macho blaxploitation hero Shaft during the wild-goose chase after corner boys in 3.1 ("Time after Time"), discussed in chapter 2, by playing Isaac Hayes's "Theme from *Shaft*" and acting "cool" during the car chase.

57. Looking down a gun at Proposition Joe, Omar orders Joe to "resist your natural inclination to do anything twisted up in this here play [the robbery of Marlo's supply]. You feel me?" (4.11, "A New Day"). In another instance he more casually explains to his lover Reynaldo that life on the rip and run has grown too easy: "It ain't what you takin', it's who you takin' it from, ya feel me?" (4.3, "Home Rooms").

58. Brown, "Neoliberalism and the End of Liberal Democracy," 46.

59. Ibid., 46.

60. Ibid., 47–48.

61. Ibid., 50.

62. Ibid., 59.

63. It seems that only the politicians, black and white alike, prove thoroughly bad. Along with Norman Wilson, Tommy Carcetti's black deputy campaign manager, we may initially have guarded hope for the white ethnic Carcetti. In the end, however, we agree with Norman's summary judgment of the entire breed of politicians: "Sooner or later they all disappoint" (4.13, "Final Grades").

1. His regular station is replaced, insultingly, by *A Prairie Home Companion*.

2. Brooks, *The Melodramatic Imagination*, 29.

3. Ibid.; Williams, *Race Card*, 28–42.

4. See Hale, *Making Whiteness*, 295.

5. Christine Gledhill writes, "If realism's relentless search for renewed truth and authentication pushes it toward stylistic innovation and the future, melodrama's search for something lost, inadmissible, repressed ties it to an atavistic past" (*Home Is Where the Heart Is*, 31–32). Elisabeth Anker echoes this when she argues that "left melancholy" is a structure organized by loss.

6. Art director Vincent Peranio, who has also done the art direction for all of John Waters's movies and for the television series *Homicide*, retrieved the faded, soiled, and ripped crushed orange velvet couch from a dumpster on the first day of scouting for *The Wire*. It was used in the pilot and then, inadvertently discarded. It had to be rebuilt for the rest of the series. "Giving Props to Baltimore," welcometobaltimorehon.com/vincent-peranio-giving-props-to-baltimore, accessed November 30, 2013.

7. In an astute video essay titled "Style in *The Wire*," Erlend Javik has noted that the series "subverts and refunctions" the most familiar figure of American domesticity: the couch on which so many "American families" and "friends" have congregated.

8. Addicts whom D'Angelo would like to treat more humanely.

9. This is very much like the problem of melodrama in colonial situations like Latin America, East Asia, and Africa: to long for the good home of the past is to long for things that one does not necessarily want: slavery, oppression, paternalism. Yet one cannot help but feel a certain nostalgia for home. One needs the structure of affect of the good to build on in the future.

10. Jameson, "Realism and Utopia," 372.

11. As discussed in chapter 3, Jameson praises *The Wire* as exceptional mass culture because it ceases "to replicate a static reality, or to be 'realist' in the traditional mimetic and replicative sense," and because it attends to "transformation, to human projects," to "the working out of Utopian intentions that are not simply the forces of gravity of habit and tradition" ("Realism and Utopia," 371). Now, Jameson's praise of *The Wire* for its "Utopianism" would seem to challenge what he argues elsewhere in the article—that the failure to imagine interesting villains has spelled the "end of melodrama and end of mass culture itself." Such, at least, is my reading of the article: melodrama rises again from the ashes of our boredom to reinfuse (what to me is lowercase) utopian energy into a new serial televisual form in the reinvention of melodrama.

Bibliography

Alff, David M. "Yesterday's Tomorrow Today: Baltimore and the Promise of Reform." In *The Wire: Urban Decay and American Television*, edited by Tiffany Potter and C. W. Marshall, 23–36. New York: Continuum, 2009.

Alvarez, Rafael. *The Wire: Truth Be Told.* New York: Pocket Books, 2004.

Anderson, Elijah. *Code of the Street: Decency, Violence, and the Moral Life of the Inner City.* New York: W. W. Norton, 2000.

Anderson, Paul Allen. "'The Game Is the Game': Tautology and Allegory in *The Wire.*" *Criticism* 52, no. 3–4 (Summer/Fall 2010): 373–398.

Anker, Elisabeth. "Left Melodrama." *Contemporary Political Theory* 11, no. 2 (May 2012): 130–152.

———. *Orgies of Feeling: Melodramatic Politics and the Pursuit of Freedom.* Durham, NC: Duke University Press, 2014.

Aristotle. "Poetics." In *Aristotle: Poetics; Longinus: On the Sublime; Demetrius: On Style.* Edited and translated by Stephen Halliwell, 1–142. Cambridge, MA: Harvard University Press, 1995.

Balukhatyi, Sergei. "Russian Formalist Theories of Melodrama." Translated by Daniel Gerould, In *Imitations of Life: A Reader on Film and Television Melodrama*, edited by Marcia Landy, 118–134. Detroit: Wayne State University Press, 1991.

Bandes, Susan. "And All the Pieces Matter: Thoughts on *The Wire* and the Criminal Justice System." *Ohio State Journal of Criminal Law* 8, no. 2 (2011): 435–445.

Bazin, André. *What Is Cinema?* Vol. 1. Edited and translated by Hugh Gray. Berkeley: University of California Press, 1967.

Beck, Eric. "Respecting the Middle: *The Wire*'s Omar Little as Neoliberal Subjectivity." *rhizomes* 19 (Summer 2009). www.rhizomes.net/issue19/beck .html.

Bennett, Drake. "This Will Be on the Mid-Term. You Feel Me?" *Slate*, March

24, 2010. www.slate.com/articles/arts/culturebox/2010/03/this_will_be_on
_the_midterm_you_feel_me.html.

Bentley, Eric. *The Life of the Drama*. New York: Atheneum, 1964.

Borden, Christine. "Cross Cutting in *The Wire*: The Journalist's Editorial Comment." Unpublished paper.

Bordwell, David. *The Way Hollywood Tells It: Story and Style in Modern Movies*. Berkeley: University of California Press, 2006.

Bordwell, David, Kristen Thompson, and Janet Staiger. *The Classical Hollywood Cinema: Film Style and Mode of Production to 1960*. New York: Columbia University Press, 1985.

Boynton, Robert. *The New New Journalism: Conversations with America's Best Nonfiction Writers*. New York: Random House, 2005.

Brooks, Peter. *The Melodramatic Imagination: Balzac, Henry James, Melodrama, and the Mode of Excess*. New Haven, CT: Yale University Press, 1976.

Brown, Keffrelyn, and Amelia Krahe. "Sociocultural Knowledge and Visual Re(-)presentations of Black Masculinity and Community: Reading *The Wire* for Critical Multicultural Teacher Education." *Race Ethnicity and Education* 14, no. 1 (2011): 73–89.

Brown, Wendy. "Neoliberalism and the End of Liberal Democracy." In *Edgework: Critical Essays on Knowledge and Politics*, 37–59. Princeton, NJ: Princeton University Press, 2005.

———. "Resisting Left Melancholy." *boundary 2* 26, no. 3 (Fall 1999): 19–27.

Buckley, Matthew. "Refugee Theatre: Melodrama and Modernity's Loss." *Theatre Journal* 61, no. 2 (2009): 175–190.

Bugliosi, Vincent. *Outrage: The Five Reasons Why O. J. Got Away with Murder*. New York: Norton, 1996.

Burke, Alafair. "I Got the Shotgun: Reflections on *The Wire*, Prosecutors, and Omar Little." *Ohio State Journal of Criminal Law* 8, no. 2 (Spring 2011): 447–457.

Caldwell, John. *Televisuality: Style, Crisis, and Authority in American Television*. New Brunswick, NJ: Rutgers University Press, 1995.

Chaddha, Anmol, and William Julius Wilson. "'Way Down in the Hole': Systemic Urban Inequality and *The Wire*." *Critical Inquiry* 38, no. 1 (Autumn 2011): 164–188.

Chekhov, Anton. "Letter to Aleksandr Semenovich Lazarev (pseudonym of A. S. Gruzinsky)," Cited in *Russian Literature in the Nineteenth Century*, by Leah Goldberge, 163. Magnes Press, Hebrew University, 1976.

Clandfield, Peter. "'We ain't got no yard': Crime, Development, and Urban

Environment." In *The Wire: Urban Decay and American Television*, edited by Tiffany Potter and C. W. Marshall, 37–49. New York: Continuum, 2009.

Cormier, Harvey. "Bringing Omar Back to Life." *Journal of Speculative Philosophy* 22, no. 2 (2008): 205–213.

Crary, Jonathan. *Suspensions of Perception*. Cambridge, MA: MIT Press, 2000.

Dickens, Charles. *Bleak House*. New York: Literary Guild of America, 1953.

Dissanayake, Wimal, ed. *Melodrama and Asian Cinema*. Cambridge: Cambridge University Press, 1993.

Doxtater, Amanda. "Figuring Danish Melodrama: Performance, Pathos and Volition in Carl Th. Dreyer's Work and Films." PhD diss., University of California, Berkeley, 2011.

Ellis, John. *Visible Fictions: Cinema, Television, Video*. New York: Routledge & Kegan Paul, 1982.

Elsaesser, Thomas. "Tales of Sound and Fury: Observations on the Family Melodrama." *Monogram* 4 (1972): 2–15.

Ericson, Richard V., and Kevin D. Haggerty, eds. *The New Politics of Surveillance and Visibility*. Toronto: University of Toronto Press, 2006.

Falzon, Mark-Anthony. *Multi-Sited Ethnography: Theory, Praxis and Locality in Contemporary Research*. Surrey, England: Ashgate, 2009.

Farhi, P. "A Television Trend: Audiences in Black and White." *Washington Post*, November 29, 1994.

Feuer, Jane. "The Concept of Live Television: Ontology as Ideology." In *Regarding Television: Critical Approaches—An Anthology*, edited by E. Ann Kaplan, 12–22. Los Angeles: American Film Institute, 1983.

Fiedler, Leslie. *The Inadvertent Epic: From "Uncle Tom's Cabin" to "Roots."* New York: Simon & Schuster, 1979.

Foucault, Michel. *Discipline and Punish: The Birth of the Prison*. New York: Vintage, 1995.

Fuller, Jennifer. "Branding Blackness on US Cable Television." *Media, Culture and Society* 32 (2010): 285–305.

Gaines, Jane. "The 'Melos' in Marxist Theory." In *Hidden Foundation: Film and the Question of Class*, edited by David James and Rick Berg, 56–71. Minneapolis: University of Minnesota Press, 1995.

Gallo, Phil. "HBO Puts Straight Dope in Its 'Corner.'" *Variety*, April 17, 2000.

Gendelman, Norman. "Zero-Degree Seriality: Television Narrative in the Post-Network Era." In *Time in Television Narrative: Exploring Temporality in Twenty-First-Century Programming*, edited by Melissa Ames, 69–81. Jackson: University Press of Mississippi, 2012.

Gledhill, Christine. "Christine Gledhill on *Stella Dallas* and Feminist Film Theory." *Cinema Journal* 25, no. 4 (Summer 1986): 44–48.

————. "The Melodramatic Field: An Investigation." In *Home Is Where the Heart Is: Studies in Melodrama and the Women's Film*, edited by Christine Gledhill, 4–42. London: British Film Institute, 1987.

Goodman, Tim. "Yes, HBO's 'Wire' Is Challenging. It's Also a Masterpiece." *San Francisco Chronicle*, September 6, 2006.

Haggerty, Kevin. "Tear Down the Walls: On Demolishing the Panopticon." In *Theorizing Surveillance: The Panopticon and Beyond*, edited by David Lyon, 23–45. Portland, OR: Willan, 2006.

Hale, Grace Elizabeth. *Making Whiteness: The Culture of Segregation in the South*. New York: Pantheon, 1998.

Halliwell, Stephen. *The Poetics of Aristotle: Translation and Commentary*. Chapel Hill: University of North Carolina Press, 1987.

Hansen, Miriam. "The Mass Production of the Senses: Classical Cinema as Vernacular Modernism." In *Re-inventing Film Studies*, edited by Christine Gledhill and Linda Williams, 332–350. New York: Bloomsbury, 2000.

Harvey, David. *A Brief History of Neoliberalism*. New York: Oxford University Press, 2005.

Heilman, Robert. *Tragedy and Melodrama: Versions of Experience*. Seattle: University of Washington Press, 1968.

Hornby, Nick. Interview with David Simon. *Believer*, August 2007. www .believermag.com/issues/200708/?read=interview_simon.

Hughey, Matthew. "Cinethetic Racism: White Redemption and Black Stereotypes in 'Magical Negro' Films," *Social Problems* 56, no. 3 (2009): 543–577.

Hynes, James. "Educational TV." *Salon.com*, September 20, 2006. www.salon .com/2006/09/20/the_wire_4/.

Jameson, Fredric. "Cognitive Mapping." In *Marxism and the Interpretation of Culture*, edited by Cary Nelson and Lawrence Grossberg, 347–365. Chicago: University of Illinois Press, 1988.

————. "Realism and Utopia in *The Wire*." *Criticism* 52, nos. 3–4 (Summer/ Fall 2010): 359–372.

Kinder, Marsha. "Re-Wiring Baltimore: The Emotive Power of Systemics, Seriality, and the City." *Film Quarterly* 62, no. 2 (Winter 2008–2009): 50–57.

Klein, Amanda Ann. "'The Dickensian Aspect': Melodrama, Viewer Engagement, and the Socially Conscious Text." In *The Wire: Urban Decay and American Television*, edited by Tiffany Potter and C. W. Marshall, 177–189. New York: Continuum, 2009.

Kraniauskas, John. "Elasticity of Demand: Reflections on *The Wire*." In *The Wire: Race, Class, and Genre*, edited by Liam Kennedy and Stephen Shapiro, 170–194. Ann Arbor: University of Michigan Press, 2012.

La Berge, Leigh Claire. "Capitalist Realism and Serial Form: The Fifth Season of *The Wire*." *Criticism* 52, nos. 3–4 (Summer/Fall 2010): 547–567.

Lanahan, Lawrence. "Secrets of the City: What *The Wire* Reveals about Urban Journalism." *Columbia Journalism Review*, January/February 2008, 23–31.

Lavik, Erlend. "Style in *The Wire*." www.vimeo.com/39768998.

Lee, Spike. "Thinking about the Power of Images: An Interview with Spike Lee." Interview by Gary Crowdus and Dan Georgakas. In *Spike Lee: Interviews*, edited by Cynthia Fuchs, 202–218. Jackson: University of Mississippi Press, 2002.

Lipsitz, George. *How Racism Takes Place*. Philadelphia: Temple University Press, 2011.

Love, Chris. "Greek Gods in Baltimore: Greek Tragedy and *The Wire*." *Criticism* 52, no. 3–4 (Summer/Fall 2010): 487–507.

Lyon, David. "The Search for Surveillance Theories." In *Theorizing Surveillance: The Panopticon and Beyond*, edited by David Lyon, 3–20. Portland OR: Willan, 2006.

Marcus, George E. "Ethnography in/of the World System: The Emergence of Multi-Sited Ethnography." *Annual Review of Anthropology* 24 (1995): 95–117.

———. *Ethnography through Thick and Thin*. Princeton, NJ: Princeton University Press, 1998.

Marshall, C. W., and Tiffany Potter. "'I Am the American Dream': Modern Urban Tragedy and the Borders of Fiction." In *The Wire: Urban Decay and American Television*, edited by Tiffany Potter and C. W. Marshall, 1–14. New York: Continuum, 2009.

Martin, Brett. *Difficult Men*. New York: Penguin, 2013.

Marvell, Andrew. *Andrew Marvell: The Complete Poems*. Edited by Elizabeth Story Donno. New York: Penguin, 1976.

McMillan, Alasdair. "Dramatizing Individuation: Institutions, Assemblages, and *The Wire*." *Cinephile* 4, no. 1 (Summer 2008): 42–50.

Michaels, Walter Benn. "Going Boom: The Economic Collapse Points Up How Little Our Literary World Has to Say about Social Inequality." *Bookforum*, February/March 2009. www.bookforum.com/inprint/015_05/3274.

Miller, Arthur. "Tragedy and the Common Man." In *The Theatre Essays of Arthur Miller*, 2nd ed., edited by Robert A. Martin and Steven R. Centola, 3–7. New York: Da Capo, 1996.

Mittell, Jason. "All in the Game: *The Wire*, Serial Storytelling, and Procedural Logic." In *Third Person: Authoring and Exploring Vast Narratives*, edited by Pat Harrigan and Noah Wardrip-Fruin, 429–438. Cambridge, MA: MIT Press, 2009.

————. *Complex TV: The Poetics of Contemporary Television Storytelling.* 2012. mediacommons.futureofthebook.org/mcpress/complextelevision/.

————. "Narrative Complexity in Contemporary American Television." *Velvet Light Trap* 58 (Fall 2006): 29–40.

————. "*The Wire* in the Context of American Television." In *The Wire: Race, Class and Genre*, edited by Liam Kennedy and Stephen Shapiro, 15–32. Ann Arbor: University of Michigan Press, 2012.

Moore, Lorrie. "In the Life of *The Wire*." *New York Review of Books*, October 14, 2010.

Nannicelli, Ted. "It's All Connected: Televisual Narrative Complexity." In *The Wire: Urban Decay and American Television*, edited by Tiffany Potter and C. W. Marshall, 190–202. New York: Continuum, 2009.

Newcombe, Horace. *TV: The Most Popular Art.* New York: Anchor, 1974.

Newman, Michael Z. "From Beats to Arcs: Toward a Poetics of Television Narrative." *Velvet Light Trap* 58 (Fall 2006): 16–28.

Nietzsche, Friedrich. *On the Genealogy of Morals and Ecce Homo.* Translated by Walter Kaufmann and R. J. Hollingdale. New York: Vintage, 1989.

Nussbaum, Martha. "The Morality of Pity." In *Rethinking Tragedy*, edited by Rita Felski, 148–169. Baltimore: Johns Hopkins University Press, 2008.

O'Sullivan, Sean. "Broken on Purpose: Poetry, Serial Television, and the Season." *Story Worlds* 2 (2010).

Peterson, James Braxton. "The Depth of the Hole: Intertextuality and Tom Waits's 'Way Down in the Hole.'" *Criticism* 52, no. 3–4 (Summer/Fall 2010): 461–485.

Postlewait, Thomas. "From Melodrama to Realism: The Suspect History of American Drama." In *Melodrama: The Cultural Emergence of a Genre*, edited by Michael Hays and Anastasia Nikolopoulou, 39–60. New York: St. Martin's, 1996.

Potter, Tiffany, and C. W. Marshall, eds. *The Wire: Urban Decay and American Television.* New York: Continuum, 2009.

Read, Jason. "Stringer Bell's Lament: Violence and Legitimacy in Contemporary Capitalism." In *The Wire: Urban Decay and American Television*, edited by Tiffany Potter and C. W. Marshall, 122–134. New York: Continuum, 2009.

Richmond, R. "Black Fare Makes $ense for HBO." *Variety* 213, February 24, 1997.

Rotella, Carlo. "The Case against Kojak Liberalism." In *The Wire: Race, Class, and Genre*, edited by Liam Kennedy and Stephen Shapiro, 113–129. Ann Arbor: University of Michigan Press, 2012.

Schaub, Joseph Christopher. "*The Wire*: Big Brother Is Not Watching You in

Bodymore, Murdaland." *Journal of Popular Film and Television* 38, no. 3: 122–132.

Sconce, Jeffrey. "What If? Charting Television's New Textual Boundaries." In *Television after TV: Essays on a Medium in Transition*, edited by Lynn Spigel and Jan Olsson, 93–112. Durham, NC: Duke University Press, 2004.

Simmons, Bill. "B.S. Report Transcript: Barack Obama." The B.S. Report, *Grantland*, March 1, 2012, www.grantland.com/blog/the-triangle/post /_/id/18690/b-s-report-transcript-barack-obama.

Simon, David. Interview by Jesse Pearson. *Vice*, December 2, 2009. www.vice .com/read/david-simon-280-v16n12.

———. *Homicide: A Year on the Killing Streets*. New York: Henry Holt and Company, 1991.

———. "Introduction." In *The Wire: Truth Be Told*, edited by Rafael Alvarez, 2–34. New York: Pocket Books, 2004.

———. "Letter to HBO." In *The Wire: Truth Be Told*, edited by Rafael Alvarez, 35–40. New York: Pocket Books, 2004.

———. "The Metal Men." *Baltimore Sun Magazine*, September 3, 1995, 6–18.

Simon, David, and Edward Burns. *The Corner: A Year in the Life of an Inner-City Neighborhood*. New York: Broadway Books, 1997.

Singer, Ben. *Melodrama and Modernity: Early Sensational Cinema and Its Contexts*. New York: Columbia University Press, 2001.

Smith, Adam. *An Inquiry into the Nature and Causes of the Wealth of Nations*. Edinburgh: Adam and Charles Black, 1863.

Sypher, Wylie. "Aesthetic of Revolution: The Marxist Melodrama." *Kenyon Review* 10, no. 3 (Summer 1948): 431–444.

Talbot, Margaret. "Stealing Life: The Crusader behind 'The Wire.'" *New Yorker*, October 22, 2007. www.newyorker.com/reporting/2007/10/22/071022fa _fact_talbot.

Thompson, Kristin. *Storytelling in Film and Television*. Cambridge, MA: Harvard University Press, 2003.

Toscano, Alberto, and Jeff Kinkle. "Baltimore as World and Representation: Cognitive Mapping and Capitalism in *The Wire*." *Dossier*, April 8, 2009. dossierjournal.com/read/theory/baltimore-as-world-and-representation -cognitive-mapping-and-capitalism-in-the-wire/.

Vasudevan, Ravi. *The Melodramatic Public: Film Form and Spectatorship in Indian Cinema*. New Delhi: Permanent Black, 2010.

Vint, Sherryl. *The Wire*. Detroit: Wayne State University Press, 2013.

Warshow, Robert. "The Gangster as Tragic Hero." In *The Immediate Experience. Movies, Comics, Theatre and Other Aspects of Popular Culture*. Cambridge, MA: Harvard University Press.

Williams, Linda. "Mega-Melodrama! The Vertical and Horizontal Suspensions of the 'Classical.'" *Modern Drama* 55, no. 4 (2012): 523–543.

———. "Melodrama Revised." In *Refiguring American Film Genres: Theory and History*, edited by Nick Browne, 42–88. Berkeley: University of California Press, 1998.

———. *Playing the Race Card: Melodramas of Black and White from Uncle Tom to O. J. Simpson.* Princeton, NJ: Princeton University Press, 2001.

———. "Ethnographic Imaginary: The Genesis and Genius of *The Wire.*" *Critical Inquiry* 38, no. 1 (Autumn 2011): 208–226.

———. "Tales of Sound and Fury" Signifying . . . Something." Forthcoming.

Williams, Raymond. *Television: Technology and Cultural Form.* New York: Routledge, 1974.

Wolfe, Tom. "The New Journalism." *Bulletin of the American Society of Newspaper Editors*, September 1970, 18–22.

Zurawik, David. "'The Wire' Loses Spark in Newsroom Storyline." *Baltimore Sun*, December 30, 2007. www.baltimoresun.com/entertainment/bal-al .wire30dec30,0,266826.story.

Index

Mad Men (television series), 46, 140
"magical Negro" image in film and television, 186–87, 190, 242n25, 243nn30–32
Malcolm X, 197
Marcus, George, 14–15, 239n15
Marimow, Bill, 28–29
Marker, Chris, 1
Marshall, C. W., 92, 101, 103, 231n32
Martin, Trayvon, 187
Marvell, Andrew, 48, 224n15
mass culture: tragedy and, 101–3; *The Wire* as, 4
Matheson, Carrie (character on *Homeland*), 139
McCullough, DeAndre, 24, 39–41, 57, 71
McCullough, Gary, 23–24, 26–29, 31, 33, 39–41, 42, 68, 71, 89, 165, 174
McMillan, Alasdair, 148
McNulty, Jimmy (character on *The Wire*): class structure and, 208; Omar and, 199, 201, 202, 204; as recurring character, 49, 85, 91, 153–54, 194–95, 214–15; on season 1 of *The Wire*, 16–17, *17*, 86, 141–45, 151, 174; on season 3 of *The Wire*, 59–60, 63, *63*, 65, 67, 69, 71, 97, 100, 103; on season 4 of *The Wire*, 71–72, 146; on season 5 of *The Wire*, 82, 117, 119–21, 129, 145, 150, 204, 211, 213
media: racial spectacle in, 180–81; season 5 of *The Wire* focus on, 72, *73*, 74, 116–36, 236n31; tragedy and, 101–3
Mehserle, Johannes, 187, 234n36
melodrama: ethnography and, 14–15, 28–35; family melodramas, 115–16; history of, 112–13, 229n13, 230n21,

234n16, 235nn21–22, 246n9; home imagery in, 215; liberalism and, 103–4; music in, 107–12; negative stereotypes of, 107–8; race and racism in, 177–82, 187–90; realism and, 107–36; scholarship on, 83–84; school melodramas, 139–40, 153–72, 239n16; suffering in, 34–35; television serials as, 45–49, 107–36; tragedy vs., 86–89, 104–6, 231nn47–51, 232n1; *The Wire* as, 4–7, 80–83, 90–106, 113–36
"The Melodramatic Field" (Gledhill), 83
"The Metal Men" (Simon news series), 21–30, *22*, 37, 39, 45, 61, 69
Metz, Christian, 232n1
Michaels, Walter Benn, 3, 29
Miller, Arthur, 92–93, 102–3, 231n32
Mills, David, 38, 39, 49, 53, 56
Minella, Vincente, 114
miscegenation: film representations of, 179–80; in *The Green Mile*, 184–87
misogyny, in *The Wire*, 161, 166, 182
"Mission Accomplished" (season 3 Wire episode), 154
Mittell, Jason, 189, 223n6, 226n11
Moby-Dick (Melville), 72, 223n2
modernity, melodrama and, 112–13
Moore, Lorrie, 29, 227n16
"Moral Midgetry" (season 3 episode of *The Wire*), 96, 111
Moreland, Bunk (Wire character): addiction of, 110; endurance on series of, 71; goodness of, 176; moral code of, 120; murder of Stringer Bell and, 100; Omar and, 193; in season 3, 63, *63*; soft eyes policing of, 6, 157–58

poetics of seriality, 51
police: allure of surveillance technology for, 143–53; morality in institutions of, 119–36, 244n45; racism and, 176, 183–87; schooling of, 154–55; in Simon's journalism, 13–14, 26–28, 30; as *Wire* characters, 6
police procedural genre: *Homicide* series as, 37, 53; network series in, 46; surveillance and technology and, 145–53; *The Wire* as example of, 4, 15–19, 53, 79–106, 119–36
Polish dockworkers, in *Wire* season 2, 18
"Poot." *See* Carr, "Poot" (character on *The Wire*)
Postlewait, Thomas, 235n20
Potter, Tiffany, 92, 101, 103, 231n32
power, surveillance and, 141–53
"power of the gun" motif, in *Homicide* television series, 55–56
PowerPoint presentations, in "Boys of Summer" (season 4 *Wire* episode), 71–72, *73*
Precious (film), 239n16
Price, Richard, 2
Production Code (Hollywood), 179–80, 182, 242n16
Proposition Joe. *See* Stewart, Joseph ("Proposition Joe") (character on *The Wire*)
Pryzbylewski, Roland (character on *The Wire*), 6, 59, 82, 152–53, *153*, 157–72
Pulitzer Prize, in season 5 of *The Wire*, 117

race and racism in *The Wire*, 2, 5–7, 173–209; contemporary versions of "Tom story" and, 182–87

Rawls, Bill (character on *The Wire*), 63, 82, 208, 212–13
Ray, Satyajit, 102
"React Quotes" (season 5 *Wire* episode), 197
realism: serial melodrama as, 107–36, 235n20; in *The Wire*, 26–27, 220–21
"Reformation" (season 3 *Wire* episode), 193
"Refugees" (season 4 *Wire* episode), 158
Re-Wired for Change, 240n4, 240n20
Rich Man, Poor Man (television series), 45
rifle-shot journalism, 19–29, 38, 56, 117, 129, 220–21
Robert's Rules of Order, 60, 65, 96
Roots (television series), 44, 44–45, 179–80, 185, 187
Rotella, Carolo, 86
Royce, Clarence (character on *The Wire*), 58, 82, 110, 176
Royo, Andre, 195
Russell, Beadie, 161, 166–67

school system: melodramas about, 139–40, 153–72, 239n16; in *Wire* season 4, 6, 19, *20*, 32, *73*, 118, 152–72
Sconce, Jeffrey, 46, 73
segmentation in television serials, 49–76
segregation, images in *The Wire* of, 174–76, 240n6
self-righteousness, in season 5 of *The Wire*, 118
September 11, 2001, attacks, surveillance technology and, 144–45
serial television: beat structure in,

51–52; black families in, 44; episode length and structure, 49–50;
episode structure on, 49–51; evo-
lution of, 45–49; network serials,
45–46; as realistic melodrama,
107–36; *The Wire as*, 16–18
Sex and the City (television series),
39
Shaft (film), 60
Shapiro, Steven, 232n36
Sherrod (character on *The Wire*), *126*,
126–28, 154
Simmons, Bill, 173, 223n1
Simon, David, 3–4; at *Baltimore Sun*,
11–12, 17, 21–27, 116–18, 130–31,
224n6; comments on *The Wire* by,
79, 119–20, 123, 236n29; *The Corner* television series and, 43–44;
ethnography in work of, 11–16;
Homicide television series and,
37–39, 49, 53, 56; on journalism,
28–35, 220–21, 224n27; "Letter
to HBO" by, 44, 225n4; television
writing by, 37–38, 53, 125–27; on
tragedy, 79, 104–6, 228n2
Simpson, O. J., 180, 183, 241n10
Singer, Ben, 112–13
single-sited ethnography, Simon's
work and, 14–15
Sirk, Douglas, 103, 114
slave morality, Nietzsche's concept
of, 113
slavery, in melodrama, 178–80, 182,
215
Smith, Adam, 100–101, 232n40
Snoop. *See* Pearson, Felicia "Snoop"
(character on *The Wire*)
Snot Boogie. *See* Betts, Omar Isaiah
(Snot Boogie) (character on *The
Wire*)

Sobotka, Frank (character on *The
Wire*), 82, 121, 133, 214; as tragic
figure, 92–93, *94*, 95, 97, 99–101,
103–4
social justice: failure on *The Wire* of,
2, 4–5, 86, 101–6, 121–36; in melodrama, 114–16, 124–25; racism
and, 174–209; recognition of good
and evil and, 113; *The Wire* as tool
for, 240n20
"Soft Eyes" (season 4 *Wire* episode),
152, 157–72
soft eyes in *The Wire*, 5–6, 152, 157–
72, 237n34
Sohn, Sonja, 240n4, 240n20
The Soloist (film), 234n7
The Sopranos (television series), 39,
46, 49, 51, 75
Southland (television series), 85
spatial imaginaries in *The Wire*, 174–
209, 215–16
spy melodrama, 170–72
Staiger, Janet, 232n1
Stand and Deliver (film), 239n16
Stanfield, Marlo (character on *The
Wire*), 176; Barksdale and, 61; in
final episode, 134; as kingpin, 176,
193; Omar and, 197; ruthlessness
of, 194, 216; in season 4, 160; in
season 5, 82, 110, 117, 119, 121–22;
as serial killer, 122; surveillance of,
144–46, 148, 150
Stewart, Joseph ("Proposition Joe")
(character on *The Wire*), 59, 95,
134–35, 245n57
Stowe, Harriet Beecher, 7, 89, 178
Stuff White People Like (blog),
44n40
"Style in *The Wire*" (Lavik), 75
Sue, Eugene, 74

suffering: of innocence, 89; in melodrama, 34–35, 112–15; tragedy and,
102–6; on *The Wire*, 131–36
Sun Magazine, 27–28
surveillance: foiling of, in *The Wire*,
147–53, *149*; in *The Wire*, 5–6, 139–
53, *146*, 199–204, *200–203*, 219–20
Sydnor, Leander (character on *The
Wire*), 59–60, 65, 69, 176

*Tally's Corner: A Study of Negro
Streetcorner Men* (Liebow), 14
"The Target" (season 1 episode), 16,
84–85, *85*, 89–90, 141–42, 151, 154
technology, in *The Wire*, 140–53
television seasons, characteristics of,
49–76
television writing, Simon's development in, 37–39
"televisuality" of *The Wire*, 75,
228n40, 236n29
Templeton, Scott (character on *The
Wire*), 117, *117*, 119, 121, 128–29,
209, 213
temporal signifiers, in television
series, 50
30 Rock (television series), 49
Thompson, Kristen, 232n1
"Time after Time" (*The Wire* season 3 episode), 56–74, 192, 228n33
The Titanic (film), 89
To His Coy Mistress (Marvell), 48,
226n12
Tom/anti-Tom stereotypes: contemporary versions of "Tom Story"
and, 182–87; in film and television,
179–80
"Took" (season 5 *Wire* episode), 72
Toscano, Alberto, 236n29
Tosha (character on *The Wire*), 204
To Sir, with Love (Clavell), 239n16

tragedy: melodrama vs., 107–8, 116–
36, 229n13, 232nn47–51, 233n2;
The Wire characterized as, 2–5,
79–106, 133–36
24 (television series), 50, 139, 141
Two and a Half Men (television
series), 49

Uncle Tom's Cabin (Stowe), 7, 89,
178–80, 234n15
The Unforgiven (film), 231n28
"Unto Others" (season 4 episode),
158, 191
Up the Down Staircase (novel and
film), 239n16
USA Patriot Act, 151, 238n12
utopianism, on *The Wire*, 80–82,
100, 113, 220–21, 246n11

Valcheck (character on *The Wire*),
152, 208–9, 213
Variety, review of *The Corner* in,
43–44
Vaughan (character in "Bop Gun"
Homicide episode), *53–54*, 53–56,
64, 66–68
victim heroes on *The Wire*, 88, 195–
96, 234n8
A View from the Bridge (Miller), 93
villainy, on *The Wire*, 81–83
von Trier, Lars, 89

Wagstaff, Calvin ("Cheese") (charac-
ter on *The Wire*), 134, 176
Wagstaff, Randy (character on *The
Wire*), 132, 150, 159–60, *160*, 162,
164, 176
Waits, Tom, 109, 148
wakes, on *The Wire*, 204–9, *205*
Wallace (character on *The Wire*):
D'Angelo and, 155–57; killing of,
96, 105, *105*, 122–24, 132–33, 162,